THE AMERICAN FAMILY

The AMERICAN FAMILY

Historical Perspectives

★ ★ ★

Edited by Jean E. Hunter & Paul T. Mason

Duquesne University Press
Pittsburgh, Pennsylvania

Published by:

Duquesne University Press
600 Forbes Avenue
Pittsburgh, Pennsylvania 15282

Library of Congress Cataloging-in-Publication Data

The American family : historical perspectives / edited by Jean E. Hunter and Paul T. Mason.
p. cm.
Selected proceedings of the Twenty-Second Duquesne History Forum held Oct. 26–28, 1988 in Pittsburgh.
Includes bibliographical references (p.) and index.
ISBN 0–8207–0219–6 (cloth) : $44.50
1. Family—United States—History. I. Hunter, Jean E., 1943– . II. Mason, Paul T., 1938– . III. Duquesne History Forum (22nd : 1988 : Pittsburgh, Pa.)
HQ536.A5466 1991
306.85'0973—dc20 90–21135
CIP

Printed in the United States of America

Contents

Editors' Preface

The American Family: Historical Perspectives is a collection of articles on a wide range of topics, discussing important aspects of American family life since colonial times. As is true of all the other essays but one, John Demos's introductory essay, "Family History's Past Achievements and Future Prospects," was presented at the 1988 Duquesne History Forum. It provides an overview of the impressive developments in the field during the past 20 years, while also describing some of the pitfalls that family historians must avoid in the future. The other 12 essays, chiefly the work of the most recent generation of family historians, demonstrate the diversity of methods, evidence and findings that makes family history such a lively and challenging undertaking.

Building on the work of earlier historians, many of these articles examine current theories about family history. Cynthia A. Kierner investigates the role of the family in a colonial business and the changing roles of family members, especially women. Ross W. Beales shows the impact of economic considerations on the life course of the boys of a New England farm family. David W. Robson describes the relationship of a father and his adult children, examining theories about the changing dynamics of family interaction. Linda W. Rosenzweig looks at mother-daughter relationships, questioning the supposition that they became more problematic at the end of the nineteenth century. David McBride studies the health problems of urban blacks and the growing emphasis on the family as a solution. Judy Barrett Litoff and David C. Smith offer a case study of a World War II courtship that both supports and challenges current theories. Jean E. Hunter investigates the changing ideologies of marital roles in post-World War II America by looking at a long-running feature in the *Ladies Home Journal*.

Other essays use the methods developed by family historians to look at new subjects. Stefan Bielinski examines the families of

Albany's early Dutch settlers to provide greater understanding of community development and social change. Charles Steffen, by studying the testamentary documents of eighteenth century Baltimore, finds evidence of a more equalitarian approach to children's inheritances. Virginia G. Crane, discussing the Lynches of South Carolina, describes the creation of an elite family. Marvin L. Michael Kay and Lorin Lee Cary seek to uncover the African roots of slave family practices in colonial North Carolina. Richard J. Altenbaugh examines the role of the family in the acculturation of Mexican immigrants by comparing their experiences with those of Italians.

The essays in *The American Family: Historical Perspectives* range widely in content and approach, but each illuminates the dynamic and exciting nature of family history as it comes to maturity.

The editors want to thank the staff at Duquesne University Press for all their assistance and support. And we also want to thank the hundreds of historians who have come to the Duquesne University History Forum over the past 23 years.

Jean E. Hunter
Paul T. Mason

Introduction

Family History's Past Achievements and Future Prospects

John Demos

The following reflects the text of a plenary address given by Mr. Demos at the Duquesne History Forum in October 1988.

I have a special feeling about this occasion—this edition of the Duquesne History Forum—and it's a good feeling. The Forum has a well-established, and well-deserved, status as a bellweather of scholarship, and the decision of the organizers this year to put *family history* out front is significant. For those of us who have been workers in this field of family history for a long time, it can be seen as a seal-of-approval of what we've been doing—or even as a *rite de passage* to mark our subject's coming of age.

I want to begin by taking you back to about the time this "baby" was born. And let me say right off that I make no claim of paternity for myself. At most, I happened along soon after the birth: the baby was squawling somewhat (as babies sometimes do), and I was among those who supplied some cuddling and comforting—and perhaps even a little wet-nursing. (Forgive the family metaphors; in the present context they are irresistible!)

Actually, though, I do think that family history *had* a father—or, to be more gender-neutral about this, a chief *parent*—namely, the brilliant French historian, Philippe Aries. I wonder how much Aries is read and remembered among younger workers in family history nowadays. It's not easy to reconstruct, almost 30 years after the fact, the impact of Aries's extraordinary book published first in France under the title *L'enfant et la vie familiale sous l'ancien regime*, and then in English translation as *Centuries of Childhood: A Social History of Family Life*. (In fact, it is hard to find citations of the book in recent scholarship—as I learned when I was trying, a few days ago, to recover the French title for the purposes of this talk. I went through the notes and bibliographies of half a dozen new studies in family history before I came upon what I needed.)

How quickly we forget! For, in its time, *Centuries of Childhood* was a blockbuster: *big sales*, I believe (at least for a work of history), *admiring reviews* (and not just in the scholarly journals), lots of *enthusiastic discussion* (and not just among historians). The book's central idea—that premodern childhood was different from, and in a sense more "childish" than, what is generally the case today—was something to grip the imagination. Right or wrong—and for the moment I take no position on that—this was an idea to think about, to argue about, and even to organize a new research field about. In its intellectual scope and sweep, its ingenious marshalling of sources, its whole spirit of open inquiry, *Centuries of Childhood* invited vigorous response; and it certainly got response in the years that followed.

To be sure, the substance of the response was not uniformly the same. There were critics, at least a few, from the outset. And gradually, as time passed, admiration was mixed with a growing skepticism. My own view, for what it's worth, is that Aries erred more by way of overstatement than of outright misinterpretation; and if so, it certainly wouldn't be the first time a master idea has been overstated. In any event, it largely stuck where it fell, and even where it was attacked and finally discredited, it had the effect of stimulating much further thought and study. I think it's not too much to say that many of us might not be here today, battling in the trenches of family history, if *Centuries of Childhood* hadn't come along when it did.

There were, of course, other early contributors-to-the-cause—even some "grandparents" of family history. Peter Laslett and his colleagues in the Cambridge Group for the Study of Population and Social Structure pioneered the demographic side. Strictly speaking, they were not pioneers, for they were building, in part, on still earlier work by demographic historians associated with the *Annales* school in France. There was also Edmund Morgan, whose study of *The Puritan Family* is now almost 50 years old. The publishing history of that work is itself a comment on the development of the field. Conceived and carried out as a doctoral dissertation around 1940, it found its way into print in serial form (and very obscurely) in successive numbers of the *Bulletin* of the Boston Public Library in 1942–43. I've never asked Professor Morgan about this directly, but I assume there was initially no interest in the manuscript among regular publishers. By the late sixties, however, much had changed. Family history was alive and well and growing fast, and *The Puritan Family* was reprinted—actually printed for the first time as a book—in the Harper Torchbook Series. And it's still going strong today; indeed, most of us would love to be receiving Morgan's royalties checks for it. One more title should be mentioned, while I'm at it: Bernard Bailyn's *Education in the Forming of American Society* (1960). This was a little book that set a large and influential agenda for scholars, roughly over the succeeding decade. Another curiosity there, reflecting the uncertain early prospects of the field: a work of family history, at least in large part of family history, masquerading as *education* history.

So, how did it look in those early days? What *were* the prospects, the problems and the preoccupations of that little band of scholars who were drawn to the cries of the "infant" family history? There was, at the start, a powerful sense of new life to be cherished—or, if I may change the figure at last—new territory to be explored. Family history began, like many other seemingly fresh forms of research, as a gap-filling enterprise. Scholarship abhors gaps in knowledge—which is why scholars, as individuals, love to find them—and family life in the past seemed to be just that. And yet a good deal of popular lore and a certain amount of academic sociology were already established before any historians arrived. This was not proper *scholarship*, but something else that needed to be dealt with before we "professionals" could do our thing. Strange as it may sound now, one even had to make a primary case that the family *has* a history—in the same sense as other cultural institutions—with ups and downs, ins and outs. This was a special problem with the "popular lore," and I remember encountering it when talking to "popular" audiences: it involved an assumption that the family was somehow "universal"—which meant, in effect, *trans*-historical. (The one added wrinkle, there, was a sometimes related assumption of gradual decline and decay from seemingly "golden age" beginnings.) Sociological theory, for its part, offered another set of assumptions that were equally problematic: no golden age and no underlying universals, but an insistence on a *process* of unidimensional change—from the allegedly "extended family" form of premodern times to the nuclear pattern of our own times. I'm exaggerating and oversimplifying as I summarize here, but I hope the point is clear. In entering this new territory, historians encountered a good deal of "underbrush" that had to be chopped out before orderly cultivation could begin. At least we experienced it that way.

Other problems of the entering phase? Well, of course, there were problems of conceptualization: how to *define* the family in a way that would make for smooth research operations. On the whole, the debate about definitions led to a tacit strategy of tolerance: let scholars define the terms in their own ways, so long as they are clear about their terms. I call that tolerance, but maybe it's only side-stepping. Problems, also, of sources: could one find what was needed to reconstruct the story of the family's changing past, especially in its more private and interior aspects? At first, that issue appeared to center on the *conundrum* of prescription *versus* behavior, norms and values *versus* experience. There were lots of sources on the "prescriptive" side—books of domestic and child rearing advice, for example—but what did they really tell us about actual, lived experience? I remember, in this connection, an important cautionary article by Jay Mechling, called "Advice to Historians About Advice to Mothers." The title itself was rather chilling.

I want to say, in looking back now from the vantage-point of 20 or 25 years later, that the problem of sources has turned out better than we initially thought—that evidence, particularly on the behavioral side, has been fuller and more revealing than we expected. Here are two small and specific examples, more or less from my own experience. I remember when I was first working on Plymouth Colony families, in the mid-sixties: I became interested in the matter of weaning. It seemed to have some possible significance, from both a demographic and a pyschological point of view. I could see some demographic grounds for speculating that the weaning of those infants, in those families, typically occurred around the age of 12 months. Birth intervals (the time between the arrival of one baby and of the next) averaged about 24 months. Since lactation has a well-known contraceptive effect, and since it would take at least a month or two to start a new pregnancy, the numbers themselves suggested the 12-month weaning age. These were grounds for speculating, as I say, but not for *proving* anything. In fact, there were other possible explanations of the same demographic facts:

for example, what anthropologists call a *post-partum sex taboo*. This means a pattern of sexual abstinence for a certain period following a new birth. So, there was no sure way to decide *between* these alternatives, and thus no way to know how long breast-feeding lasted, and when weaning occurred (and under what conditions). I thought we'd never know; I couldn't imagine finding hard evidence of actual cases. But I was wrong—there *is* evidence of actual cases. Admittedly, they make a rather motley assemblage—mere fragments, when considered one by one—yet they do add up. And now we have whole journal articles, based on this evidence, and giving us a much sharper picture of this little corner of family history than once seemed possible.

Another corner—not so little—where I also underestimated the possibilities: the historical study of courtship. I remember when Ellen Rothman, then a graduate student of Brandeis, picked that as her dissertation topic. *Great*, I thought, some deeply important issues there, but then on *second* thought: would she find sufficient evidence? Wasn't that too private and personal a part of experience—anybody's experience, past or present—to have left the sort of traces that we historians require for our work? I worried and kept my fingers firmly crossed while my student set out over the countryside on a tour of local historical societies, courthouses and (I think) at least a few proverbial trunks-in-the-attic. I needn't have worried. When she returned, she was loaded with good materials, mostly from personal correspondence. Nineteenth century Americans, it turned out, had committed to paper some remarkably specific and "sensitive" parts of their courtship experience. It was not everything we'd like to know—scholars, of course, never feel they have enough—but, in this case, there was more than enough for a fine dissertation and then a first-rate book. Indeed, Rothman's book *Hands and Hearts* stands, in my mind, as a kind of monument to persistence—and to hope—in our field.

There were problems, too, with the *boundaries* of the field: where it stopped and other areas began. An especially tricky one was the boundary between family history and women's history. The stakes there ran to competing turf-claims, and to ideology as well. There was a period in the early and middle seventies when ideological correctness seemed to require a denial of any possible overlap here. A connection between women and the family must not be assumed: that was a point of feminist orthodoxy (with which I, at least, felt some sympathy).

And yet in practice—which is to say, in history—the two very often went together. And what about the history of childhood? Is that always, and necessarily, a subfield of family history? And the history of the later life-course, including middle and old age? And things like sex history and the history of love more generally? The answers one gave to such questions were inevitably somewhat fuzzy. Mostly, I suppose, one put one's head down and followed the trail of one's evidence even when it led in a direction out of family history as narrowly conceived.

There were problems, or at least questions, of method. And they were *big* questions. The study of family life has been elaborately pursued, in some cases for quite a long time, on the other side of a lot of disciplinary frontiers: in psychology, for example, and sociology, and anthropology—and even in literature and philosophy. There were many opportunities, many *reasons,* for historians to borrow. Yet the intellectual coinage—not to mention goals and strategy—was frequently not the same, so one had to be careful. This is not, I think, the place to begin a lengthy discussion of interdisciplinary history—that's something that goes far beyond family history—but we can't avoid noticing that research on the family has been a principal means of infiltrating interdisciplinary methods into historical studies at large. (Take quantitative methods, for instance.)

Finally, on the problems list, we have the whole business of the relationship between family history and other more well-established and traditional branches of history. That issue struck me very forcibly on one particular afternoon in the late sixties. I received a phone call from a historian much my senior—in fact, everyone was my senior then—and he put a question to me. He was part of the program committee for the meetings of the American Historical Association that year, and he wanted to organize a session to reflect the new work in family history. His idea was to explore the possible relationship—perhaps even the *causal* relationship—between American child rearing patterns in the late nineteenth century and the rise of the progressive movement in American *politics* in the early twentieth century. Did I think there *was* such a relationship? Did I know anyone studying it, who, in short, might contribute to the hoped-for session? The question blew me away. I had no idea what to say; I think I mumbled something to the effect that research in family history "hadn't gotten that far." There is no strong reason to conceal the identity of the caller: it was Carl Degler (now of Stanford University). I want, in fact, to mention Professor

Degler, because he subsequently was a very distinguished recruit to the cause of family history. He wasn't part of it at the time of the AHA-program call; he signed on later and, indeed, became a leader. After all, the quality of "recruits" says something about the importance—and the success—of the cause itself, and family history has been notably fortunate in this respect. When people with the stature of Carl Degler sign on, it helps to build confidence to say nothing of adding strength to the overall ranks.

But back to Professor Degler's 1968 question: After I had demurred as gracefully as I could, and had calmed down a bit, I realized that it was a reasonable *kind* of question to ask. It was reasonable, in short, for "political history" to expect some help from this newfangled work in family history—reasonable, at the very least, that there should be links between our field and the others. Family history seemed, at that point, to be running a separate course of its own making. But eventually that would have to change—wouldn't it? It felt like an important challenge then, and I must say it still feels like a challenge today. I'll come back to it, a little more, later on.

Perhaps this is enough historiographical time-travel for one evening; I want now to shift *out* of reverse gear and talk with you about where we seem to have arrived more or less at the present time. Let me do that by sketching a kind of map-of-the-territory that I've used to organize my own thinking for quite a number of years. Like all maps, mine is a device—a tool—designed to serve a set of quite pragmatic purposes. Another historian would surely draw it differently; this is *my* map, nothing more. Moreover, it has come to me not through any sudden epiphany, nor as the deductive outcome of one or another theory; rather, it's a response to what I think I've *seen* out there on the surface of the scholarly landscape. It aims simply to cover the ground, at least as much as possible.

It divides the territory into five "provinces" or subsections. The first one includes a variety of questions about the composition of families: how many its individual members typically are—and who—all that sort of thing. I put this first not in the sense of its being most important, but rather because it does seem to have a certain logical priority over the others. You have to identify the players before you can put them into action (so to speak). And, in fact, there is an element of historiographical priority here as well: a disproportionate amount of research energy has been directed to this particular subsection, especially in the early years. If its substance—its subject—is family composition (broadly speaking), its chief method has been demography. Study has been piled on study, truly all around the world. Large international conferences have been devoted to such questions as "mean household size," and whole legions of younger scholars have chained themselves to computers in pursuit of technical expertise. The gains from all this are indisputable: gains of substance; gains, too—quite dazzling gains—in refinements of method. On the side of method we've started with grade school arithmetic—that's where I dropped in and soon dropped out—and moved to statistics, and then to elaborate computer models. With respect to substance, we now have a good fix on all the main contours of the story: not just "mean household size," but age of marriage, fertility and mortality rates, illegitimacy, and so on. (By "the story" I mean change-over-time in the major sectors of the Euro-American world since about the sixteenth century.) And the work is still continuing—though it's gradually moving, I would say, toward some lesser contours. There are still certain knowledge gaps to be plugged, especially about the demographic behavior of various smaller and off-center groups *within* the total historical population. But I'd be surprised if new work changes our basic sense of the story.

In fact, the very success of the demographic approach has itself become something of a problem. I remember a conference in the mid-seventies where speaker after speaker referred to "demographic history" and "family history" in the same breath, as if family history *was* demographic history and nothing more. I remember an invitation, four or five years ago, to serve on a small panel of judges that would review articles published in *The Journal of Family History* during the preceding decade and award prizes to the best two or three. I had, once upon a time, read that journal avidly; then my interest had become sporadic—and now I realized why. A good 80 percent of the articles it had published fell into the demographic/quantitative category. When I asked the editor why, she replied that those proportions reflected the nature of their submissions; she wished it were otherwise, but what could one do? The lasting effect of going through the whole ten years' worth of articles was a kind of mind-numbing: I retained and remembered some interesting points of method but very little of substantive *results*.

I don't wish to be heard as opposing demographic study all through—just the pattern of an 80 percent imbalance. We have (again, in my opinion) gone somewhat overboard in this direction, probably because the evidence is fuller and sharper than is the case with some other directions, and also because the methods and strategies seem so pleasingly systematic and sure. I've always thought that demographic work was essential for establishing certain vital, numerical benchmarks in family history. But when you've got those in hand, you need to move on.

In fact, demographic practitioners have *tried* to move on—to extend their range beyond the benchmark business—but I think with very dubious results. Stated differently, they have tried to move beyond their initial (and appropriate) focus on issues of family composition to other issues of an entirely different sort. But here, I submit, they overstep. Can we really go from changing rates of illegitimacy, for example, or rates of "bridal pregnancy," to conclusions about changes in authority patterns within the family as a whole? Can we really use infant mortality rates to develop an argument about the emotional investment of parents in children? Can we really regard child *naming*—another cultural practice that can be organized and analyzed in very precise fashion—as a measure of individualized attachment in family relations? Claims have, in fact, been made, and arguments advanced, on each of these counts. Yet each involves a leap of inference—a leap from quantities to *qualities*—that seems to me unwarranted.

Let me switch to the second of the subsections on my family history map. And let me call it, simply, "ideology." There is nothing fancy or mysterious about this one; in a sense, it's the most old-fashioned piece of the larger territory. The issues are: ideas about the family, values attaching *to* the family, attitudes toward the family, "norms," expectations, images and so on. What, in short, does the family *mean* to people, in one or another historical setting? That is the underlying question. The Aries book *Centuries of Childhood* landed mostly here, as did a number of important subsequent studies. (I think especially of the work of Christopher Lasch.) But, on the whole, the results—and, indeed, the *effort*—in this particular area have been surprisingly thin.

One reason for this is, I would guess, a lingering doubt—a kind of skittishness—caused by the prescription *versus* behavior dichotomy of which I spoke earlier. Prescriptive evidence has come to be regarded as suspect—indeed as the province of old-fashioned scholarship, while behavior holds the center of the scholarly stage. Yet prescription and behavior do not really form a dichotomy at all. Prescription is itself a *form* of behavior, and something that surely influences *other* forms in all sorts of ways. The lines of influence may often be indirect and even very crooked—we're not talking about reflexive exchange here or simple stimulus-response—but the fact of "influence" can hardly be doubted. And, for what it's worth, I would urge family historians to overcome the fear of being thought old-fashioned, and then to plunge into prescriptive sources—sermons, advice books, popular fiction, whatever—and take seriously the full range of "ideological" constructs in and around our subject.

Actually, the process of study here—the strategies, the methods—are not so unsexy as they might initially seem. Interdisciplinary borrowing should be no less appropriate and helpful than in our other subsections; there is certainly much relevant work in contemporary anthropology ("reading culture," as one recent book title puts it), in sociological studies of ritual, and even in the new literary criticism. There are some signs already of new effort by family historians in the "ideology" area: the recent work by Jan Lewis, for example (including a stunning piece, not yet published, on changing notions of "mother love.") Could anyone seriously doubt that the ideology of mother love has been a major force in the lives of millions upon millions of women? And, in somewhat different ways, surely a major force on men's lives, too?) I think, in this same connection, of Dallett Hemphill's work on the history of etiquette, some of which was presented at a session here earlier in the day. Still, while there are signs of change, signs of renewed interest in "ideological" materials, we need to do more, much more.

Moving right along, we come to subsection three on my map, which I'll call *structure*. This is obviously critical, and I think its main internal features are fairly obvious, too: power and duty, responsibilities and roles, "status" and "function", who's-in-charge here and who-isn't—you get the idea. How do we take hold of these issues? Again, there are some obvious dividers with which to begin: for example, age and gender. Much progress has been achieved in this area, especially by scholars who focus on the experience of women. Indeed, this is a major point of intersection between women's history and family history. Intersection has led increasingly to collaboration, with clear benefits for both sides. I'm not going to linger over details of progress—they are mostly quite well-known—but I do want to mention what I see as a further opportunity for historians of family structure. I mean the application in our research of concepts and methods borrowed from *family systems theory*. This is not, incidentally, a new idea with me; I noticed in the Forum program a session on the topic "Family History and Family Therapy." I couldn't attend, but I suppose what happened was some exploration of possible exchanges between the two fields. Anyway, that sort of exploration *ought* to happen, more than it has so far. I know of just *one* historian who has sought and obtained actual training in family systems theory, and she has done some very promising things with it. What these people on the other side of this particular interdisciplinary bridge have to tell us is precisely about the family as a *system*: how all the parts interact and continually reshape one another. It may not sound like big news as I briefly allude to it here. I can only say, on the basis of some limited experience of reading systems theory (and also of watching videotapes of treatment situations) that it does seem different, and "deeper," than what we historians are doing, and we can probably learn from it.

Subsection four is what might be called "affect," the whole emotional dimension of family life. I see this as a virtual disaster area so far. Not for lack of *effort*, but rather because the effort we've made (again, so far) has been fundamentally misguided. We do have a kind of "consensus view" as to the chief outlines of the story; it's a highly "progressive" view, according to which emotional experience has been getting better and better. One scholar has referred to it as a "love-up, anger-down" model of change over time; another wrote baldly of the "Bad Old Days" of affective impoverishment (everything in the premodern era), as contrasted with the Good New Days—and Good *Feelings*—of our own time. The details are vivid and sometimes rather gory. Premodern marriage, for example, was supposedly full of wife-beating (and maybe even some husband-beating); the partners came together, in the first place, not so much from loving sentiments as from a sense of instrumental advantage. By the same token, premodern child rearing is supposed to have been widely infused with practices that *we* would regard as child *abuse*. I'm exaggerating again, and even caricaturing, in order to make a point—but not an awful lot. There are voices of doubt about the "progressive" view, but they are so far quite faint and few.

I don't really know how and where all this got started, and maybe it doesn't matter. What does matter is that we have taken a very wrong track, and we need, at least in my judgement, to start over. We have to deal, first of all, much more carefully and more *intelligently* with evidence of emotional experience. Indeed, we have to be clear about what constitutes good evidence here. Some of the difficulty and some of the error in recent years has come from that same excess of zeal about demographic evidence of which I spoke earlier. To repeat just one example: does a high risk of infant death necessarily mean that parents would not have allowed themselves to become deeply attached to their own infant children? I think the inference could as easily go the other way: that is, toward *more* attachment—or at least more anxiety (and thus more direct involvement)—wherever the infant seems to be seriously in danger. There have been other errors, other forms of misconstrued evidence. Material from premodern diaries, for instance. Often you do find, in such diaries, references to the death of spouses or children that seem remarkably brief, thin, laconic in tone. But does this really imply lack of *feeling* (lack of love, lack of grief) in the diary *keeper*? My own sense is that most premodern people did not use diaries to record powerful feeling of *any* sort; and if so, what this is all about is less the history of emotion than the history of diary keeping.

There are, however, possibilities for doing better with this part of the enterprise—possibilities of getting closer to the actual center of past emotional life. As to evidence, personal documents are surely the front line of research. *Diaries* themselves become much more useful as one moves nearer to the present. *Personal correspondence*, too, as I've already mentioned when referring to courtship history. *Court records*, I think: at least for early America, the file papers of local courts show ordinary people acting—and emoting—in all sorts of seemingly humble, but nonetheless significant, settings. The list of these possibilities can certainly be lengthened, with special entries that might apply to one or another particular place—notarial records, Bibles, travel accounts and so forth. Admittedly, it looks like a grab-bag, all-in-all. It's messy, and it's incomplete. But it's what we've got, and at least it's *on the subject*. That may be the most important point of all.

But evidence is not, in fact, our only difficulty here. Emotional experience is intrinsically hard to handle even where there is lots of evidence—hard to sort out, hard to organize, hard to analyze in any "systematic" way. We all *have* emotions of our own, and there is a corresponding risk of subjective distortion in what we read (and infer) about past emotional life.

In addition, there is the matter of terminology, the words and phrases threaded all through our everyday discourse and the discourse of our forebears. Too *many* words and too variable (even slippery) in their shades of meaning for us to use them effectively in our research. It's for this reason that we must, I think, decline a "common sense" and "common language" approach to emotion history and adopt, instead, a stance based on theory. For some years I've been advocating one particular brand of "affect theory," associated with the work of the psychologist Sylvan Tomkins. Tomkins identifies eight "primary affects" (as he calls them) and works out many permutations and combinations starting from there. I won't describe the further details now—there simply isn't time—but if you liked, you could look it up. In a way, the use of *any* theory would be an improvement on the present situation—any set of reasonable (and consistent) principles for bringing a little more order out of a generally prevalent chaos. If we don't do *something* of this sort, I fear that chaos will prevail in the realm of "affect history" more or less indefinitely.

The last part of my map is a little different from the others. It's not a subject in the same sense, not (in terms of the metaphor) a "territory" at all. Rather, it's like a stream whose sources and headwaters rise separately in each of the other subsections and then flow right out of family history, eventually to join the great river that is historical scholarship at large. This is the business of linkage between our research and all the other scholarly currents, political history, intellectual history and so on. This was the point of Professor Degler's question to me years ago: what about child rearing practice in relation to progressive politics? As I've already said, it was a *fair* question—and a challenge. In fact, I think family historians have been responding to the challenge for some time—slowly, incrementally, but more and more effectively. A few examples from American family history: Philip Greven's book *The Protestant Temperament,* an ambitious and stimulating attempt to marry family history with religious history; Mary Ryan's *Cradle of the Middle Class,* with its skillful interweaving of several different historical threads (family, class, religion and governance); Tamara Hareven's *Family Time and Industrial Time,* a major contribution to the scholarship of family, immigration and work. The list could be lengthened, but you see the point already. There isn't any grand synthesis of family history and other history, but the links are growing in a kind of natural way as the field itself grows. And that, I suppose, is the way it ought to happen.

I could fuss with this model a little more. There are some things I haven't quite squeezed in. One omission that especially troubles me is the material basis of family life—the "stage" and the "props" and all the other tangible accoutrements: domestic architecture, furnishings, clothing, household implements, even (I suppose) food and drink. This is important stuff, no doubt about it—and the evidence is, at many points, quite abundant. I'm not sure that this is a subject area in quite the same sense as family composition, ideology, structure and so forth; in fact, it might better be broken up and grafted onto those other primary areas as the specific evidence may dictate. But better still *not* to fuss; instead, let me use my concluding minutes to try to get a view of the entire terrain.

So, again: where are we at this point, and where are we heading? Some of the early problems—what looked like problems 20 years ago—seem quite different now. We don't worry much about confronting and clearing away the underbrush of traditional myths and lore on the history of the family; that task has more or less been completed. We don't worry so much about problems of definition; that task, too, was intrinsic to the earliest phase. We're not so concerned with turf struggles and boundaries, with where family history as such leaves off and other adjacent histories begin. On that score we can see ourselves as marching in the ranks of a much broader movement. When someone draws an historiographical bead on the late twentieth century—say, 50 years hence—surely he or she will give pride of place to the *study of private life*. Most of the history that historians did, before 1950 or so, was about public life—not all, but most of it. And now the balance has clearly and massively shifted. That's what the broader movement is all about, and family history has been right in the thick of it.

Two problems remain and loom large now—probably more than two, but these especially trouble *me*. One is the problem of dealing with *change*. Change, after all, is central to our understanding of history, our interest in history and our whole enterprise of scholarship. Yet *family* history, as carried out so far, has not done justice to the element of change. Many of our proudest accomplishments—our most "successful" studies—are focused on a single time or period. We are better at making historical snapshots than full-scale moving pictures. Snapshots are all right; indeed they have their own kind of importance. But we have to do more. First, we have to find better ways to *describe* change—that's hard enough—then we have to *explain* it. What causes change in the family? And what about the family itself as a *cause* of change in other sectors of experience? I expect that progress with these questions will come especially from further "linkage" studies—the family and economics, the family and the environment, the family and public policy and so on.

The second problem that increasingly concerns me is very different. It's the problem of *presenting* our work, of finding a "voice"—words and images and tone—appropriate for what we have to say. There, too, I don't think we've done especially well so far. Part of the problem is the prominence of quantitative study in a good deal of our work; it's always hard to write from numbers. Another part is our use (at least sometimes) of social science *theory* which also raises obstacles to successful prose. And by "successful" I mean more than simply "clever" and "prettified"; for, surely, in all historical writing "success" *involves* more than marshalling facts and expounding arguments. There are *nuances*, refinements of color and shading, the interplay of surface and depth—all of which express the evocative side of our task—in family history no less than in other research areas. (No less, and quite possibly *more*.) In my personal view, one of the finest of all books on American family history is Wallace Stegner's novel *Angle of Repose*. And I'd say a similar thing about David Bradley's novel *The Chaneysville Incident*, in relation to black family history. Both these works are, in fact, based on extensive knowledge of *actual* history: Stegner worked from a large family archive in the Stanford University Library, and Bradley is a professional historian. Yet both authors achieved something more than what was there on the surface of the documents themselves. They belong, I think, on our list of exemplary models.

This sounds a little down-side, and it's not the note on which I wish to end. Problems we do have, but how could it be otherwise? In fact, this glass is half *full*—more than half. We've got much to feel good about, and, of course, much work yet to do. If anyone had suggested to me in 1968 that we'd be meeting here in 1988, on the topic of family history, under the distinguished auspices of the Duquesne History Forum, I'd have offered a very large bet against it. But then, I suppose, historians are always lousy forecasters (and worse gamblers). I'm glad I was wrong.

1

The New Netherland Dutch

Settling In and Spreading Out in Colonial Albany

Stefan Bielinski

Several thousand men, women and children came to the Dutch colony of New Netherland before 1664. The New Netherland Dutch sought to replicate their native cultive in America and thus relied on a strong family as the basis of their society, and New Netherland flourished because the original settlers were able to raise large families. Their descendants followed the frontier west, leaving their cultural imprints on communities across the continent. Until recently, our knowledge of these pioneers has been more or less confined to a number of amusing anecdotes and oft-repeated cliches. However, a remarkable last decade of serious scholarship on the Dutch in early America has transformed our understanding of their contributions to the birth and development of the American nation and particularly of the role of non-English people in that drama.[1] For almost a decade now, the experiences of the New Netherland-era settlers, their families and their descendants have been major concerns of the Colonial Albany Social History Project, a New York State Museum-sponsored research and field services program formed to study the founding, growth and development of community life in the city of Albany during the seventeenth and eighteenth centuries.[2]

At the outset, two specifications are necessary regarding place and people. What constituted "colonial Albany" can be defined by understanding that those living within Albany's municipal boundaries were accorded opportunities to engage in trading and market activities that made their lives and expectations substantively different from the farmers and marginal people of the surrounding countryside. The city charter of 1686 codified the distinction and gave the city fathers legal sanctions with which to remind transgressors of Albany's unique commercial and political status.[3]

Having defined the place, the social historian then poses the question of "Who were the people of colonial Albany?" The names of Philip Schuyler, Philip Livingston and Philip Hooker are among those that spring immediately to mind, as their contributions have pervaded all forms of traditional historical exposition. These notable individuals were the community's leaders, and their prominence in any discussion of Albany history is indisputable. At the same time, one of the chief ambitions of the Colonial Albany Project has been to understand and incorporate the contributions of the lesser-known members of the community—the rank and file artisans and laborers, the mothers and keepers of the community's domestic economy, the children—who were more numerous than any other group, the infirm and incapable (all of whom did not perish and who sometimes managed to live long if undistinguished lives), and that of older residents, slaves, soldiers and transients. Considered together, these more ordinary townspeople or preurban cityfolk were not only the most typical but also the soul of the colonial community.

However, on the surface, the ordinary people of colonial Albany do appear to have constituted a silent majority. Most of them never wrote as much as a letter; their material legacy has not been preserved as historic buildings or in other collections of material culture. Consequently, their stories often have been missing from the historical narrative. To correct this deficiency, the Colonial Albany Project has developed an approach to research designed to comprehend their lives and keep them from getting buried under the more highly acclaimed and well-documented achievements of the members of Albany's elite.

The initial research objective was to identify by name every person who lived in the city of Albany from the time of the formation of the community during the mid-seventeenth century to the coming of the Industrial Revolution about 150 years later. Albany residents were named on census, tax, voting, membership and activity lists as government, business and interest groups sought to involve either all or select households within the community in their programs and activities. An information file was established on each individual identified as an Albany city resident.[4] By naming the heads of households, we then had the tip of the community iceberg.

Marriage, church and legal records identified their spouses—and a file was created for each person who married an Albany resident. Albany and regional church records and historical materials on more than 300 family groups have yielded demographic information on the children of each Albany couple. A file was created for each child born to Albany parents before the end of 1800 and who was not named already on the survey and marriage documents.[5]

Activity and membership information and demographic data were consolidated in single cases when justifiable. The names of unrelated boarders, tenants and other transient residents who were neither heads of households nor born to Albany parents, and the names of servants and slaves have been recovered from documentary resources including survey lists and the records of political, judicial, business, and social institutions and organizations. The remaining pieces were added to the community's social mosaic when a biographical file was established for each of these individuals.

By the end of 1988, the Colonial Albany Project had identified almost 16,000 different people as Albany residents through 1800. Since 1981, project members have been collecting and evaluating information from the documentary record of the residents' lives to achieve a research goal of a complete and comparable lifecourse biography for each person who lived in the colonial community.[6]

This research strategy works well for colonial Albany because from its early days, everyday life in the upriver community was participatory. All of the major community activities involved large portions of the city's population. In local government, for example, from the mayor and the city fathers to contractors and licensees, each resident was expected to take part—to make a contribution. Records were created to document each person's participation—and much of this information has survived—although not always in orthodox ways.[7]

During the project's early days, we sought to establish a starting point or benchmark for the study of the Albany community. A baseline date would facilitate the identification of issues, and then comparisons of conditions and developments in the city at different points in time. We were challenged to find the earliest historical document that encompassed the Albany community by accounting for all those living in the city at a particular historical moment.

After evaluating each of the extant surveys, the census of householders in Albany County taken in June 1697 was selected as the base historical document. The enumeration named the principal personage or head of the house, described the household in terms of men, women and children, and also provided some information on ethnicity.[8]

A social profile of Albany at that time has been enhanced by two detailed maps made of the community by the English; by more than a dozen supporting survey documents including assessment rolls, lists of subscribers, supporters and members; by a complete set of city government minutes, payment accounts, real property, court and probate records; and by the archives of the Albany Dutch Reformed Church—which counted more than 80 percent of the city's householders as members.[9]

Except for the English soldiers garrisoning Fort Albany (which overlooked the community), the Native American fur traders who sometimes lived in the huts that were falling into disrepair beyond the western wall of the stockade (but who never were considered members of the community), slaves (who constituted a significant minority group) and unattached transients, the census of 1697 appears to have accounted for most of the regular residents of the Albany community.

Aside from the aforementioned categoric exclusions, Governor Benjamin Fletcher, who ordered the census, could expect that the total of 714 individuals approximated the number of people living in the city. Most conspicuous on the census are the names of mayor Dirck Wesselse Ten Broeck and recorder Jan Janse Bleecker, both of whom had lived in the community for many decades and who stood out as the patriarchs of large Albany families. Next in prominence were the city homes of treasurer Johannes Becker, Jr., high constable Anthony Bries and marshall James Parker. Found throughout the list were the households of each of the six city aldermen, six assistants, three constables, three firemasters and three assessors. All but two of these 26 community leaders were drawn from the established families of the community. Most of them had been born in the Albany area and were linked by birth, marriage and interest to a large portion of the overall community. The participatory nature of local government in colonial Albany is underscored by the fact that the households of these city officials also accounted for almost a fifth of the city's population—giving one out of every five Albany households a direct voice in their municipal government.

By the end of the seventeenth century, colonial Albany had been a family-based community for many decades. By 1697, the children of the children of the original settlers of the Dutch town of Beverwyck (Albany's ancestor) were beginning to have children of their own. In that census year, more than two-thirds of Albany's 174 households included children. This prevalence of family-style living made the single and unattached the exceptions. Eleven homes were shared by newlyweds; three housed childless couples of childrearing age; another six sheltered older couples who had been born before 1650. While more than 100 different surnames appeared on the census, eight families were particularly well-established in the city and accounted for over 25 percent of the households. Without exception, the founders of each of these clans first came to the upper Hudson during the New Netherland era.

The descendants of Philip and David Schuyler were the most numerous. In 1697, nine Schuyler-named households stood out as prominent landmarks on Albany's best streets. Because the city Schuylers totalled 38 people (or about five percent of the community total), any discussion of family life in colonial Albany rightfully begins with them. In 1697, the Schuyler matriarch was European-born Margarita Van Slichtenhorst, the 69-year old daughter of a Rensselaerswyck director, mother of ten, and widow of Philip Pieterse Schuyler—a carpenter turned fur trader, landlord and founder of Albany's first family. In 1697, Margarita Schuyler was the most fortunate of Albany's 19 widows as she was settled in a comfortable home on the south side near the *Stadt Huys* or city hall. These days, she less frequently stayed at the family farm located a few miles upriver on the "Schuyler Flats." However, Margarita was able to draw on the farm's resources and derived additional income from another city house up the hill near the English fort.

At the northern end of Albany's water-level boulevard was Catharina Verplanck, the daughter of a New Amsterdam family, who had married the younger Schuyler emigré in 1657. Like her sister-in-law, widow Catharina was alone in her north side home while four of her sons prospered in the city. A third Schuyler widow, Alida, a younger Van Slichtenhorst daughter, had married the eldest son of David and Catharina Schuyler. Widowed early, she was left to raise seven children in a modest first ward house.

All of these Schuylers were able to build on the legacies left behind by their original settler-ancestors. After the three prominent Schuyler widows, six Albany-born sons of the first Schuylers stood out on the census as Albanians of the first rank. Pieter Schuyler, first mayor of the city, judge, diplomat, soldier, landowner and member of the governor's council, was Albany's best-known native son. Although his career reached far beyond the city limits, in 1697 his south side home near the Ruttenkill bridge was an Albany landmark that still buzzed with the business of government, commerce and the church. Pieter Schuyler's younger brother, Johannes, who had married the widow Elizabeth Staats Wendell in 1695, headed Albany's largest household of 11 children when the new family came together in the Schuyler house at the corner of State and Pearl streets. An alderman in 1697, Johannes Schuyler was a successful trader and landholder who would become mayor of Albany in 1703. David and Myndert Schuyler, younger sons of David Pieterse, both lived on State Street where they also engaged in trade (buying and shipping farm and forest products), administered their inheritance acreage, and waited for their turns at community leadership positions. In both cases, this included the city mayoralty.

An extraordinary four of the six Schuyler sons living in the city in 1697 had or would be recognized as Albany's businessman of the year—the criterion a royal governor used most often for selecting the city's mayor. The remaining Schuyler householders, Jacobus and Abraham—also sons of David and Catharina—were merchant/shippers who maintained separate residences near the home of their mother. The Schuylers were exceptional in that the legacies of their Dutch forebears enabled so many descendants (nine households identified on the census) to prosper in the emerging regional opportunity center of Albany. Each of these city Schuylers was able to parlay his father's achievements in the fur trade, commerce and landholding into a substantial fortune that not only made theirs the leading Albany family in 1697 but provided a foundation for wealth and community leadership for years to come.[10]

Their unparalled stature enabled the Schuylers to enhance the family fortune through marriage. Both Schuyler men and women consistently married members of the best Albany and regionally prominent families. In 1697, two of the daughters of the first Schuylers were included on the census as wives of established Albany businessmen—Robert Livingston and

Willem Claese Groesbeck. The value and significance of the Schuyler presence in these households cannot be underestimated. For example, Philip Pieterse Schuyler's daughter, Alida, was the widow (and heir) of Dominie Nicholas Van Rensselaer and the wife of Robert Livingston—whose new kinship connections helped him become Albany's wealthiest entrepreneur. Alida Schuyler often acted as the head of the State Street household and also of an extensive regional estate, as Livingston was absent more often than not. Much of her enterprise was intertwined with that of her brothers and cousins, the Schuylers.[11]

Second to the Schuylers in community prominence were the offspring of Evert Janse Wendell whose six buildings housed 24 city residents. Evert Janse, a one-time Friesian cooper, had lived in the community for more than four decades. Once active in church and civic affairs, in 1697 he was in his 90th year. Three of his sons resided in Albany, two of whom were merchant/traders—the other a simple shoemaker. The then deceased eldest son, Johannes, had been one of the first aldermen in 1686 and was appointed mayor by Jacob Leisler in 1690. In 1695, Johannes Wendell's widow, the above-mentioned Elsie Staats, married Johannes Schuyler. With her ten Wendell children, she joined the Schuylers in their State Street townhouse. These and the other children of Evert Janse's children would make their marks in the commercial centers of Albany, New York, New Jersey and Boston in the years to come.[12]

In terms of community prominence and prevalence, the Schuylers and Wendells stood out as Albany's elite families. However, several other New Netherland-era emigrés must be considered just behind them in a comprehensive survey of the colonial city's leadership. The Ten Broecks, Bleeckers and Hansens represented a significant portion of Albany's wealth and influence. Their prominence was based on the maturation of each founder's economic success in the upper Hudson region over the preceding half-century.

Mayor Dirck Wesselse Ten Broeck, the son of a West India Company soldier, used his facility with native American languages to become a leading trader on the Beverwyck fur market. At the same time, Dirck Wesselse was among those who understood that fur trading prosperity would be short-lived. During the first three decades of English rule, he diversified his activities and was able to follow his patron and mentor, Robert Livingston, into extensive land holdings, including an estate south of Kinderhook. Unlike Livingston—who, despite his marriage and often-demonstrated community spirit, was perceived as an English placeman—Dirck Wesselse was both elected and appointed to important leadership positions. By 1697, he had held office on the city, county and provincial levels. By the end of the century, his 11 children had intermarried with the better families of the region, although most of them chose more rural locations. His eldest son, Wessel—a baker and sometime trader—was the only member of the third generation of the Ten Broeck family to be named on the census. Like his father, Wessel Ten Broeck was active in community affairs and would be elected an alderman that fall. Several of Ten Broeck's descendants would be accorded Albany's highest status, the mayoralty, in the future.[13]

Recorder or deputy mayor Jan Janse Bleecker arrived in New Netherland during the 1650s. He too was one of Albany's first city officials, having been named alderman and treasurer in 1686. Before his death in 1732, Jan Janse would hold every political office—although that career would not peak for another decade. This one-time cobbler was able to parlay success in the fur trade into landholdings that included several lots within the city of Albany. In 1697, he was still an active trader, but he could rely more on his real estate holdings for consistent income. At that time, only the oldest of his 11 children was established in the community. Soon, however, the other sons would spread out in the city as the Bleeckers maintained their privileged position, successful in landholding and commerce. Members of this family were fixtures on North Pearl Street for the next century.[14]

Living in the family home near the north end of Market Street was alderman Hendrick Hansen. This 37-year-old son of a just-deceased New Netherland fur trader had inherited most of Hans Hendrickse's holdings. By 1697, he too was prospering after making the transition from the fur trade to commodities export and the management of the family's country real estate. This pillar of the community would be named mayor of Albany in 1698. His European-born mother, Eva De Meyer, had lived most of her life in the Hudson Valley. In 1697, "Effie Hanse" and one servant were identified on the census and occupied a more modest house next door to her other son, the merchant Johannes Hansen, also near the north wall of the city stockade.[15]

Wealth, civic responsibility and a prominent presence in

multiple households distinguished the Schuylers, Wendells, Ten Broecks, Bleeckers and Hansens from most early Albany families. However, other regionally prominent New Netherland-era families were represented on the census of 1697 by only one household. These families less frequently achieved leadership status and should be regarded as special cases. Thirty-year-old Hendrick Van Rensselaer was a first ward alderman, proprietor of what would become the Claverack Manor, and a future member of the provincial assembly. His aldermanic seat was in recognition of overall family stature. Yet the exclusively real property basis of the Van Rensselaer fortune made it difficult for them to assert any leadership in city business or government. Albert Ryckman, the son of an original settler, was the city's most successful brewer and a perennial alderman representing the third ward. The three grown sons living with him in 1697 soon would establish themselves in Albany trades. In 1702, Albert Janse's long service was recognized when the governor apointed him mayor of Albany. However, no other brewer or tradesman would be so honored.[16]

Other wealthy, prominent, yet not prolific New Netherland-era Albanians whose families were represented by only one household in 1697 included treasurer Johannes Becker, Jr.; Pieter Van Brugh, an overseas merchant and three-term mayor whose marriage to Sara Cuyler produced no male heirs; Johannes Appel, a former treasurer and sheriff who also owned land in New York and Schenectady; Johannes Teller, the only remaining member of a once-large fur trading family; Pieter Bogardus, a longtime Albany resident who spent his last years in Kingston; and Marte Crieger, Maes Cornelise Van Buren and Willem Van Allen—all of whom relocated to country farms with the "Peace of Ryswick" in 1697. The families of each of these sons of New Netherland settlers disappeared from Albany rolls with their deaths.[17]

After the above-named, exceptional Dutch-ancestry families who were able to reach or momentarily touch (like Albert Janse Ryckman) the community's economic summit, came the body of city residents who were able to remain solvent in the Albany economy after the decline of the fur trade by establishing themselves in a trade or needed service activity. The census of 1697 identifies more than a hundred of these Dutch-ancestry householders who were able to pass on at least a part of their legacy to succeeding generations. By the end of the seventeenth century, those who achieved everything but great wealth and leadership status were emerging in the preurban community as members of a "middle class."

Almost as well established demographically—yet prominent in ways substantially different from the Schuylers and Wendells—were the Bradts, Rosebooms and Visschers. Together accounting for 70 individuals (about one-tenth of the city's total), these three families provide outstanding examples of more typical Albany households, as their crafts, trades and service orientations made them the backbone of an evolving community economy. Like most Albany family groups, the Bradts, Rosebooms and Visschers retained some involvement in the Indian trade—although only Ariaantie Visscher, the widow of Harmanus Wendell, her brother Johannes Visscher, Johannes Bradt and Hendrick Roseboom, Jr. could be called primarily fur traders. Instead, each of these city-based families was beginning to exhibit an area or areas of special interest and skill that would have been less likely choices during the heyday of the fur trade.

Ariaantie Visscher Wendell and Johannes Visscher were among the children of Harmen Bastiaense, a Dutch emigré who had spent much of the past 50 years as an Albany carpenter. By 1697, Harmen Bastiaense had died, and his widow, Hester Dircks, lived on in the family home near the Dutch Reformed Church. Five of their sons and a daughter were counted as heads of families within the city stockade. These American-born adults had found success in resource processing and service activities and would be known in years to come by the name "Visscher." Although Ariaantie and Johannes still clung to the fading Indian trade, the other Visscher children had abandoned the quest for furs and instead made sawmilling, brewing and shipping their major enterprises. While other formerly successful Dutch fur trading families were forced out of the Albany community by competition and market conditions, the Visschers flourished by embracing more logistically feasible and readily marketable activities.[18]

The four Roseboom sons named on the census spread out from Hendrick Janse's trading house at the north gate and adapted their business activities from a native American to a colonial clientele. The Bradt family moved from shady fur trading practices and suspect loyalties to the building trades, transportation and positions of trust in local government and the Dutch Reformed Church. These New Netherland-era families represented successful variations on the adaptation theme. Incidentally, in 1697, Hendrick Janse Roseboom, the New Netherland emigré, still lived in his landmark trading house at the end of Pearl Street, but he had long ceased to be an important trader. And Barent Bradt, who made the trip to America with his parents on the *Rensselaerswyck* in 1637, still was living just outside the north gate. By 1697, Bradt's four sons and a nephew, Wouter Vanderzee, had established themselves within the city stockade and were involved in successful business and service careers.[19]

The Lansings best exemplified the Dutch-era emigrés who made a broadly based impression on the character of the community. The family matriarch, Elizabeth Hendricks, came to New Netherland with her husband, Gerrit Lansing, about 1640. By the late 1670s, widowed and the mother of seven surviving children, she was remarried to Wouter Albertse Vandenuythof, an Albany baker. By 1697, she was deceased; however, three of her sons, a grandson and Wouter Albertse were identified as heads of Albany households living on the north side of the city. Son Gerrit had married Wouter Albertse's daughter, begun baking and was a major competitor for municipal and military business. Jan, still a fur trader, was a city alderman who was able to acquire additional acreage in the region. Hendrick Lansing, a butcher, also owned another tract outside the city. Abraham, the youngest, had just set up his home near the north wall. The three Lansing daughters had married Albany residents, but only Hilletie, the widow of Willem Ketelhuyn, was alive in 1697.

Each of these Lansing households offered a service needed by the people of the growing region. Their children built on their fathers' practical career choices, intermarried with most other Albany families, and consequently became the largest and most solidly established family in eighteenth century Albany.[20]

Many of the remaining Dutch-ancestry families with more than one household identified on the census of 1697 resembled the Lansings in their community experience. Few of these rank-and-file city residents achieved great wealth, and only the exceptions would be elevated to leadership positions. Although these Dutch-ancestry householders had settled into lives that would remain substantially stable for another half-century, others were unable to continue city traditions with their offspring. Some original emigrés, like the carpenter Claes Ripse who would live into the eighteenth century in the comfort of his Pearl Street home, watched his children achieve great prominence elsewhere, as did his son, Rip Van Dam, a New York City merchant and acting governor. And the family name disappeared from Albany annals when Claes Ripse's daughter married Hendrick Hansen. Paulus Martense Van Benthuysen, a wheelwright and long-time city resident, saw his three sons leave Albany and become farmers. Leendert Philipse Conyn, a master tailor, had also lived in the community since the 1650s. His death in 1704 left no descendants in the city.[21]

The New Netherland families that flourished in the colony's second city were able to find life in Albany after the decline of the fur trade. The key to their sustenance was the flexibility to adapt to service—whether it was in a trade or craft, transportation, processing operations (tanning and milling), preparation of building supplies (sawing and brickbaking), or filling in as contractors of the city government, the Indian commissioners, or at the fort. The Ketelhuyns, Marselises, Van Nesses, Groesbecks, Van Iverens and Van Deusens—each with three or more name-identified households in the city[22]—and the De Foreests, Fondas, Gansevoorts, Outhouts, Quackenbushes, Slingerlands, Teunises, Vanderpoels, Vanderheydens, Van Hoesens, Van Schaicks, Winnes, Witbecks and Wyngaerts—with one or two named-households each[23]—had survived the transition on these terms. However, generally speaking, these New Netherland-era families tended to move into the countryside as farmland became available during the eighteenth century.

Having accounted for about three-fourths of the 175 heads of city households in 1697 by identifying them as New Netherland-era settlers and their descendants, two groups of residents have not been mentioned. These merit special consideration. First, 15 heads of families were either singled out on the census or clearly can be connected to non-Dutch origins. These English, Scot, Irish, French and Spanish ancestry householders established themselves in the community after 1664. Several of the non-Dutch first settlers, including William Hogan, Joseph Yates, Thomas Williams, Pierre Villeroy (de Garmo), Joseph Janse Van Zandt and Robert Livingston, founded permanent city families.[24]

The remaining ten households might have been considered with one of the groups discussed earlier. However, each of these families is exceptional. Godfredius Dellius, the Dutch Reformed minister for the past decade, was a pillar of the Albany community. Although John Miller served as the Anglican chaplain at the fort, Dellius was the only full-time cleric to serve a diverse Christian population. In 1697, many Albany people belonged to Dellius's congregation, and most residents of the greater region received either spiritual or social services from the Dutch church located in the middle of the community's principal intersection.

The Reformed Church, however, did not represent an ideal situation for many of the New Netherland-background families who were not of Dutch ancestry. Members of the La Grange, Van Zandt, Hallenbeck, Witbeck, Pruyn, Evertse, and even the Gansevoort and Winne families, in addition to most of the British background householders, often were uncomfortable with Reformed liturgy and sometimes felt alienated from the church-centered business and social life enjoyed by the majority of their still Dutch-speaking neighbors. By the end of the century, the Lutheran and Catholic householders either became active members of the principal church (like the Bradts, Douws, Gansevoorts and Pruyns) or moved out of Albany and into the countryside. English speakers (who married local women) either accommodated language and cultural barriers or endured spiritual frustration until the establishment of St. Peter's Anglican Church almost two decades later.[25]

The more newly arrived but of New Netherland stock, however, found life in Albany somewhat more hospitable. Barent and Hendrick Ten Eyck were identified on the census of 1697 as sharing a home on the hill in the second ward. These determined young men were beginning careers in a traditional Albany activity, the Indian trade. However, that enterprise had become increasingly more labor-intensive, and most Albany men sought less arduous career paths. Thus, the Ten Eyck brothers were able to gain a foothold in a commercial activity that had been jealously guarded only a few years before. Living next door was their widowed mother, Geertruy Coeymans, the daughter of a Rensselaerswyck family who had married a shoemaker from New York City two decades earlier. Her third son, Coenradt, had been sent to New York to learn the silver trade. He would return home to enjoy a half-century of success and prominence as Albany's leading silversmith.

The father of these opportunists, Jacob Ten Eyck, was one of several Dutch-ancestry opportunists who had relocated to Albany after 1664. Chiefly because of demographics and the preemption of the best opportunities by the community's entrenched families, these post-New Netherland Dutch emigrés would not challenge either the Schuylers and Wendells for leadership, or the Visschers and Lansings in the community's traditional trades. Instead, they sought new opportunities and to fit in. Three decades later, the Ten Eycks had been joined by the Cuylers and Beekmans in establishing a small but solid presence in the city's business and service industries. These newcomers had joined the Dutch community's mainstream, as established Albany families across class lines found these Calvinists to be suitable spouses for their children.[26]

Jacob Staats and Hendrick Van Dyck, Albany's physicians in 1697, were sons of New Netherland-era surgeons who headed small but vital family groups. In the years to come, the Van Dycks, in particular, were distinguished as surgeons in Schenectady and Kinderhook as well as in Albany where a "Dr. Van Dyck" was a constant on city rolls.[27]

A final point concerns the flexible nature of life on the northern frontier. Several contemporary observers noted that King William's War had caused a population decline in New York's frontier region. However, that ebb may have been more of an adjustment as some settlers did move—although often not very far. Ryer Jacobse Schermerhorn and his brother, Cornelis, both had been prominent residents of the village of Schenectady. Ryer had already served two terms in the provincial assembly and later would return to Schenectady where his real estate ambitions provoked great controversy. Cornelis moved out to Livingston Manor after 1720. In 1697, these two survivors of the Schenectady Massacre of 1690 were listed in adjoining houselots in Albany's second ward. Many of the 22 city households with more than one adult male were swelled with refugees from Schenectady and other outlying areas.[28]

The census of 1697, which included all these families, has provided a rationale for studying the socioeconomic composition of the city of Albany. A set of historical records closely connected to the status of the community as a chartered city has enabled contemporary historians to understand significant features of their lives. This survey of the city's population in 1697 has demonstrated great continuity between old and new and has shown that most of these Albany people traced their family roots to New Netherland days before 1664.

In 1697, a number of New Netherland-era emigrés were still living in the city of Albany. However, all but the youngest of these were quite old and had matured beyond an active involvement in business or community activities. For the most part, the people of colonial Albany in 1697 were the American-born children of these original settlers, and their children as well.

Many of their American-born offspring became established in New York and New Jersey communities, of which colonial Albany provides a well-documented example. Those who prospered did not forget the culture of their forebears and retained many Dutch legacies for generations to come. However, those who succeeded were able to adapt their Dutch heritage to new challenges and opportunities. In the process, they and their families became American.

2

The Evolution of a Family Business

The Livingstons of Colonial New York

Cynthia A. Kierner

The Livingstons of New York were among the most notable of America's early entrepreneurial families.[1] The colonial Livingstons were merchants and landlords, shipowners and shopkeepers. They were among the leading millers in New York, and they owned and operated the colony's most productive ironworks. The Livingstons were also land speculators and land developers. By the eve of the Revolution, their collective holdings totaled more than a million acres, including the family manor in the Hudson River Valley.[2]

During the colonial era, the development of the Livingstons' family business mirrored the evolution of New York's economy and society. The example of the Livingston family suggests that the two most significant changes occurring in colonial businesses were the growth and diversification of a family's enterprises and the progressive decline of female involvement. These two changes were interrelated. Prosperity and economic growth brought colonial entrepreneurs financial security which, in turn, enabled them to develop a new "high style" culture that included ornamental wives and daughters.[3] This cultural transformation brought about changes in education; colonial elites encouraged both sons and daughters to pursue genteel accomplishments, in addition to their more practical occupations. But once their education was completed, eighteenth century women increasingly abstained from the ungenteel world of business, while their husbands, sons and brothers continued to work to expand their family's enterprises.

The Livingstons' family business had originated in a partnership formed in 1679 when Alida Schuyler of Albany married Robert Livingston, a recent immigrant of Scottish extraction. A member of Albany's most influential family, Alida gave Robert the connections he needed to become a person of consequence in the colony. Her brothers became his trading partners and political allies; Alida herself became his most trusted business manager and adviser. By 1686, Livingston had persuaded Governor Thomas Dongan to grant him 160,000 acres in the Hudson River Valley.[4] This land became known as the Manor of Livingston, and it eventually became the cornerstone of the Livingston family business.

In building up his entrepreneurial concerns, Robert Livingston relied heavily upon Alida's services as merchant, business agent and estate manager. Robert also left the family business in Alida's hands during his own frequent absences—testimony as to the high regard he had for his wife's business judgment. Livingston traveled twice to England and spent a total of more than five years there trying to collect government debts owed him. Even when he was not abroad, he spent an average of three to four months each year in New York City, attending to his political and business interests. In 1698 and 1717—both very busy years for him politically—Robert spent nine and eight months, respectively, in the provincial capital, leaving Alida to supervise their business interests at the Manor and in Albany County.[5]

During most of their 45-year partnership, Robert and Alida shared the responsibilities entailed in running a growing family business. While Robert normally attended to their import and export interests in Manhattan, Alida handled their northern enterprises. She routinely shipped furs and surplus flour, bread and lumber to Robert downriver in New York City; he returned the family sloop to her laden with textiles, sugars and other imported goods, which she then distributed to their stores at Albany and the Manor. Alida also supervised the milling of grain and baking of bread at Livingston Manor. While Robert's political influence had brought them military provisioning contracts, it was Alida who filled these contracts by overseeing both the production and distribution of foodstuffs and other merchandise.[6]

Alida's position in the Livingston family business was both permanent and ongoing; she was more than a "deputy husband" who filled in for her spouse by doing "man's work" under unusual or extraordinary circumstances.[7] But Alida was the only Livingston woman who played an integral role in the family's entrepreneurial activities. While she shared with Robert the responsibilities of managing their growing commercial and industrial concerns, her daughters and granddaughters were, at most, marginal figures in the family's business enterprises. Alida taught her own daughters, Margaret and Joanna, the skills they needed to be competent deputy husbands. Each of Robert and Alida's four sons at some time served as their parents' commercial agent, but their sisters learned only the most basic business skills, so that they could engage in trade if the interests of their family required it.

Surviving letters do indicate that both Livingston daughters were thoroughly acquainted with their husbands' affairs. Margaret, the elder sister, actually began trading on her own during the frequent absences of her husband, Colonel Samuel Vetch, and she continued trading intermittently after Vetch's death in 1732. Margaret's family and business associates neither condemned nor applauded her commercial activities; as a widow with young children, she was merely filling in for a permanently absent husband and father.[8] Moreover, the Livingston men seemed to consider their wives and sisters both capable and knowledgeable, despite their limited business experience. For instance, Robert and Alida's son Philip respected the judgment of his wife, Catrina Van Brugh, whose advice was instrumental in persuading him to erect an iron forge at the Manor in the 1740s. "I am doing all I can to Satisfy your good mother about the building of this forge," wrote Philip to his eldest son, "and [I] am perswaded you will do any reasonable act to Satisfy her [as well]."[9]

The decline of female entrepreneurship in the Livingston family was symptomatic of a gradual drift toward more rigidly defined sex roles throughout colonial America. In New York, however, this trend was compounded and reinforced by the imposition of English law after the conquest of New Netherland in 1664. While Roman-Dutch law had allowed married women to sue and be sued in court, to own property and engage in business with complete autonomy, English common law deprived wives of these fundamental legal rights. Under the common law doctrine of coverture, when a woman married she forfeited her legal identity, which was subsumed under that of her husband.[10] In New York, however, legal change did not always cause social change: decades after 1664, Robert routinely consigned cargoes to Alida and she continued to act as his attorney and to provision local troops, even if Robert's signature was required on the actual contract. Still, the strictures of coverture, if enforced, did force women merchants to rely on their husbands and sons in certain instances, thus legitimizing and reinforcing the trend toward limiting women's involvement in the affairs of the business community.[11]

In the Livingston family, as in many other colonial families, demographic development and family structure were still more important than legal strictures and social customs in determining the scope of women's economic activities. By European standards, early colonial society was relatively fluid and underdeveloped. Consequently, during the early colonial period, women's entrepreneurial activities were less a strident defiance of the common law than a way of adapting to unusual social conditions. Seventeenth century Chesapeake women shared their husbands' business responsibilities because kin of either gender were scarce in this demographically unstable region. Later, growing kinship networks replete with male relatives undermined women's economic importance, as sons and brothers replaced wives and daughters in the family-run plantation economy.[12] Likewise, Robert and Alida shared the management of their family's business interests, but their son Philip shared his commercial responsibilities not with his wife, but with his sons and brothers.

By setting up storehouses at the Manor, New York and Albany, by investing in ships and building mills, and by seeking tenants to cultivate the family land, Robert and Alida Livingston laid the foundations for a family business that would grow to magnificent proportions in future generations. Their son, Philip, inherited his parents' entrepreneurial talents and ambitions. Under his aggressive leadership, the second and third generations of Livingstons improved and expanded the family business begun by Robert and Alida. The parents had built mills and engaged German refugees as tenants to begin developing their landed estate; Philip added more mills, and he and his son Robert recruited tenants from Scotland and the German states in order to increase their trade by augmenting their land's productivity.[13]

Philip expected all six of his sons to take their places in the family commercial network. As both a father and prospective employer, he took a keen interest in his sons' commercial education and used his considerable personal influence to secure them apprenticeships in prestigious trading establishments. He personally trained his first and fourth sons—Robert and Philip, respectively—for the Albany trade, using his influence to get the elder son passes to trade in Canada and the younger son clerical posts in Albany's local government.[14] Two other sons, John and Peter Van Brugh Livingston, went to London and apprenticed in the office of Samuel Storke, Philip's longtime trading partner. Peter later moved on to Jamaica to learn the sugar business and became, for a time, his father's West Indian agent.[15] Philip's fifth son, Henry, studied French at New Rochelle and served a commercial apprenticeship in Boston; he also toured Europe, presumably to cultivate business connections. Of Philip's six sons, only William did not become a merchant. After a disastrous apprenticeship in his father's store, William became a student in the office of James Alexander, New York's most prominent lawyer.[16]

Although all of his sons except Henry settled in New York City, Philip probably had envisioned a far-flung commercial network with his sons acting as his agents and trading partners throughout Europe and America. Philip had educated his sons to play specialized roles in his growing business in order to make his trade more self-sufficient and systematic. Albany, New York, the West Indies, London and Boston were his main commercial outlets, and Philip had trained at least one son to specialize in each of these branches of trade.

Philip also tailored his sons' commercial training to suit New York's changing economy. Although he himself was one of the colony's leading fur traders, he recognized that the fur trade was declining by the time his own sons were coming of age.[17] These changing economic circumstances shaped Philip's plans for his sons' futures. Only Robert, the eldest, had been trained extensively in the fur trading business; he had completed his education by 1727, before the outlook for the Albany fur traders became so dismal.

Philip had long been involved in the grain trade; but by the late 1730s, wheat and grain products accounted for the bulk of his export business. Since New York's growing population was producing more grain than ever before, exporting foodstuffs became a lucrative business for the colony's merchants—particularly for those who, like Philip Livingston, owned tenanted estates in prime grain-producing regions. Moreover, the grain trade's potential for growth seemed limitless since grain, unlike furs, was not among the articles enumerated by the Navigation Acts for export to England exclusively.

Concentrating upon the grain trade enabled Philip to experiment with new trade routes, take advantage of his landed estate, and compensate for the decline of his trade in furs. During the middle decades of the eighteenth century, Philip and his sons diversified their business by experimenting with new markets that introduced different commodities to their trade. For instance, Philip's extensive trade with the West Indies led to his involvement in the African slave trade. In the 1730s and 1740s, he was one of New York's leading importers of slave labor from the sugar islands, and he was also one of few New Yorkers who imported slaves directly from Africa before the abolition of the Spanish Asiento in 1748. In 1738, Philip bought a one-third share in a voyage to Guinea, where two hundred slaves were purchased and consigned to his son Peter Van Brugh Livingston and his partner in Jamaica. After 1748, New York's direct trade with Africa grew significantly. Philip and his sons continued to be among the colony's leading traders with that continent.[18]

The Livingstons also expanded their trade into new markets in Europe and America. By the 1740s, southern Europe and the Wine Islands were increasingly important markets for colonial grain exports. Philip and his sons used the English contacts they had made during their fur trading days to exploit Europe's demand for American foodstuffs. For instance, Samuel Storke of London informed them when the Iberian grain crops failed; they were therefore able to tap that market ahead of their competitors. On such occasions, the Livingstons either shipped their grain directly to Spain or Portugal, or they sent it to Storke who forwarded it to his agents in Gibraltar, Barcelona and Cadiz.[19]

Like many other colonial merchants, Philip Livingston and his sons also expanded their coastal trade, and they used this growing trade with the mainland colonies to complement their European commercial interests. For instance, in 1741 Philip sent bread and flour to Newfoundland. There, his cargo was exchanged for fish, which was later traded for wine in Madeira. Philip sold his wines locally, or he re-exported them elsewhere. In 1740, he shipped grain and wine to South Carolina to be traded for rice, which he, in turn, exported to Amsterdam.[20]

Each of Philip's sons at some time acted as his agent, supplier or business representative, but the two oldest—Robert and Peter Van Brugh—were involved most extensively in their father's commercial enterprises. Beginning in 1734, the Livingston brothers handled the Manhattan end of their father's business, in addition to pursuing their own independent trade. Meanwhile, Philip attended to the family's northern interests, just as his mother Alida had done a generation earlier. He supplied the produce for his sons to export and sold imported goods at his stores in Albany, Schenectady and the Manor.[21]

Robert and Peter disposed of their father's grain, lumber and furs, and they shipped West Indian sugar products and English manufactures back to him in Albany. Typically, they traded foodstuffs for sugar and coin or bills of exchange, which they then used toward purchasing English goods that would be marketed in New York or Albany County. Peter left for Jamaica in 1736 and for several years acted as agent at Kingston.[22] Robert, who remained in New York City, corresponded regularly both with his father and with Samuel Storke in London. After the dissolution of their partnership in the late 1730s, Robert and Peter continued to act separately as their father's New York agents, shipping his grain and flour to the West Indies and Europe.

Under Philip's leadership, the Livingston family business thus grew and prospered. The family's trade also became more diverse, penetrating new markets and embracing new commodities. Philip also expanded the family's shipping interests and the Manor's milling facilities. But most importantly, in the early 1740s, Philip built New York's first permanent ironworks at Ancram on Livingston Manor.

By the middle decades of the eighteenth century, many colonial merchant-entrepreneurs were diversifying their businesses by developing industrial sidelines to complement their trading interests.[23] Few, however, were as ambitious as the ironworks at Livingston Manor. In 1741, Philip estimated the cost of building and stocking his Ancram ironworks at more than £6000, New England currency. Nevertheless, he believed that "the Iron Manufactory is the most advantagious business if well managd" and that success in that industry would enable him to spend most of his remaining years at the Manor, where he would "Enjoy [his] Brook . . . & lay up an Everlasting treasure" to ensure his family's financial future. Consequently, Philip erected one blast furnace in 1743 and one forge two years later; his son Robert added at least two more forges, both located at the Manor.[24]

The ironworks quickly became an integral part of the Livingstons' family business. In the 1750s, the Ancram furnace turned out nearly 500 tons of pig iron each year, making it New York's most productive iron-making facility. During this period, the Manor forge refined 1,302 tons of pig iron into bars and converted 65 tons to other castings. The Livingstons cleared a profit of roughly 80 percent on each ton of pig iron they sold. In the 1760s, Philip's son Robert estimated the weekly profits of the iron-making and milling operations at £100, which, he believed, was "more than any [other] Gentleman in America can this day say."[25]

When Philip died in 1749, Robert inherited both the Manor and his father's position as *de facto* head of the family business. Like his father, he relied heavily upon his kin—first his brothers and later his sons—to run the Manhattan end of his trade. As Robert admitted to his brother Peter in 1751, "I am out of the way of trade and herefore am the more obliged to you."[26] Peter marketed his brother's grain and iron products, much as he and Robert had done earlier for their father. As they came of age, Robert's sons began to replace their uncles as his commercial agents.

We know little about the types of apprenticeships that Robert's sons served, but is clear that the third lord of the Manor did expect his sons to work as merchants or lawyers after they completed their formal college educations. In 1763, for instance, he advised his son Walter to return home from Cambridge because—after four years abroad—"its high time for him to be in away of business." Walter returned to New York the following year and took his position in the family business, acting as his father's commercial agent.[27]

Three generations of Livingstons believed that youth was a time "to prepare for future usefulness" and that a proper education was one that prepared young people to lead "useful" adult lives.[28] Usefulness meant industry, self-reliance and success in one's calling. The callings of the Livingstons and their social peers became more varied and complex over the course of the colonial era. Robert and Alida's children had been called to be merchants and merchants' wives; their grandchildren and great-grandchildren were expected not only to work in such practical occupations, but also to act as gentlemen and ladies, leaders and ornaments of their increasingly stratified and complex society.

The Livingstons and their peers continued to view education

as practical training for future success, but their definition of success became broader as their class began to assume the cultural posture of a provincial aristocracy. While they continued to seek and to value diligence and material success, these eighteenth century New Yorkers also became preoccupied with the aristocratic concept of *noblesse oblige*. They came to see themselves as a distinct governing class and, accordingly, they sent their sons to college to acquire both the knowledge and the public demeanor that would set them apart from their social inferiors. Philip Livingston had sent four of his six sons to Yale because he believed that a liberal education could turn young men into public-spirited community leaders. Comparing New Yorkers unfavorably to New Englanders, he noted that "we have not such a publick Spirit here as you have among you nor ever will unless we have Some of your Education." Philip hoped his sons' business apprenticeships would bring them success in trade; he hoped that their experience at Yale would enable them to become part of a new class of public-spirited gentlemen-leaders.[29]

During the second quarter of the eighteenth century, the education of young men and women also developed an ornamental aspect, a result of the gentrification of Anglo-American elite culture.[30] Changes in the education of young women were more substantial because the roles and functions of colonial women were changing more dramatically. A woman's duties as wife and mother were constant, but her additional responsibilities changed over time. The education of young women evolved to accomodate these changes. Once men began delegating their business responsibilities exclusively to male relatives, women's public duties became primarily social, not economic. By mid-century, hospitality and sociability were particularly desirable female attributes. Because Alida Livingston had supervised her family's growing enterprises at Livingston Manor, she could justifiably scold her husband for sending her unannounced guests. In 1722, when Robert sent an unexpected visitor to Alida at the Manor, she sought lodging for her guest elsewhere and carried on with her business. Such a reaction would have been unthinkable for later generations of Livingston women, who were not overwhelmed with business responsibilities. By the Revolutionary era, grace and gentility had become the American gentlewoman's most admirable qualities. In 1778, Henry Beekman Livingston rejoiced in the marriage of his cousin, Robert Cambridge Livingston, to Alice Swift because the bride was "an amiable young Lady who will be an ornament to our Neighborhood."[31]

By the middle of the eighteenth century, the education of the daughters of the elite was diversifying in order to prepare them to fulfill new social responsibilities. Although the Livingston daughters continued to learn reading, writing and traditional domestic skills, their parents now deemed lessons in French, music and dancing equally useful. Some parents regarded their daughters' education as an especially important matter. Philip Livingston made a provision in his will for educating his unmarried daughters, Alida and Catharine, aged 21 and 16, respectively, when he died in 1749. Robert Livingston sent his youngest daughter, Alida, to spend a winter with a married sister in New York City, where he expected her to "improve" herself and "not Spend her time Idlely." Robert's granddaughter was sent by her parents to Philadelphia in 1781 because "she wanted this opportunity of polite Company to give her the Accomplishments which tho' inferior to those of the Mind are essential to her Rank."[32]

Young gentlemen also came to value ornamental learning during the closing decades of the colonial era. Formerly the bastions of studious ministerial candidates, colonial universities became finishing schools for the sons of the provincial gentry during the eighteenth century. The third lord of Livingston Manor wanted all of his sons to attend college and required that their childhood tutor have not only a liberal education, but also "Something of the Gentleman in his Behavior." New Yorkers established King's College in 1746 partly in response to the gentry's desire to give their sons fashionable university educations.[33]

Economic growth and diversification had underwritten the development of this new high style culture that enjoined both men and women to be genteel, while widening the cultural gulf between the sexes and their ideal roles and functions. Changes in the education of young men show how late colonial elites sought to combine gentility with entrepreneurship. Contemporaneous changes in women's education reinforced a growing trend toward sex-specific work and set a precedent for separating the genteel sphere of womankind from men's ungenteel and competitive business world.

The development of the Livingstons' family business thus illustrates some of the dominant trends in early American social history. Economic growth and diversification had resulted in increased social stratification, as merchant-entrepreneurs like the Livingstons emerged as the main beneficiaries of nearly a century of Anglo-American prosperity. Financially secure entrenched elites, in turn, embraced a new class-specific genteel culture that denoted their new sense of social superiority. High style culture relegated women to the kitchen and the drawing room, thus reinforcing the demographic developments that had hastened their departure from the counting house. The Livingston family story also shows the increasing rigidity of sex roles in provincial America, at least within the ranks of the colonial elite. In the nineteenth century, these tendencies would crystallize into an ideology of separate spheres that would become an integral part of the social ethic of middle-class America.

3

Inheritance Patterns among the Chesapeake Gentry

The Case of Colonial Baltimore County, Maryland

Charles G. Steffen

When the descendants of the colonial Chesapeake gentry set out to reconstruct their lineages after the Civil War, they conjured up the image of a golden age of rolling plantations, dutiful bond servants and easy gentility. It seemed that the men who ruled this society came from long-established families, some of whom could trace their ancestry to English Cavaliers. While Thomas Wertenbaker exploded the Cavalier connection many years ago, scholars continue to accept the notion of intergenerational continuity among the gentry.[1] Bernard Bailyn and others have made a powerful case that sometime around the turn of the seventeenth century the leading gentry families of the Chesapeake coalesced into a stable economic elite that preserved their preeminent position until the Revolution, and probably beyond.[2] Like father, like son—this is the essence of what we might call the *continuity interpretation* of the Chesapeake gentry.

The continuity interpretation rests in part on the gentry's inheritance strategies. A man composing his will walked a narrow line between two competing priorities. First, he wanted to ensure that at least one of his heirs received a large enough bequest to keep his family name at the pinnacle of society, and the obvious way to do this was to leave the lion's share of the estate to the eldest son as a trustee for future generations. But for a variety of reasons, primogeniture was risky. If the favored son turned out to be a spendthrift or a fool, he could easily squander his patrimony and undo the careful planning of his father. Worse, the son could die unexpectedly and without a will, an ever present possibility in the colonial Chesapeake. Then the estate would become mired in the probate courts where impatient creditors, dubious kinsmen and a long line of fee collectors threatened to ravage a lifetime of work.

The competing consideration arose from the natural affection men felt for their wives and children, an affection that sometimes found expression in the principle of partibility, in which the estate was divided among many heirs. No man relished the idea of condemning his younger children or widow to a life of penury, even to ensure the perpetuation of the family fortune. The expectation that sons and daughters should marry within their own social class often required fathers to make substantial dower payments to their daughters either at the time of the wedding or afterward, which reduced the portion available to the eldest son. And besides, it was only prudent to spread property among several heirs in the hopes that at least one would make something of himself. In short, the prospect of dying forced rich men to make a difficult choice between primogeniture and partibility.

What did they do? In his recent study, *Tobacco and Slaves,* Alan Kulikoff speculates that families in Prince George's County, Maryland, who practiced partible inheritance had a difficult time hanging on to their gentry standing because their children received moderate-size estates that could not support the appropriate lifestyle.[3] Since most gentry families in Prince George's kept their status generation after generation, Kulikoff's analysis suggests that some form of primogeniture prevailed at the highest level of society. Yet what little direct evidence we have points to partible inheritance as the dominant pattern among the gentry. In an analysis of wills in Albemarle County, Virginia, Daniel Blake Smith states that 63 percent of testators who died during the second half of the eighteenth century bequeathed land to all of their sons. The figure was probably higher for the gentry, since they had more land to give. Smith sums it up this way: "While fathers may have occasionally given slightly larger, more valuable parcels of land to one son—usually the eldest—the central tendency was to provide for all sons as equally as possible."[4] In short, the gentry of Albemarle County practiced inheritance strategies that seemed to undermine intergenerational continuity.

What we know about the internal dynamics of the gentry family also points toward partible inheritance. Smith argues that the eighteenth century witnessed a dramatic alteration in family relations among the gentry, centered on an intensified emotional intimacy within the household. As the terrible mortality rates of the early period declined, it became possible for parents and children to develop stronger bonds of affection. Pursuing an inheritance strategy that favored one child over another—that is to say, one son over another—threatened the basic tenets of this newly emerging domestic pattern.

Jan Lewis takes issue with Smith's emphasis on affection as the dominant motif of family life, but she reaches similar conclusions with respect to inheritance.[5] In *The Pursuit of Happiness,* Lewis contends that gentry families strove to preserve domestic tranquility inside their homes by restraining emotional excess and by observing a code of formality that kept family members from getting too close. The relations between parents and children resembled a business contract; each party agreed to fulfill certain obligations, usually material in nature. Sons expected parents to fulfill parental responsibilities by providing them with a bequest, just as parents expected financial support from their children in their old age. A father who gave everything to one son not only reneged on his part of the contract with his other sons; he jeopardized the domestic peace that the gentry were intent on maintaining. Thus, whether we view Smith's affection or Lewis's tranquility as the bedrock of family life, these studies suggest that the gentry had developed a set of values that favored partible inheritance over any form of primogeniture.

In this paper, I examine inheritance patterns among the gentry of colonial Baltimore County, Maryland. I conclude that gentry on the northern frontier of Chesapeake society adopted the principle of partibility, fully aware that the result would be a fragmentation of the paternal estate. A word like egalitarian seems strangely out of place in the colonial Chesapeake, but it fits a pattern of inheritance that threatened to transform a rich man's children into middling planters and erase the family name from the ranks of the gentry. Whatever the underlying causes of partible inheritance, it amounted to a radical redistribution of wealth for each generation and drastically reduced the chance that sons would inherit the economic standing of their fathers. In a sense, men of wealth sacrificed their class interests to secure economic security for their children.

But just who were the gentry? The one thing a gentleman had to have was wealth. Fortunately, the information on wealth-holding in the colonial Chesapeake is immense. The Maryland probate courts kept careful records of estate inventories, listing every bit of personal property people owned at their deaths, right down to the last six-penny nail. The chief problem in using the inventories is the omission of land. Some historians have attempted to estimate the value of landholdings, but with limited success. We often do not know exactly how much land a person owned, and we rarely know what improvements had been made to the property. The omission of land from the inventories is a drawback but not a fatal one, for the people who owned the most personal property also owned the most real property.

In this study, I have defined the gentry as those individuals who owned the largest personal estates at their deaths. Identifying these people involved four separate steps:

1. I calculated the estate value for every decedent who died in Baltimore between 1660 and 1776 and whose inventory was recorded in the county court.[6]

2. I did the same for all Baltimore residents whose inventory appeared in the provincial but not in the county court.[7]

3. I adjusted the estate value for price inflation with a deflator generously provided by Lois Green Carr and Lorena Walsh of the St. Mary's City Commission.

4. I selected the richest ten percent of decedents for the period before 1690 and for each succeeding decade until 1776.

The result was 1,810 Baltimore County inventories for the entire colonial period, yielding a total of 180 individuals whom I have labeled gentry. Drawing the cutoff point at ten percent is admittedly arbitrary. Although very few historians have been willing to venture an estimate on the number of gentry families in any one county at any one time, no one has suggested that they comprised over ten percent of the population. My estimate might well err on the liberal side and include some men who hovered around upper-middling status or who fell outside the privileged circle altogether. But closing the door at five percent or two percent would mean running the risk of excluding some who clearly moved among the county's leading families. All in all, ten percent strikes me as a reasonable figure. Of the 180 gentry, 114 left wills in the probate courts.[8] What follows is an analysis of those wills.

An analysis of inheritance must begin with demography because the size and composition of families made certain strategies impossible and others inevitable. The data assembled from wills indicates that mortality rates were declining in eighteenth century Baltimore, certainly for children and probably for adults, with the result that stable nuclear units eclipsed the assortment of relatives and acquaintances that had made up earlier households.[9] One piece of evidence is the increase in the number of children mentioned in the wills. The 32 gentry who died between 1676 and 1720 listed a total of 73 children, or 2.3 per testator. This figure suddenly jumped to 5.7 in the 1720s and never dropped below 3.2 in any decade before the Revolution. During the entire period 1720–1776, 376 children appeared in 82 wills, an average of 4.6 per testator, twice the level of the earlier years.

A second indication of falling mortality rates is the relative number of testators who died with mature children. Before 1720, 43 percent of testators (ten of 23) with offspring whose ages can be identified had at least one child who was either married, over the age of twenty, or named as executor of the estate. The 1720s again represented a demographic watershed, for six of seven gentry wills recorded in that decade referred to mature children. Between 1720 and 1776, 74 percent of the wills (39 of 53) contained references to adult children, and in only one decade during that period did testators with minors outnumber those with older sons and daughters.

Thus as the eighteenth century unfolded, more and more gentry fathers sought to balance the competing demands of their wives, sons and daughters for a share of the estate. They usually owned enough to whet the appetite of every potential heir, but the most coveted prize was the "dwelling plantation." Just what did this term mean? Sometimes it was used to refer only to the main house itself and the furnishings inside; for most testators, however, the dwelling plantation consisted of the house and outbuildings, together with the adjoining fields, meadows and timber reserves that comprised a part of the total landed estate. In nine wills that described the land attached to the dwelling plantation, the acreage ranged from 150 to 600, and averaged 361. It was possible to identify the recipient of the dwelling plantation in 88 of the 114 wills. The following analysis focuses on 70 wills in which testators were married and had at least one child, since in these cases we can see how they balanced the claims of rival heirs within their own families.

The most general answer to the question of who got the dwelling plantation should come as no surprise—the children did. In 66 cases, a son or daughter received the plantation; in the other four, a grandchild was the lucky one. Nor is it any wonder that sons did better than daughters. Throughout the colonial period, sons kept a steady grip on the dwelling plantation—and even tightened it. Before 1720, 63 percent (12 of 19) of the testators gave the plantation to their sons, while during the next 56 years, the proportion increased to 86 percent (44 of 51). Yet the assumption that sons should succeed to the plantation upon their fathers' deaths was even stronger than these figures suggest, for eight of the ten daughters who inherited had no brothers. In other words, daughters got the plantation only when there was no son available, and sometimes not even then.

But even when a father decided to bequeath the plantation to a son, he usually had several from which to choose. Only 23 of the testators could ignore the problem altogether because they had only one son or all daughters. While the eldest son would seem the predictable choice, most fathers did the unpredictable and attempted to treat their sons evenhandedly. Indeed, 12 testators found the notion of setting one son above another so troubling that they bequeathed the plantation to two or more sons as joint owners. And in 14 of the remaining wills where the ages of the male heirs could be identified, younger sons received the plantation nine times and eldest sons only five. Despite the deepest cultural traditions proclaiming the preeminence of the first-born, gentry fathers seemed determined to launch each of their sons with an equal stake.

Yet the wills tell only part of the story. Long before a father considered making a final testament, he might lay out a plantation for his son. Sometimes these gifts were formally recorded in the court together with any special stipulations, but more often the exchange occurred little by little as the son steadily assumed more responsibilities around the plantation. It is impossible to determine how many sons received such gifts, but the frequent allusions to them in the wills suggest that the practice was common. Twenty of 42 testators who could be identified as having at least one adult child indicated that one or more of their sons had already received their portion. And the actual number was undoubtedly greater. Testators might fail to mention earlier gifts, creating the impression that a son had been dispossessed, or they might use their wills to confirm gifts that had already been in the son's possession for years.

These inheritance patterns suggest that the intergenerational tensions scholars have uncovered in the New England colonies had no counterpart among the Baltimore gentry. By the early eighteenth century, many older settlements in New England and elsewhere were facing land shortages that seriously threatened the prospects of young people on the threshold of adult life. As farms shrank to less than 100 acres, fathers could no longer afford to establish all of their sons on land carved from the family's holdings.[10] The result was that young men in their early twenties had no choice but to continue working on the farm under their parents' watchful eyes, all the while postponing the day they would marry, start a family, and join the ranks of freeholders. In these circumstances, fathers had the kind of patriarchal authority the Old Testament said they ought to have; and the unwillingness of many fathers to relinquish control over the land, even when they were too old to work it, kept their children in a state of economic dependency. Gentry sons in Baltimore would not have understood the predicament facing these Yankee boys, for their fathers encouraged them—or perhaps *pushed* them—to stand up on their own.

The dwelling plantation was the main prize but not the only one. Beyond the immediate vicinity of the home fields stretched additional acres cutting across parishes and even spilling over county lines. The largest estates were like a microcosm of the local economy: roughhewn farms producing corn and tobacco, outlying quarters containing a few cleared fields, forest tracts awaiting ax and hoe. There was much here to entice a hopeful heir. To inherit a farm or quarter transformed a young man's prospects overnight and spared him years of backbreaking labor. For an expectant heir dreaming of the day he would become a full-fledged planter, the land outside the dwelling plantation was the ticket to independence and respectability.

Fathers faced a familiar dilemma. Should they keep their sprawling estates largely intact by leaving everything to one or two heirs, or should they break up their holdings and distribute the pieces more widely? Most chose the second course. Above all else, elite testators wanted their children to settle in the shadows of the home plantation, raising their own offspring on land encrusted in family tradition. Tearing a once proud estate into pieces must have disheartened many testators composing their final testament, but they willingly paid the price to keep their children—especially their sons—nearby. During the entire colonial period, 97 percent of sons mentioned in the wills (203 of 209) received a landed bequest or had been endowed with land sometime earlier. And at least one of the six landless sons was either physically or mentally incapacitated, forcing the father to leave his entire estate to a younger son on the condition that he care for his needy brother. Another son who did not receive land was William Buchanan, the youngest child of Dr. George Buchanan, who directed his wife to "provide for him as to make him equal in fortune with the rest of my Children."[11] To father and son alike, land was an unquestioned birthright.

Daughters did not automatically inherit, as did their brothers, but they too claimed a large share of the landed estate. Testators could have turned their daughters away with a simple cash payment, a family heirloom or a slave, since it was common practice for females to inherit personal property exclusively. Yet 45 percent of the daughters (89 of 196) received land at their fathers' deaths or sometime earlier. A daughter who was an only child or who had only sisters could count on land as a virtual certainty, and even married women had a one in three chance of getting land, though they had probably received some form of dower payment on their wedding day.

What kind of land did daughters receive, and how much? Did daughters get sizable tracts or just a few scraps of the land that remained after their brothers had hauled in the choice pickings? Since testators never mentioned land values in their wills and rarely described improvements on their property, the question of the quality of land is beyond our reach. However, the occasional references the wills make to the size of tracts leave little doubt that male heirs obtained more than their sisters. Judging from five wills that specified the acerage of the landed legacies, female heirs received one-half to two-thirds less than males. It would be a mistake, however, to assume that daughters were saddled with a few stone-filled acres that no one else wanted. On the contrary, in these five wills daughters received an average of 414 acres—a handsome bequest by any standard.

Not all daughters were given land, but they all got something. Nearly 90 percent of the 107 daughters who did not obtain a landed legacy received personal property of some type, and of the 12 who went away with nothing or only a few shillings to buy a mourning ring, 11 were married women whose portion could have been awarded years earlier. Nor did a bequest of land exclude a daughter from receiving additional personal property. All but two of the daughters who were given land also inherited cash or moveables, usually a share of what remained of the estate after the legacies and debts had been paid off. Testators did not list the value of their bequests, so it impossible to measure quantitatively how daughters did compared to sons. Yet what indirect evidence can be extracted from the wills shows that daughters did remarkably well in the face of the most stubborn social and legal traditions consigning them to subordinate status.

Their mothers also did remarkably well. The law guaranteed that no widow would go away empty-handed, entitling her to one-third of the estate's personal property outright and one-third of the real property during her lifetime. Nothing prevented a man from giving his widow more, and most did. Of the 83 widows with children, two-thirds received property in excess of their dower rights. The prospect of having to pack up her belongings and find another place to live must have frightened every wife, and most husbands did what they could to smooth the transition to widowhood. Twenty-nine widows were guaranteed the right to occupy the dwelling plantation during their lifetime, and another 13 could remain there until they remarried or until the principal heir became an adult.

Another area in which widows fared well was as executors of their husbands' estates. A testator might insert into his will a thousand contingency provisions and last-minute codicils, but the fact remained that the document was only as good as the executor named to enforce it. An executor had to combine sound judgment and good faith, so that the spirit of the will would prevail even when unforseen circumstances arose. It was a solemn trust, and to fill it, most men looked no farther than their wives. The widow was appointed as sole executor by seven of 12 men who died without children, and by 35 of 83 with children. Although the relative number of sole executors declined after 1720, it would be wrong to infer that the status of widows was slipping. The eighteenth century witnessed a decline in mortality rates, leading to an increase in the number of mature sons old enough to administer the estate. Not surprisingly, fathers shifted more and more responsibility onto the shoulders of their adult sons, but even when the first-born son was named as executor, he usually shared the responsibilities with his mother. Testators with children made their widows sole or coexecutors in 70 percent of the wills before 1720 and in

65 percent afterward; the absence of any significant change suggests that wives continued to play a key role in estate management.

There is an egalitarian theme that continually surfaces from the wills; this reached a culmination of sorts in the independence struggle. Only four testators who had wives and children divided their estates evenly among all their sons and daughters, and all of them died in the decade preceding 1776. The first was David McCulloch, who in 1766 ordered his executors to liquidate his entire estate within seven years, including two lots in Joppa Town where his "dwelling House" was located.[12] The proceeds from the sale were then to be divided equally among his wife, son and two daughters. McCulloch added that if his wife was pregnant at the time of his death and gave birth afterward, then this child, too, could claim a share.

By the 1770s, this type of will was becoming commonplace. Of the nine wills recorded between 1770 and 1776, three called for a measure of equality in the distribution of legacies among heirs. Like McCulloch, William Cockey directed that his house in Baltimore Town be sold for the payment of debts, while the residue of his land was to go to his wife, son and daughter.[13] Barnet Haltzinger also ordered his executors to sell everything and pay each of his children L200, except for a married daughter who received only L20 because she had presumably received her portion earlier.[14] Samuel Owings did not go quite this far, but he too provided that upon the remarriage of his widow, his dwelling plantation was to be divided evenly among his five sons and four daughters.[15] What motives lay behind these bequests? Perhaps we catch a glimpse of shifting values in the will of Roger Boyce, who four years before independence asked his executors to avoid any "ostentation" at his funeral and to "have the good sense and discernment to prefer the American new way of mourning."[16] By dealing with his own heirs on a basis of equality, this proponent of the republican ideology demonstrated his beliefs through his own actions.

As has been noted, a gentry father did not have to wait until he died before giving his children land. He could do it earlier, either informally through a private understanding or in a deed of gift registered at the county court.[17] The deeds of gift in the land records probably represent only a fraction of what fathers actually gave to their children, but they illuminate a number of key questions: What kind of property was given? Who received it? And what stipulations, if any, did fathers attach to their gifts?

These deeds offer one more bit of evidence that elite fathers attempted to produce independent sons who, from a relatively early age, could assume the rights and responsibilities of manhood.

During the entire colonial period, about one in five members of the gentry recorded deeds of gift at the court. Not surprisingly, the seventeenth century witnessed very few instances of gift-giving, probably because parents died at an early age before their children needed a stake to launch their careers. But with the general drop in mortality rates during the eighteenth century, more and more mature sons had to have land to start plantations, while their sisters required dowries to attract suitable husbands. Thus while only 11 percent of the gentry who died before 1700 recorded a deed of gift, the figure rose to 19 percent for the period 1700 to 1729 and peaked at 26 percent between 1730 and 1759. Then the trend broke off, with gift-giving falling to 15 percent between 1760 and 1776. One possible explanation of the reversal was the movement away from dowry payments, a change that historians have associated with the rise of the nuclear family and individual autonomy on both sides of the Atlantic.[18] While the elite made a total of eight gifts to their sons-in-law exclusively or to their sons-in-law and daughters jointly, none of these dower payments came after 1760.

Gentry fathers, it seems, were free to reward whomever they pleased, but in fact their largesse rarely extended beyond the circle of immediate family members. Not surprisingly, sons fared better than everyone else. Of the 65 deeds of gift recorded before 1776, 36 went to sons. Three sons received what every young man hoped for, a fully developed plantation or a combination of land and slaves. In 1749, for example, Dr. George Buchanan gave his son Lloyd a plantation together with livestock, tools, plows and 50 barrels of Indian corn to keep his animals alive. A plantation without fieldhands would soon go to ruin, so George included a slave family of one man, one woman and two boys who could bring in a harvest of about 5,000 pounds of tobacco per year and provide a source of future workers. The plantation had at least one barn, for George said he intended to keep the tobacco hanging in it. Although the tract itself contained only 150 acres, Lloyd undoubtedly knew that it was part of a larger estate that his father planned to give him. When George died a year after making the gift, he left a will bequeathing Lloyd an additional 579 acres, two slaves and one lot in Baltimore Town. And at his mother's death in 1758, this lucky son acquired possession of the main dwelling plantation that his father had built decades before.[19]

Even if most gentry sons did not amass the possessions of Lloyd Buchanan, they fared well enough. Twenty-two sons received land without the capital to develop it, but they could probably have borrowed tools and laborers from their fathers, who usually lived a short distance away. For ordinary planters, even a few dozen acres would have been a windfall, but gentry sons needed much more to maintain the social position they had inherited. Their fathers did not disappoint them. In 21 of the 25 deeds where sons received land, we know how many acres changed hands. The mean gift equalled 505 acres, while half of the sons received more than 300 acres. That these gifts were considerable is suggested by the fact that 19 of the gentry sons' land holdings were enough to put them in the top half of the county's landholders.[20] Whether they could make it to the very top depended on careful management of their property, prudent investment of their money and a bit of luck—but certainly gentry fathers had pointed their sons in the right direction. The size of these gifts remained stable at about 300 acres throughout the colonial period, more than enough for a self-supporting plantation. Landed gifts averaged 277 acres before 1709, and 272 between 1710 and 1759. Although the figure jumped to an average of 963 acres between 1760 and 1776, the increase resulted from two huge gifts of over 2,000 acres each. Putting aside these exceptional cases, the average dropped to 270 acres and fell in line with the earlier period.

Daughters were not entirely left out of the gifts, but they did not enjoy the generosity shown to the sons. Only ten daughters got something from their parents, and what they received did not match their brothers' gifts. Only three of ten got land, compared to two-thirds of the sons. These landed gifts averaged an impressive 507 acres, equivalent to what sons received, but it does not follow that the seven daughters who only received slaves or slaves and chattel considered their gifts second-rate. A young woman looking to get married stood a much better chance of finding a husband if she could add a few hands to his workforce. Indeed, if he lived at the other end of the county or outside Baltimore altogether, a distant tract of land under the supervision of unchecked overseers might seem more trouble than it was worth. Slaves had a distinct advantage over land—they were movable. Some of the gifts to daughters were outright dower payments. Gentry fathers who made presents to their sons-in-law or to their sons-in-law and wives jointly did so in order to enhance their daughters' marriage prospects. Yet while finding his daughter a suitable husband weighed heavily on a father's mind, he did not want to pay more than he had to. Of the five sons-in-law who received gifts, three were given land in the county and one in Baltimore Town. The average size of the rural tracts was only 149 acres, less than a third of what gentry sons or daughters received. Likewise, in the three cases where gentry fathers gave land jointly to their son-in-law and daughter, the gift averaged only 157 acres.

No one gave more or bigger gifts than Charles Ridgely, Sr. It would be wrong to present this powerful man as typical of the gentry—the scale of his operations dwarfed nearly everyone else's—but his story reveals how determined wealthy fathers were to make their children economically independent. In 1721, at the age of 18, Ridgely married Rachel Howard, and together the couple raised a family of two sons and three daughters. By the late 1740s, he had amassed an estate of around 7,000 acres and began distributing parts of it in deeds of gift to his children. The first gift went to his eldest son John, then in his mid-twenties. John's gift included 260 acres on the Patapsco River and the family plantation Charles had spent two decades building. The deed stipulated that at John's death, the plantation would descend to his son Charles. This grant was just a portent of things to come, for 22 years later Charles added between 2,000 and 3,000 acres to John's estate.[21]

Next came his recently married daughter Achsah, who in 1753 received almost 1,000 acres scattered between the Patapsco and Gunpowder. That same year, Charles gave 300 acres to his second daughter Pleasance, on the condition that it go to her daughter Elizabeth Goodwin at her death; another gift of over 600 acres would pass to her other daughter Rachel Llyde Goodwin when Pleasance and her husband died. Pleasance also had a son, William Goodwin, who in 1770 received 260 acres from his grandfather. By 1760, Ridgely's second son, Charles, Jr., was 27 years old and took possession of 2,000 acres on the upper reaches of the Gunpowder. Only one child remained, the youngest daughter Rachel, and in 1767 she and her husband received 433 acres on the condition that it go to their son William Lux at their deaths. While we cannot know the innermost thoughts of Charles Ridgely, this land-hungry gentleman seems to have been driven by a desire to surround himself with children and grandchildren securely established on their own estates. By his death in 1772, he had given away 6,000 to 7,000 acres to five children and five grandchildren.[22]

Clearly, the inheritance strategies pursued by all members of the gentry played a large role in determining whether sons and daughters would keep their places at the top of society once they struck out on their own, or lose those positions to others. If fathers had chosen primogeniture, they would have increased the chances of keeping at least one member of the family in the ranks of the gentry. Yet, as we have seen, they did not choose this path. Partible inheritance distributed the wealth of the gentry among many children, and while it reduced the likelihood that any one of them would slip too far down the social ladder, it also made it more difficult for the children to match the economic achievements of their fathers. Although the subject falls outside the scope of this paper, my investigation suggests that most of these children, indeed, became what might be best described as middling or upper-middling planters.

4

The Lynches of South Carolina

Traditional Elite and the New Family History

Virginia G. Crane

The Lynch family of South Carolina resembled most other colonial elite families in that they were a home-grown aristocracy, beginning with an immigrant of modest middle-class resources and moving upward by the third generation to wealth, status and public prominence. Thomas Lynch, Jr. (1749–1779) signed the Declaration of Independence, and his father Thomas Lynch, Sr. (1727–1776) was a leader of the Continental Congress. For those reasons, the Lynches, in the third quarter of the eighteenth century, became part of that constellation of first families of Carolina revered for their participation in the hallowed patriot enterprise.

Southern elite families have been rather fully treated in traditional genealogies and patriotic "great man" histories. They have, as well, been analyzed by modern scholars who have focused on the ideology and political and economic roles of the patriarchs of that order, on the femme covert status and the role and values of the matriarchs, and on the world made by the slaves of the planter class. If those same patricians and their servants are viewed through the prism of the new family history, a different portrait emerges of a private world of individuals bound by kinship, proximity and identity who, over time, shaped and were shaped by the public world of money, power and institutions.

Recent New England, Chesapeake and general studies have used historical demography, career line analysis, prosopography, community and life cycle analysis, cliometrics, statistical genealogy, aggregate analysis and modernization theory; these provide some models that can be applied with benefit to all colonies and to the upper class as well as to nonliterate or immigrant populations. A family history approach to communities with slim extant literary sources has revealed much about neglected segments of society.[1] The Lynches invite that kind of treatment because, despite their status and the public prominence of two of their members, comparatively few original Lynch materials survive, as they have been lost through the accidents of time.[2] Thus, unlike other families of the Carolina elite, the Lynches have not been exhaustively studied.

Family history in recent years has become a "sophisticated, technical and downright arcane area of research";[3] but it is still accessible enough to afford the student of an elite family like the Lynches (a family without a rich literary record) techniques for delineating the structure and function of the family; its power distribution and roles; cohesion and continuity; inheritance patterns; image, identity and external relations; as well as its household size and composition, fertility/mortality rates, and some of the family's other quantitative boundaries.

The South Carolina branch of the Lynch family began just seven years after the colony was established. Jonah Lynch and his wife Margaret Johnson, with their two young sons, Johnson and Thomas, migrated as a family with two servants from Galway, Ireland. They arrived in South Carolina in April 1677. Two years later, Jonah began to acquire land on the east branch of Cooper River and there, at a place called Wattesaw, he established the first Lynch plantation in Carolina and renamed it The Blessing. He soon established a reputation as an "ingenious" planter, producing barley for malt. He acquired the utensils and equipment for making English beer and ale and became a brewer for profit. Jonah and Margaret Lynch no doubt suffered the trauma of uprooting and transplanting that migrants to America experienced, but they started their life in the new world with some capital, a near guarantee of upward mobility in the seventeenth century. They became Carolinians, and Jonah served his community as a captain of the provincial militia. He had apparently learned a lesson in the old world about the importance of keeping a family estate intact, and when he died he followed the practice of primogeniture and left his property to his older son Johnson. Johnson had no surviving male heirs, so the family name was continued by the second son, Thomas.[4]

Men without inherited property had few problems acquiring a personal estate in early eighteenth century Carolina, and when Thomas Lynch (1675–c.1738) came of age, he began to acquire land and established a plantation in Christ Church Parish. He also worked as a courier in the Indian trade to Charles Town and was active in provincial and parish politics and government, serving as justice of the peace, commissioner of the high roads, and as captain and later colonel of militia. He was also a member of the Proprietary Commons House of Assembly, and in that body he became involved in the struggle against the Lords Proprietors that ended with South Carolina becoming a royal province in 1719. A decade after that, he was elected to the Third Royal Assembly but did not serve, refusing to take the state oaths required of assembly members because swearing on the "Holy Evangelists" was against his conscience.

When Lynch was 45 years old and the colony was celebrating a half century of existence, he changed the direction of his career toward specialization in rice planting. Beginning in 1718 and continuing through the South Carolina land boom of the 1730s, he acquired 15,000 acres of choice tidal marshes and swamplands on North and South Santee River in Craven County. His interest in the Santee flowed from his pioneering experiments in transferring rice cultivation from inland swamps to tidal river marshes, and the Santee River was eminently suited to that new method of production. Lynch bought slaves, eventually acquiring about 183, and with their labor built seven productive rice plantations on his vast holdings. Among the plantations, three became prominent in family history: Peachtree, Hopsewee and Fairfield. On a high bluff overlooking the Santee delta at Fairfield, he built a six-room, two-story clapboard house. Weeping willows and mock orange, live oak and Spanish moss, and the luxuriant green of spring rice complemented the simple lines of the Fairfield residence. The West African slaves on the plantation performed hoe and stoop labor in the snake-infested waters of the fields, and their productivity relieved the Lynch family from manual labor, shielded them from having to develop a Puritan-like work ethic, and poured treasure into the family coffers.

Colonel Lynch had two wives and eight children. When he was over 30, he married Margaret Fenwick; they had a daughter Margaret, born about 1710. The first wife died young, and

Lynch chose Sabina Vanderhorst (1696?–1778?) as his second wife. The bride was about 16 and the groom was 37. The couple had two boys who died early, but the third son, Thomas, survived to adulthood. There were also four daughters—Mary, Sabina, Sarah and Elizabeth. By the act of naming, Colonel Thomas of the second generation thus honored his parents Jonah and Margaret, the first generation immigrants. He honored himself, the founder of the family fortune, and insured his own immortality by giving his name to the son who survived and became famous.

Thomas Lynch I died about 1738 at age 63, a score of years beyond the average mid-eighteenth century lifespan of 45 years. He left no will, suggesting a sudden and unexpected death. His wife Sabina apparently lived on for another 40 years and died at age 82, a remarkable longevity record for an eighteenth century southern woman who had experienced at least seven live births and possibly more. Despite those two records of physical endurance, the second Lynch generation in America—like the first—produced only one son who survived to adulthood, married and produced one surviving son.[5]

Thomas Lynch II* (1727–1776) was born when his father was 52 years old. The child was 11 when his father died. That was the usual age of transition from childhood dependence on maternal care to a new era of paternal training and education. Thomas did receive an education, and he and his sisters apparently continued to live with their mother Sabina at the Fairfield plantation. When he came of age, Thomas, as the favored male child and his father's namesake, apparently received the bulk of the Lynch property.

He came to maturity in the 1740s just as South Carolina was "brought to the Brink of Ruin" by King George's War. The war and an overproduction of rice brought on a depression that caused a 70 percent drop in rice prices between 1741 and 1746. Young Lynch must have cast about for alternative ways to make a profit during the rice depression, and he found them in the mercantile business, in the production of indigo and in land speculation. Between 1748 and 1774, he received land grants that totaled over 11,000 acres. Much of this land was in Prince George Winyah and St. James Santee parishes adjoining his

---

* Thomas Lynch II is the same individual referred to as Thomas Lynch, Sr. earlier. (See page 41.)

inherited rice empire in Craven County. Other parcels, though, were scattered throughout South Carolina, Georgia and East Florida.

In 1745, Thomas Lynch married money. Elizabeth H. Allston, a rice heiress, became his bride when she was 17 and the groom was a year older. They lived at Hopsewee plantation on the Santee across from Thomas's widowed mother's home at Fairfield. Between 1747 and 1749, Thomas and Elizabeth had three children. Sabina, the oldest, was named for her paternal grandmother at Fairfield, and her younger sister was called Esther. The first son in this generation was named Thomas for his father and grandfather. Birth spacing close together—three children in three years—was unusual for the time and suggests that Elizabeth may have used a slave wet nurse for her babies, thereby losing lactation as a birth control technique. The early pregnancies were perhaps too much for the adolescent bride, and she died while her three offspring were still quite young. In 1755, her 28-year-old widowed husband took as his second wife 19-year-old Hannah Motte. Hannah was one of 21 children of a wealthy Huguenot merchant-banker in Charles Town. The following year, she had a baby and the child was named Elizabeth Motte Lynch. Hannah had only this one child though she outlived her husband and married again—a fertility record that was unusually low for a white woman of her time.

This third generation of the Lynch family lived at Hopsewee plantation until 1762 when Thomas sold that place and moved the family across the river to Peachtree plantation on Lynches Island, South Santee. In 1762, Thomas, at age 35, was one of the richest planter-merchants in South Carolina. As a visible display of that vast wealth, he added an architectural jewel to the economic gold of Peachtree. He had an ornate manor house built there and furnished it with the costly objects that befitted a noble family—albeit an American one without title.

Peachtree was located a few miles from the plantations of other rice lords, and it was near the old coastal community of Georgetown where Lynch had a number of connections. He served there as justice of the peace and as a commissioner to regulate the pilotage and to supervise the building of a jail and courthouse. He was a founder and first president (1755–1757) of the Winyah Indigo Society, a club incorporated by area planters for the purpose of increasing the production of indigo. The Lynches and Mottes were Anglicans, a socioreligious identification expected of the low country elite, and Thomas Lynch was a builder of two churches on the Santee. Despite this local public service and modest institution building in the neighborhood, Lynch and the Santee elite were not "buttressed by institutions." Rather, they were a "self-created and self-disciplined" rural gentry who lived by their own code of individualism, peer group taboos and prescriptions.

The Lynches and other Carolina families like them were not isolated in their rural kingdoms; they lived half their lives in Charles Town, their second home. Thomas Lynch, in keeping with his place in low country society, had his plantation carpenters build him a fine dwelling house there, constructed of black cypress cut from his Santee lands. Its stable was filled with elegant equipages and well-bred horses. Even more than Peachtree, the town residence was elaborately furnished. Well-crafted family plate and linen, marked with the family crest, were all about the place to ornament, to announce wealth and to link the self-made Carolina family to an ancient and legendary past. One family tradition has it that the entire profit of the Lynch plantations for a year was invested in silverware and table linen. Damask tablecloths—two of which survived until the Civil War—were custom woven in Ireland for use on "state occasions." They had the Lynch coat of arms in the center, family crest and motto in each corner, a border of Maypop blossoms around the edge, and an overall pattern of shamrock, rose and thistle. Such a tradition suggests that, by the third quarter of the eighteenth century, the third generation of Lynches in America had emerged from the past of immigrant Jonah Lynch's modest entrepreneurial grasping after land and the first Thomas Lynch's acquisitive-productive achievements to a glorious present of lordly wealth, both inherited and made. With that wealth, Thomas Lynch II acquired the decorations, heraldic paraphernalia and conspicuous consumption habits of the late colonial Carolina aristocracy, a group that yearned for identification with the British elite.

Lynch also had mercantile investments and a shipping business in Charles Town and was thus actively involved in the business life of the city. He was a founding member of the Charles Town Library Society and a pew holder at St. Michael's Church—one of the highest status congregations in the city. He was an active competitor and gambler at the racetrack. As in Georgetown, so in Charles Town he involved himself with a gentlemanly modicum of local government obligations, serving as justice of the peace and commissioner for construction of the Exchange and Custom House. He apparently preferred provincial public service to work in local government, however, and set a record for long-term membership in the Commons House of Assembly. For a full generation, 1752–1776, he served in all but one Assembly.

In Revolutionary era politics, Thomas Lynch was one of those planter-patriots who advocated home rule but not natural rights. He served as one of three South Carolina delegates to the 1765 Stamp Act Congress, and during the five years after that was so active in local radical politics that the royal lieutenant governor identified him as a first mover in the "grand machine" of resistance to British policy. On a family summer visit to Boston in 1773 (to escape the heat of Charles Town and the swampy Santee), he met John Adams. Adams found him to be a "hearty friend to America, and her righteous Cause." The following year, South Carolina sent Lynch as one of its delegates to the Continental Congress in Philadelphia, and Hannah and Elizabeth accompanied him to the north.

In that summer of 1774, Thomas looked much older than his 46 years. He was plain; he wore his hair straight and adopted a garb of simple style, cut from the manufacture of American looms. Either patriotism or his own personal taste prevented the wealthy planter from ornamenting himself as he did his table and sideboard. Perhaps he realized that a wardrobe would count for little—what with changes in fashion—whereas silver and damask would last indefinitely.

In the First Continental Congress, Lynch played a prominent role, and the following year he was returned as a South Carolina delegate to the second Congress, which prepared for war. In the second Congress, Lynch was not as much a champion of the radical position against the crown as he had been in 1774, and he opposed a precipitate move toward independence. He was nevertheless a staunch supporter of the Continental army when it was created under the command of George Washington (with whom he had established a "private Friendship"). His ardor for war cooled by early 1776, and he began to cast about for a "mode of application for Peace." He had little time to pursue his course toward conciliation, however, for in March 1776 he suffered a stroke. Partial paralysis and brain damage followed, and three months later, though "greatly recovered," he was still "under the direction of Doctors and Nurses."[6]

Thomas Lynch's only son, Thomas III* (1749–1779), had emerged as a public figure during the years before 1776 and was prepared, by that time, to take his place beside his stricken father in Philadelphia.

As a boy who lost his mother before he was five, young Lynch had been raised by his father and stepmother. He was sent to Georgetown to a school established by the Winyah Indigo Society, and there he demonstrated a "capacity for letters" that led his father to sketch out "schemes of usefulness and distinction" for the promising youth. According to a family tradition, the father's "fondness' and "parental affection" for his only son occupied a "large portion of the interest of his existence," and he decided that the boy should receive more than a provincial education. Thus, at the age of 13, Lynch III was sent to England to attend Eton. There, and later at Cambridge, he received a classical education and developed a passion for literature, especially Shakespeare. In keeping with that literary and scholarly interest, he began to acquire a library suitable for the needs of an educated Carolina gentleman. He made the grand tour and in England had his portrait painted—full-length in academic regalia, holding a book.

Lynch II wanted his heir apparent to return home a "finished man." The most suitable means to that end was the study of law, so he secured admission for his son to the Middle Temple of the Inns of Court. Young Lynch did not complete the legal course there; he became increasingly restive in pre-Revolutionary London and induced his father to release him from his studies and let him come home.

Almost immediately upon his return to South Carolina in 1772, Thomas Lynch III married his childhood sweetheart, "beautiful" Betsy Shubrick, his stepmother's niece. His father gave the newlyweds a plantation and the slaves on it as a gift, and young Lynch soon added to his holdings land, plantations, slaves and profits from the slave trade. With an estate well established that needed little exertion on his own part, Lynch III seemed destined for a life of ease. He was reportedly "addicted to the indulgence of that literary longing, which, when urged to an extreme, degenerated into absolute indolence." He was not inclined toward a life of action, but he soon found himself caught up in the whirl of pre-Revolutionary agitation that characterized South Carolina politics after 1773. He was elected to

* Thomas Lynch III: earlier referred to as Thomas Lynch, Jr. (see page 41).

the South Carolina Provincial Congress and was chosen captain of a provincial military corps. His father, in Philadelphia at the time, disapproved his son's accepting a captaincy in the provincials and urged him to come to Philadelphia to secure a commission for a higher rank. Captain Lynch rejected his father's suggestion and proceeded to throw himself into the task of recruiting troops for his company. A young man of Lynch's urban habits was unaccustomed to the exposure of encampments near malarial swamps, and he suffered an attack of "coastal bilious fever" that eventually "destroyed his constitution." He was still "feeble and emaciated" later that year when he was elected to the Second Provincial Congress.

When the "melancholy tidings" of Thomas Lynch II's stroke reached Charles Town, young Lynch immediately requested a furlough to go to Philadelphia. He received it and was elected a delegate to the Continental Congress to join his father there or to replace him if necessary. By the time Lynch III arrived at Philadelphia, his father's condition had stabilized somewhat, and the elder Lynch remained in the city with his son. He made clear his reservations about independence, but John Adams and others served as a sufficient counterpoise to the senior Lynch's cautious position, and the son moved with the Patriots toward a break with the crown. On July 2, Thomas Lynch, Jr., the second youngest member of the Continental Congress, voted for independence—along with the rest of the South Carolina delegation except his father—and he later signed the Declaration.

In December 1776, the Lynches left Philadelphia for home and got as far as Annapolis before the elder Lynch reacted to the strain of travel. He had a second stroke, died in his son's arms, and was buried in St. Ann's churchyard in Annapolis. He was 49 years old when he died.[7]

In the eighteenth century, a man of princely fortune sought to control his estate and family after death as he had in life, and Thomas Lynch II had used his will for that patriarchal purpose. He left his widow, for her lifetime if she remained unmarried, the use of the family town house with its furnishings, plate, horses and carriages, the use of five slaves, and an annual allowance of 1,600 pounds to be paid quarterly. That was not a generous maintenance considering that Lynch's personal estate was worth nearly 100,000 pounds at the time. He favored his only son and namesake by giving him all the family real estate, including the family's country seat at Peachtree plantation, along with all the horses and carriages, furnishings, plate and arms on all Lynch properties outside Charles Town. The slave property he divided equally among his three daughters and his son. Lynch II also sought in his will to control his heirs' very identity with a proviso that if Lynch III died without a male heir, Peachtree should go to the oldest male child born to the eldest Lynch daughter, Sabina, provided that the heir change his name to Lynch. On that point, Lynch II was explicit. He intended that Peachtree "remain for ever" in his family in the possession of a male whose name was Lynch.

Thomas Lynch III, the new master of Peachtree, had very little time to enjoy his new status as head of the Lynch family. He was ill on his arrival home from Annapolis, suffered from "severe and continued rheumatic fevers," was "deprived" of the use of his limbs, and was "habitually and constantly an invalid" for the "remnant" of his life. He retired to his plantation at age 27 and made his will. In it, he continued his stepmother's annuity until her death or remarriage. He designated his executors as guardians for his son, if he and Betsy should have one, and he instructed them to send the boy to school in England. If he died without issue, his estate, except for Peachtree, should be sold. During her widowhood, his wife would have the use of one-third of the cash from the sale of the field slaves up to a total of 70,000 pounds (later increased in a codical to 150,000 pounds), plus the use of the domestic slaves. She would also get the 20,000 pounds due her by the terms of her marriage settlement. If Betsy died without children, Peachtree would go to Thomas's eldest sister in trust for her renamed son; and at Betsy's death, the remainder of the estate would be divided equally among Thomas's three sisters. The executors were instructed to have the senior Thomas Lynch's body moved from Annapolis after the war to be reinterred in the parish churchyard at Santee with a plain marble monument erected to mark the grave.[8] Lynch III, in this legal instrument, thus followed the example of his father and others of his class in the era of the civil death laws; he denied his wife control over either his property or her children, and he placed an impediment in the way of her remarriage.

Thomas and Betsy had no children, and Sabina's husband died in 1778 leaving her also without children. Thus the future of the Lynch name was in question in 1779 at a time when the master of Peachtree was in precarious health. He decided to travel to the south of France for an extended period of recuperation, and Betsy Lynch, whose "conjugal devotion" had reportedly increased as her husband's health declined, traveled with him. They sailed from Charles Town in December 1779 and were never seen again. They were presumed to have drowned in a wreck at sea.[9]

Thomas's three sisters—Sabina, Esther and Elizabeth—thus inherited the entire Lynch fortune, a goodly sum all told. Esther never married. Elizabeth married twice, the second time to a Revolutionary War veteran, Major James Hamilton of Pennsylvania, by whom she had a son, James, and three daughters—Hannah Motte, Elizabeth Lynch and Harriot. James Hamilton, Jr. grew up to become almost as prominent in South Carolina politics as his maternal ancestors, serving the state in the nineteenth century as legislator, state senator, member of Congress and governor. Elizabeth's elder sister Sabina, whose male heir was conditionally destined to inherit Peachtree, remarried and had six daughters and a son. The young man changed his name to Lynch at his father's death and thereby, through a matrilineal line of descent, inherited Peachtree. The Lynch name died out, however, when the new master of Peachtree's only son died young without a male heir.[10]

Lynch history in South Carolina began as family history. The first generation migrated together as a household—nuclear family and servants—and later Lynches demonstrated that same cohesion. The Lynches, however, established their position in the Carolina aristocracy with money, not with family. They and their order grew powerful from the possession of land and the acquisition of labor. The errand into the wilderness for early Carolinians was not ideological; it was acquisitive, and the immigrant Jonah Lynch began his mission with 880 acres. The second generation acquired 18,100 acres, the third added 11,000 acres more, and the fourth generation inherited most of that and added another 5,000 acres to these holdings. The Lynches claimed sovereignty over a vast domain on the Santee and other rivers. With the exception of Hopsewee plantation, they gave English names to their properties along those waterways, and Lynches River, Lynches Creek, Lynches Island and Lynches Causeway reflected the family's claims to sovereignty in east-central Carolina.

The family fortune was started with initial capital brought over by the immigrant founder and was expanded not only with land grants but also with Indian trade, brewing, shipping, land speculation, and the sale of staple crops and slaves. Elite families supplied capital, innovation and management for colonial enterprise; and aggressive risk-takers like Thomas I and Thomas II expanded their family's fortunes under that system. In his middle years, Thomas I moved into experimental rice production at a new base and profited from his capitalist venture. Thomas II responded to a foreign war and a rice recession with alternative means of making money. Innovative agricultural capitalism and nonplanting enterprise, added to his other resources, soon made him one of the wealthiest members of the Carolina elite.

The family's position in society was established and maintained by the advancement through four generations from making money to enjoying it. The first generation, as immigrants, were uprooted, transplanted and acquisitive. The second experimented, expanded, exploited, built a fortune and a solid house, and entered public service. The third continued those activities, built a splendid house, and added social status, institution building and national reputation. The fourth generation, Thomas III, received wealth and status and would have devoted the energies of his mature years to literature and culture had the Declaration of Independence not intervened to convert him almost accidentally into the most notable public figure in the family's history.

The Lynches, by the third generation, participated in the world beyond the plantation with a self-confident awareness that vertical mobility was no longer possible for their family because they were already at the top of their social order. Thus, advancement could only be measured by comparison with earlier generations and by the movement of a son into a new realm of quality leisure enriched by learning and culture.

Like other elite families, the Lynches were comfortable in their society but were also set apart from it. The family circle was closed and protective. It served, along with its social class, to insulate its members from problems—except sickness and death—and to provide them with resources for adaptation and advancement.

In their political and governmental roles, the Lynches shared with the eighteenth century southern patriciate a medieval concept that power was rooted in the land and that economic status carried with it political power and responsibility. The Lynches evolved into a political force in South Carolina over three generations. The founder of the clan served as a captain of the militia; his son was a colonel and served with the militia in Queen Anne's War; his great-grandson was a captain and served in the Revolutionary era provincial army. Both Thomas I and Thomas II held office as justices of the peace and as commissioners in local government, and they served in the provincial Assembly. With that body, each rebelled against executive authority—proprietary or royal. Thomas II and Thomas III served in the Revolutionary Provincial Congress and in the Continental Congress. The "great events" of war and politics in the eighteenth century impinged on the Lynch family by depressing prices in the 1740s, by drawing Lynches into contact with Patriots after 1774, and by exposing Thomas III to a disease from which he never recovered.

In early society, the family satisfied a broad range of instrumental needs for production, education, worship, medical care and welfare. It provided access to government and society, to status and marriage. The family's functions brought its members into contact with the larger world outside the kinship circle and dictated their external relations. As has been shown, the Lynch family in the eighteenth century was quite clearly an economic unit of production, and it also achieved status in society and prominence in politics and government. Religion, however, appears not to have been a significant family function for the Lynches. Thomas I refused an Assembly seat because of religious scruples, but the daily life and behavior of later Lynches was apparently not infused with religious proscriptions or prescriptions. Furthermore, the absence of religious principle created no moral crisis for family members. Ritualistic Anglicanism was satisfactory and placed no obstacles in the way of owning and trading in slaves, gambling or indulging in an orgy of materialism. The Anglican way and the code of the gentry allowed pleasure without guilt. That code often lapsed, for some, into toleration of dissipation, but the available record suggests no severe family problems with alcoholism, duels, sexual trespasses or other such vices. Even Thomas Lynch III, who lived in aristocratic England for a time and toured decadent Europe, was said to have escaped unscathed, except for his fondness for leisure in the library.

The internal structure of the Lynch family in Carolina through four generations was certainly patriarchal. The patriarch's strategic knowledge—of production and marketing, access to land and labor, and settlement of legal questions—was valued in an acquisitive society, and his role as chief of enterprise strengthened his role as head of the family. The patriarch's sovereignty was expressed primarily through inheritance, that "vital nexus" of power in the premodern family. Primogeniture was the pattern in the first Lynch generation. Partible inheritance, so important in early New England, was not practiced by the Lynches who, instead, gave preference to male over female heirs, especially for the transmission of real estate.

Concerning the women of the Lynch family, the prevailing values were sexist, although no such concept existed at the time. Women lived in a world in which the social norm was marriage, and wealthy women were economic parasites. The perception of gender roles granted to men reason, property, guardianship of children, moral strength, legal responsibility and the right to participate in public affairs. The Lynch wives emerged from the genealogical record as individuals who were indeed denied autonomy and economic independence, but they benefited from their upper-class status. Slaves cared for them, and wet nurses apparently cared for their babies. They lived a life of luxury and had access to society. Lynch women consistently married young. Sabina at the time of her first marriage was 16 years old; Elizabeth was 17; Hannah was 19. No record exists of their pregnancies, but available genealogies indicate that they had relatively few offspring. The immigrant mother, Margaret Johnson, had two surviving children; Sabina had seven; Hannah had one, and her daughter Elizabeth had four. Thomas I's first wife Margaret had one child, and Thomas II's first wife Elizabeth Allston had three. Betsy Shubrick Lynch was married for seven years and had no children. On the basis of that limited evidence, the average fertility rate for Lynch women can be calculated at about three children each. Two wives died, but both second wives lived to see their surviving children reach maturity. In addition, the maternal Johnson and Motte family names were incorporated into Lynch naming patterns.

Patrician children like Thomas Lynch III did not have to provide parents with old age security as did sons in less wealthy families. Moreover, children of the gentry left home because of parental preference, not because of the family's need for space, food or money. Literacy was a value and a defining characteristic of the eighteenth century elite; and for the Lynches, education of the young was required. It was not a religious obligation as with the Puritans, nor did it involve a skill and time commitment for personal teaching as with isolated farm families. Rather, it involved a financial commitment made by a patriarch.

The relationship of Lynch parents and children cannot be determined for mothers and their offspring, but for fathers and sons, a "genteel" style of child-rearing prevailed. No evidence exists of the "unbounded love" and affection that theoretically constituted one element of that pattern, but neither is there evidence of a traditional Protestant imperative to control the child, to break its will, and to protect its soul. Thomas Lynch II, in his relationship with his son, fit the model of father as progenitor. He sought to insure his son's success, to shape his future on earth, to socialize him for the responsibilities of his class, and to make him into an ornament of civilization. He invested in his son's education and professional training, but instead of providing Lynch III with a professional career alternative to planting (a career that would have enabled the young man to develop his own autonomy), the law became an adjunct to planting and to amateur politics. Young Lynch appears to have been obedient and dutiful, even after his father's death, but he also demonstrated, on three occasions, significant signs of independence: his desire to be free of law school, his refusal to benefit from nepotism with a higher rank than was assigned him in the South Carolina military, and his decision to sign the Declaration of Independence despite his father's disapproval.

The Lynch family structure in the eighteenth century can best be described not as a nuclear family but as a modified extended family. Conjugal units of different generations lived separately but retained significant economic and emotional ties. The cross-generation families thus did not meet the defining factor of co-residence, but they were closely linked by Lynch identity, affection and the promise of the son's inheriting the home place (and much more) at the parent's death or the mother's remarriage. Individual Lynch households were composed of parents, children, about six or seven domestic slaves, and perhaps a tutor. They all lived in a large enough space to afford privacy and hospitality for guests. Services and simple products of industry were provided by the domestic unit. Isolation could have been a problem resulting from such self-sufficiency, but slaveowners and their servants were able to travel, and maintain residences in the city and in the north.

The absence of personal papers prevents the modern student of Lynch family history from gaining any affective knowledge about the Lynches—their emotional history—but something can be deduced perhaps from a nineteenth century descendant's references to the devotion of Thomas II for his son and of Betsy Shubrick's conjugal love for Thomas III. Moreover, the family function of providing emotional support for its members is quite clear from Thomas III's attending his sick father in Philadelphia.

If measured by the criteria of modernization theory, the Lynch family was a blending of both the traditional and modern. Patrician self-assurance, status, power and conservatism would have led the Lynches to believe that the future would be like the past, and that all members of society should know their places and stay there. They were, after all, comfortable at the top. As slaveowners, the Lynches and their slave managers would have operated not by a rule of law but by arbitrary and perhaps capricious rules made on the plantation. The code of their time was racist, sexist, patriarchal and undemocratic, so they would not have believed in equality before the law. The women and slaves of any traditional family, elite or not, manifested few if any modern values because of the eighteenth century culture lag between material and social progress. Despite such traditional characteristics, however, the Lynches also demonstrated a modern orientation that flowed from their upper-class status and access to power. The eighteenth century elite class, by its very nature, accepted both birth and achievement as means to advancement. They operated by self-interest, not submission, believing that nature and human affairs were knowable and controllable. They wanted individual development and advancement for their sons. Far from being victims of fear and fatalism, they were bold innovators who accepted new techniques and technology to change their world. They measured success in material terms, and they had less confidence than did traditional families in hope for a better world after death. They rarely suffered from a sense of powerlessness and approached most problems rationally rather than with superstition.

The intergenerational transmission of kinship, wealth, opportunity, status, houses and other material objects, as well as the family name, gave the Lynches continuity and identity for over a century. The Santee family estate and residences, especially Peachtree, provided revenue and a sense of place. Inheritance patterns kept the lands centered at Lynches Island in the hands of Lynches for four generations. Some of that real estate was sold, but most of it passed intact from one surviving son to his sole male survivor. The inability of the line to produce numerous sons who survived infancy worked to maintain the integrity of the family property. The perpetuation of an intact estate that resulted from three generations with a single male heir was reversed after 1779 when Thomas Lynch III died without children. The family name disappeared with the marriage of two of Thomas III's sisters, the death of his spinster sister and of the son of his legally renamed nephew. Despite that intergenerational discontinuity, the kinship circle in the years after 1779 retained a conscious family pride. Thomas the Signer became the reference ancestor whom all descendants—no matter that they were not named Lynch—respected as a shaper of the American nation. Thus, the symbols and relics of family permanence continued well after Peachtree and the Lynch name left the family. The engraved silver and monogrammed linen, the library, the portraits of founding generations, and Lynch as a middle name in later generations—all of those were scattered throughout the female lines after 1779 as enduring parts of the symbolic Lynch estate.[11]

One indication of the strength of the family collective memory can be seen a half century after the death of the last son of the patriarchal line. An 1847 tribute was paid to Thomas Lynch II by his grandson James Hamilton, Jr., a descendant who felt a close link to his Lynch maternal family: "I would rather have sprung, as I have sprung, from his loins, than that the blood of all the Howards should flow in my veins."[12]

The application in this essay of selected techniques of the new family history adds a bit of flesh to the bare bones of the Lynch family record. A fuller picture emerges of the patriarchy and its values, the household, the estate, and—to a limited extent—the women and children of the family. In the future, the new family history will doubtless come to inform most studies of the early southern elite in general, not just of those families with limited written sources. The new forms of data from social history, innovations in the modes of applying data, the creation of an interest in new issues not before addressed in traditional approaches, and the development of modernization theory can all add depth and dimension to the complex and profoundly important question of power distribution and the uses of power in the American past.

5

Marriage and the Family Among North Carolina Slaves, 1748–1775

Marvin L. Michael Kay and Lorin Lee Cary

Despite the harsh constraints of bondage, slaves constructed, out of their varied African pasts and American needs and possibilities, highly rewarding marital and familial relationships. This will be investigated here for slaves between 1748 and 1775 in North Carolina, a colony too often bypassed by other scholars.

Slaves lived organic lives in both a psychological and sociological sense. If they sometimes compartmentalized elements of their existence, they also attempted to integrate their experiences by comprehending the complex interrelationships that exist among institutions, roles, values and behavior. Slaves thus interwove, in complex ways, patterns of resistance and adjustment that historians commonly view as disparate responses to enslavement: murder, arson, sabotage and flight, as well as a sustaining religiosity and expansive, powerful marital, familial and communal ties.[1]

Marriage and family, profoundly satisfying expressions of sexual, parental and filial affection and love, were intimately intertwined with the primal phases of the life cycle—birth, child rearing, intergenerational culture transmission, and death. It was hardly surprising, then, that slaves attempted to implement their sense of a moral economy—a conceived right to defend traditional social patterns and values—especially as these related to marriage and the family. Despite the frequent breakup of slave marriages and families by masters, slaves rejected the treatment accorded them. Whether or not they actively resisted, they typically construed such breakups as an abuse, an attack upon cherished institutions that involved the people they loved best—spouses, children and siblings. Growing out of and incorporated within the needs and demands of slave marriages and families, therefore, were slave definitions regarding acceptable limits of treatment by masters.[2]

An analysis that stresses the autonomous roles slaves played and their effective challenge to some of the parameters of bondage must question the adequacy of the concept of "cultural hegemony" to explain the development of slave behavior, beliefs and culture. The use of the Gramscian model of cultural hegemony, with its emphasis on consent, to describe the value system and worldview of slaves—especially during the colonial period—is inconsistent with the requirements of slavery.[3] For slaves to accept the essentials of their exploiters' culture, freedom—with its opportunities and rewards—had to be offered as well as the responsibilities of disciplined labor. Such, of course, was not the case. Moreover, masters were often anxious to withhold their culture from slaves rather than to convert them to it. At no time was this more in evidence than during the colonial era. Given the formative state of slavery in much of the south—and certainly in North Carolina—masters primarily focused on establishing plantations, stocking them with slaves, and ensuring the essential power relationships necessary to maintain and extend the conditions of enslavement. Rather than even dreaming of achieving cultural hegemony to implement this, masters used forceful, coercive, direct methods of control, both cooptative and terroristic, the stress varying with time and circumstance.[4]

Looking at this issue from the vantage point of the slaves, comparatively large numbers of Africans lived in the Carolinas and Georgia through the Revolution. In North Carolina, the percentage of African-born slaves among the adult slave population ranged from about two-thirds during the years 1751–55 to one-third during the last 15 years of the colonial period.[5] Many of these slaves would have had considerable difficulty understanding even a simplified version of English. They spoke a variety of African languages, plus pidgin-creole languages that they had constructed primarily to communicate among themselves. Therefore, it would not have been easy to convert them to ruling class values.

Linguistic differences were only one manifestation of the

cultural chasm between European masters and African slaves that would have had to have been bridged before cultural hegemony could even be contemplated. There was no substantial base of shared culture upon which to build cultural hegemony. Such hegemony must evolve through cultural diffusion, but in the colonial Carolinas and Georgia the process was only in its infancy. Thus, a postulation that a hegemonic culture embraced masters and slaves in colonial North Carolina is anachronistic. Such an analysis also ignores and understates the powerful hold that African languages, institutions, values and worldviews had upon African slaves and the generations they brought forth on this continent.

Lacking the will and the capacity to establish cultural hegemony, masters used more elemental methods to maximize profits and security. Accordingly, they delegitimized slave marriages and families. North Carolina was not distinctive here for, as Orlando Patterson has persuasively argued, social death, including natal alienation, has been the definitive characteristic of slaves in all slave societies. Despite such similarities, the slave systems of North Carolina and other southern colonies on the mainland of British America were somewhat distinctive in that the slaveowners juxtaposed harshly defined delegitimations of slave marriages and families with an acceptance of viable de facto institutions. The denial of de jure status would strip slave marriages and families of their lawful capacity to protect themselves against external attack or disruption. On the other hand, de facto slave marriages and families would give the masters added leverage to induce higher slave birth rates and more productive and better disciplined slaves. Whatever the intentions of masters, slaves in the diaspora desperately tried to reconstruct marriages and families in accordance with their traditional African beliefs and practices. And although the owners' designs in the ensuing dialectic with slaves often prevailed, the marriages and families so heroically established by slaves not surprisingly served first of all their own needs, helping them to achieve lives of fulfillment while empowering them to challenge more successfully some of the bastions constructed by masters to keep slaves in "their place."[6]

Yet, slaves faced daunting difficulties in restructuring marriages and families from their African pasts. Coming from a multiplicity of cultural heritages, slaves in colonial North Carolina and elsewhere had experienced a succession of traumas: capture; separation from homelands, families and friends; hideous conditions on forced marches and during the middle passage; and finally, a series of sales. Nonetheless, slaves began the never ending process of adjusting to their new environments, resisting engulfment by the masters' power and definitions, and conjunctly constructing African-American cultures from their diverse African backgrounds as allowed, modified or redefined by the situational possibilities and needs prescribed by enslavement.

In this process, African slaves drew on memories that consisted not merely of recollections of times past but that also encompassed the habitual ways these folk understood reality.[7] Memory in this sense is important for all immigrant groups. It was especially important for this group—persons from traditional, kinship-defined societies who lived against their will among, but significantly apart from, ascendant groups whose belief patterns, mores, practices and institutions substantially differed from their own and were often denied to them.

The degree of success slaves had in replicating their pasts hinged upon the fortuitous concordance of a number of variables. For one thing, although Africans came from divergent cultural groups with distinct practices, they often shared both underlying cultural principles and particular cultural forms. Such equivalencies enabled numerous reconciliations or convergences among slaves, whether through the continuation of mutally inclusive behavioral practices, cultural syntheses, or the dominance of the practices and beliefs of particular ethnic groups.[8] Yet, the specific reconstitution and development of marital and familial forms varied among the diverse regions in America and followed different timetables within each region. This was so because treatment, labor demands, and epidemiological and demographic conditions—factors basically determined by masters and the natural environment, not by slaves—differed in time and place, as did the slaves' particular African backgrounds.

We look first at how West African marital practices fared in North Carolina. To legitimize and stabilize marriage, to symbolize the worth of the woman, to compensate her family for the loss of a valuable member, and to help guarantee that the husband will treat her properly and fulfill his obligations, almost all West African societies traditionally have required a material consideration by the prospective groom and his family. This could be paid to the prospective bride and her family in goods, in services or in kind. If paid in goods such as cloth, currency or livestock, it is called bride price, bride wealth or bride gift. If the groom labors for the bride's parents, the consideration is called bride service. Payment in kind, or exchange marriage, involves giving a woman of the groom's family, a sister or a daughter, to a relative of the bride in exchange for her. Bride price currently predominates in West Africa and probably has done so in the past. It is often supplemented by bride service but infrequently replaced by it. Exchange marriage is uncommon, although it is practiced by a number of societies on the Nigerian Plateau. The predominant mode, bride price, involves single or multiple gifts of prestige goods.[9]

Bride price, as practiced by different West African peoples, was organically interrelated with each society's diacritic implementation of polygyny, lineages, living arrangements and forms of inheritance. Since slaves could not reconstruct most of these institutional forms or patterns, they failed to interweave bride price with a host of related and defining institutions.[10] While John Brickell undoubtedly missed some of the details of the slave practice, his description of bride wealth in North Carolina during the 1730s shows that, in all likelihood, this slave institution lost many of its common African functions.[11] The abbreviated form of bride price that he saw still incorporated some essentials of West African ways. No marriage took place if the woman rejected a small gift by the prospective spouse. The smallness of the gift continued the West African practice of varying the material value of bride wealth in accordance with the comparative wealth of the different peoples involved. In the case of a marital breakup, the wife returned the gift.[12] What probably remained, therefore, was a convention slaves followed to highlight, consummate and help to solemnize their marriages.

West African practices of bride service and polygyny did not continue in North Carolina even in such attenuated forms. The limited control a man had over his labor probably ensured the discontinuance of bride service. Sex ratios in the province, despite decreasing from 153 to 125 males to 100 females during the last 25 years of the colonial period, were not conducive to polygyny's continuation. This factor, combined with the restricted physical movement of slaves, their poverty, their low density patterns, and, compared with the West Indies, their limited numbers on large plantations, made it extremely difficult for slaves to implement polygyny. Lastly, when mainland masters accepted de facto slave marriages, substantially for self-interested reasons, they probably tended to press slaves to implement monogamy, in keeping both with the masters' practices and morality.[13]

Slave monogamous marriages, however, represented something more than merely a succumbing to the demands of demography and the pressures of masters. To understand this requires a closer look at West African marriage patterns. An analysis of both eighteenth and nineteenth century documents reveals a point amply demonstrated by ethnographic investigations: wherever polygyny has been or is the "preferred" marital form, limits imposed by demographic and economic factors require the coexistence, if not numerical predominance, of monogamy.[14] Slaves coming from West Africa, then, had experiences encompassing both polygyny and monogamy and thus need not have relied upon their masters' example to institute the latter. Indeed, most male slave imports, normally young adults who had not had time to accumulate much wealth, had practiced only monogamy in Africa prior to capture. When confronted by the severely limiting demographic and social conditions in America, they tended to replicate their monogamous but not their polygynous experiences.

Owners in the southern mainland colonies simply reinforced this tendency. Albemarle Sound slave owners, Brickell observed, became involved in the marital arrangements of their slaves only to give permission for such unions or when no children had been born within a year. In such cases, planters might "oblige" slave women "to take a second, third, fourth, fifth, or more Husbands or Bed Fellows; a fruitful Woman amongst them being very much valued by the Planters, and a numerous Issue esteemed the greatest Riches in this Country."[15] However common planter-induced serial monogamy was during the 1730s in North Carolina, plantation records for the second half of the eighteenth century do not support Brickell's suggestion that owners frequently broke up and reconstructed slave marriages to impel more prolific matches. The data does support his general contention that masters had a keen interest in slave fecundity and consequently acquiesced to slave attempts to reconstitute monogamous marital arrangements.[16] Slaves did so informed by their memories and preferences within the constraints imposed by slavery.

Among these constraints, none demarcated marital and familial possibilities for slaves more precisely than did demography. North Carolina's relatively late settlement and immature slave economy, with its diversified production of tobacco, lumber products, naval stores, grains and provisions, is reflected demographically most precisely in the extremely low density patterns of its black population, by far the lowest in the south. Also, with the exception of Maryland, North Carolina had the smallest slave population and the lowest proportion of blacks in its total population of any of the southern colonies. Nonetheless, North Carolina had one of the fastest *growing* slave populations on the mainland. Moreover, by mid-century slaves in the colony had come to be as heavily concentrated on large plantations as in three surveyed tidewater counties in Maryland and Virginia. Even more surprisingly, during the 1760s the Lower Cape Fear Region, where North Carolina's slaves were most heavily concentrated on large plantations, had similar proportions of its slaves residing on plantations—from ten or more slaves up to 100 or more—as did South Carolina's lowcountry.

Sex ratios and "sex imbalance ratios" (a new scale we have constructed to measure sex disparities) reflect both the tendencies described above. A decrease in sex ratios in the province from about 153 males to every 100 females in 1751–1755, to approximately 125:100 between 1761 and the Revolution, demonstrates the increasing opportunities North Carolina slaves had to find mates and raise families. Nonetheless, sex imbalance ratios, a surer guide than sex ratios to marital possibilities among slaves on individual plantations, suggest that the proportion of slaves who could not find spouses on individual plantations varied during the years 1748 to 1772 from about one-third among slaves living in the eastern counties, to one-half in the inner coastal plain and eastern piedmont counties, to a full two-thirds in the western counties.[17]

Carrying such indicators of slave marital possibilities forward, we have calculated as precisely as possible the proportions of slaves who comprised double-headed families, single-headed families, or who had no visible family members on individual plantations during the years 1750–1775 (Table 1). Surprisingly, given North Carolina's demographic characteristics, late formation, large number of Africans, and comparative economic immaturity, slave family development in the colony appears to have been similar to that among slaves in either the Chesapeake or South Carolina on plantations of comparable size during the late colonial period. Thus, the double-headed family among slaves in North Carolina probably was the most common familial form from 1750 to 1775 *only* on estates with 16 or more slaves, with one-half to three-fifths of these slaves comprising such families. Still, families with both the mother and father present existed to some extent on all slaveholds of two or more slaves. About one-fifth to one-quarter of the slaves constituted such families on estates with two to five slaves. And while most slaves did not live in double-headed families in colonial North Carolina, an average of 35 to 43 percent of all slaves probably made up such families during the last 25 years of the colonial period.

If, despite insufficient samples, we distributed the data summarized in Table 1 into time cohorts, we would find that double-headed families increased 1.3 times from the 1750s to 1760s and 1.4 times from the 1750s to the 1770s. Given such trends, it is quite possible that by 1775 about half of the slaves in the province lived on plantations with their mothers and fathers. Yet, throughout the period reviewed, 36 to 44 percent of the slaves comprised single-headed families, and close to 22 percent lived on plantations with no parents present. The double-headed family on individual plantations, therefore, was still not the predominant institutional form in colonial North Carolina that it would become during the nineteenth century.

Patterns of familial development similar to those that occurred over time may also be discerned for the different regions of North Carolina because of variations in maturation. Between 1750 and 1775, more than two times as many slaves comprised double-headed families in the eastern regions of Albemarle Sound and Neuse-Pamlico than in the western regions (Tables 2 and 3). Indeed, only 17 to 21 percent of the western slaves lived on the same plantations as did both of their parents. The statistics for the east and the west, however, normally exhibit the same monotonic tendencies, i.e., the larger the estate, the greater the proportion of slaves comprising double-headed families.

This discussion of double-headed families, remember, refers to those that existed on individual plantations. Thus, an unknown number of the heads of single-headed households had spouses living on separate farms or plantations. Children were occasionally divided between the parents, but they were more likely to be living with the mother. In any case, the high percentages of single-headed families and unattached slaves in colonial North Carolina suggest that demographic factors prevented many slaves from marrying and forced others, both adults and minors, to live apart from spouses and families either temporarily or permanently. Although factors beyond the control

Table 1: Estimates of Slave Marital and Familial Development in North Carolina, 1750–1775

Total Slaves in Household	*N Slaveholds*	*N Slaves*	*Percentage of Slaves in Two-Headed Families: Probability A & B*	*Percentage of Slaves in Single-Headed Families: Probability A & B*	*Percentage of Unattached Slaves on Plantations: Probability A & B*	*Percentage of Slaves in Single & Double-Headed Families: Probability A & B*
1	80	80	A=0	A=0	A=100.00	A=0
			B=0	B=0	B=100.00	B=0
2–3	65	152	A=26.35	A=45.36	A=28.29	A=71.71
			B=21.80	B=49.91	B=28.29	B=71.71
4–5	22	97	A=27.08	B=54.36	A=18.56	A=81.44
			B=22.41	B=59.03	B=18.56	B=81.44
6–10	30	220	A=47.76	A=40.88	A=11.36	A=88.64
			B=39.51	B=49.13	B=11.36	B=88.64
11–15	13	165	A=48.56	A=41.14	A=10.30	A=89.70
			B=40.17	B=49.53	B=10.30	B=89.70
16–20	4	69	A=61.86	A=32.34	A= 5.80	A=94.20
			B=51.18	B=43.02	B= 5.80	B=94.20
29, 66, 32, 104	4	231	A=58.84	A=30.76	A=10.39	A=89.60
			B=48.68	B=40.92	B=10.39	B=89.60
TOTAL	218	1014	A=42.42	A=36.77	A=20.81	A=79.19
			B=35.10	B=44.09	B=20.81	B=79.19

Sources: All the wills, inventories and plantation papers used to construct these tables may be found in the North Carolina State Archives. The wills and inventories are in the following sets: Secretary of States Records—North Carolina Wills, 1663–1789, S.S. 845—873, vols. 7–35; Chancery Proceedings and Wills, 1712–1754, S.S. 878; Wills, 1738–1752, 1750–1758, 1755–1758, 1758–1773, S.S. 877, 879–81, vols. 4, 6–8; Inventories and Sales of Estates, 1714–1798, S.S. 889–905. Bertie County Wills, C.R. 10.801.1–10.801.8, vols. 1–8; Bertie County Estates Papers, C.R. 10.504.1–10.504.1.15, C.R. 10.504.1.19–10.504.1.114; Bertie County Inventories of Estates, C.R. 10.507.2. Carteret County Records, Miscellaneous Papers, 1717–1844, Book A, Records of Wills and Bonds, C.R. 19.905.1; Wills, Inventories, Sales and Settlement of Estates, C.R. 19.802.1–19.802.11, vols. 1–11; Carteret County Wills, C.R. 19.801.1, 19.905.1. New Hanover County Wills, vols. 1–5, C.R. 70.801.1–70.802.5. Northampton County Wills, C.R. 71.801.1, C.R. 71.802.1, C.R. 71.802.2. Cumberland County Wills, C.R. 29.801.1–29.801.4. Mecklenburg County Wills, 1749–1869, C.R. 65.009–65.027; Estate Papers, C.R. 065.508.3–C.R. 065.508.140. Orange County Estates Papers, 1758–1785, C.R. 73.507.1. The plantation papers used, all in the North Carolina State Archives except as noted, are: "Negroes S[arah] Allen their ages in Feby – 1761," New Hanover County; James M. Robin's Papers, vol. 1, Massachusetts Historical Society; Cullen Pollock's Will, Tyrell County, 13 August 1749, and "Lean made by Thomas Pollock Esqr. to Jacob Mitchell bearing Date Twenty-Seventh Day of March 1770," both in Pollock Papers, P.C. 31.1.

Table 2: Estimates of Slave Marital and Familial Development in North Carolina, 1750–1775 Albemarle Sound and Neuse-Pamlico Regions

Total Slaves in Household	*N Slaveholds*	*N Slaves*	*Percentage of Slaves in Two-Headed Families: Probability A & B*	*Percentage of Slaves in Single-Headed Families: Probability A & B*	*Percentage of Unattached Slaves on Plantations: Probability A & B*	*Percentage of Slaves in Single & Double-Headed Families: Probability A & B*
1	34	34	A=0 B=0	A=0 B=0	A=100.00 B=100.00	A=0 B=0
2–3	26	63	A=31.27 B=25.87	A=44.92 B=50.32	A=23.81 B=23.81	A=76.19 B=76.19
4–5	12	54	A=35.26 B=29.18	B=42.52 B=48.60	A=22.22 B=22.22	A=77.78 B=77.78
6–10	16	118	A=42.85 B=35.45	A=46.13 B=53.53	A=11.02 B=11.02	A=88.98 B=88.98
11–15	8	105	A=57.54 B=47.60	A=30.08 B=40.02	A=12.38 B=12.38	A=87.62 B=87.62
16–20	4	69	A=61.86 B=51.18	A=32.34 B=43.02	A= 5.80 B= 5.80	A=94.20 B=94.20
32, 104	2	136	A=62.29 B=51.53	A=32.56 B=43.32	A= 5.15 B= 5.15	A=94.85 B=94.85
TOTAL	102	772	A=47.86 B=39.60	A=35.21 B=43.47	A=16.93 B=16.93	A=83.07 B=83.07

Note: Karl Vezner, professor of political science at the University of Toledo, devised the SAS computer programs to construct Tables 1 and 2 and helped to develop the formulas necessary to implement Table 2.

Table 3: Estimates of Slave Marital and Familial Development in North Carolina, 1750–1775 Western Region

Total Slaves in Household	*N Slaveholds*	*N Slaves*	*Percentage of Slaves in Two-Headed Families: Probability A & B*	*Percentage of Slaves in Single-Headed Families: Probability A & B*	*Percentage of Unattached Slaves on Plantations: Probability A & B*	*Percentage of Slaves in Single & Double-Headed Families: Probability A & B*
1	27	27	A=0 B=0	A=0 B=0	A=100.00 B=100.00	A=0 B=0
2–3	24	52	A=18.95 B=15.67	A=48.36 B=51.64	A=32.69 B=32.69	A=67.31 B=67.31
4–5	3	13	A=15.16 B=12.54	B=77.15 B=79.77	A= 7.69 B= 7.69	A=92.31 B=92.31
6–10	4	29	A=31.71 B=26.23	A=40.70 B=46.18	A=27.59 B=27.59	A=72.41 B=72.41
11–15	1	11	A=59.70 B=49.39	A=31.21 B=41.52	A= 9.09 B= 9.09	A=90.91 B=90.91
16–20	—	—	— —	— —	— —	— —
21+	—	—	— —	— —	— —	— —
TOTAL	59	132	A=20.90 B=17.29	A=38.19 B=41.08	A=40.91 B=40.91	A=59.09 B=59.09

of slaves normally caused such separations, the willingness to consummate interplantation marriages and the ability to deal with living apart from loved ones significantly depended upon the slaves developing suitable compensatory social and psychological techniques.[18]

That slaves did this may be gleaned from a study of naming practices. Herbert Gutman argues that nineteenth century slaves most frequently named children for fathers because fathers "were more likely to be separated from their children than mothers." The naming process thus "confirmed that dyadic tie and gave it an assured historical continuity that complemented the close contact that bound the child to its mother."[19] Available plantation records indicate that slaves in colonial North Carolina also tended to name their children after fathers more frequently than after mothers; this occurred in 50 to 60 percent of the surveyed slave families, while only 16 to 20 percent named children after mothers.[20]

Slaves also drew upon their African memories to help sustain them in dealing with the problem of having to live apart from spouse and family. In divergent West African societies, wives and children commonly spend much of their lives separated from husbands and parents. Among the Asante and Fante of Ghana, for example, wives traditionally go to live in their husbands' compounds when first married. After wives become pregnant, they return to their matrilineal households and remain there three to four years, until they wean the child. During lactation, women may not have sex, and the husband's sexual needs are satisfied by institutionally approved extramarital sexual liaisons and polygyous relationships. New marriages may also be consummated at this time. After weaning, the wife returns to her husband's compound and sexual intercourse resumes. The child, however, remains behind to be reared by the matrilineage under the primary authority of the oldest maternal uncle, the lineage providing economic sustenance and eventual inheritance. Each succeeding pregnancy entails the same process. After menopause, wives normally return to their matrilineal homes. While the Ga, also of Ghana, practice the same sex taboos as those of their Akan speaking neighbors, their customs are patrilineal. Ga wives customarily live in their own patrilineal family compounds after marriage. Husbands, who also reside in their own familial homes, visit spouses from time to time. Children stay with their mothers until weaned and then live with their fathers and their patrilineages.[21]

While the precise practices may vary, the fact remains that wives and children in West Africa often lived apart from their spouses and fathers.[22] Such practices were sufficiently widespread to have affected the attitudes of enslaved Africans regarding spouses and children living on separate plantations. Presumably, their background made interplantation marriages and familial separations somewhat more palatable to slaves *who had reasonable access to their spouses, parents and children*. This tendency would have been prevalent during the colonial era when African immigrants and their mores and values were strongest. Even then, of course, slaves frequently had to draw upon their memories without the presence of the African infrastructures that gave meaning, identity, nurturance, support, security and satisfaction to mothers, fathers and children who formally lived apart. In time, slaves partially bridged their institutional limitations with the development of extended families and significant communal ties.

Thus far, we have only alluded to the importance and complexity of West African familial units beyond nuclear families. We now must discuss in detail why and how familial groupings such as extended families, lineages and clans either survived or succumbed to the ordeal of the transatlantic crossing to North Carolina. Understandably, individuals uprooted from African environments would strenuously attempt to reconstruct extended families given the past significance and the important functions such groups could perform for the slaves. Yet, many of the elaborate structures and patterns within which extended families existed and were defined in West African societies—e.g., lineages, clans and interrelated political institutions—could not be rebuilt in North Carolina. Slaves lacked the power to reconstruct their African political institutions, and they found unilineal descent and organizational patterns dysfunctional since slaves had to use all members of the family to the fullest extent possible. Descent, therefore, came to be cognatic, traced through *both* the maternal and paternal lines. Since clans were compromise kin groups significantly defined by existing unilineages, they, too, were not transplanted by the slaves.[23]

References to bilaterally defined extended slave families are frequently found in plantation records. Of the 57 slaves on the Allen plantation in the Lower Cape Fear county of New Hanover in 1761, for instance, 36 were members of five families, each consisting of three generations. John Walker of Wilmington, also in New Hanover County, left less detailed records about his slaves, but of the 16 listed, ten were members of a single three-generation extended family.[24]

On Thomas Pollock's plantation in Craven County (Neuse-Pamlico Region) in 1770, only five of 122 slaves seem to have had no relatives on the plantation.[25] Forty-nine slaves were members of single-headed families, and another 60 were members of double-headed families. Three of the slave families had three generations each and, most remarkable, Old George and Kate's family spanned five generations (Figure 1). The great-great grandparents, Old George and Kate, had four children, 11 grandchildren, four great grandchildren and one great-great grandchild. The family of Old Emanuel and Jenny, who had 11 children, only encompassed two generations, but a comparative name analysis of this family and that of Old George and Kate suggests that the two were related in some way. Both families named sons Emanuel and George, although in different rank orders, and two of Old Emanuel and Jenny's daughters had the same names as two of Old George and Kate's grandaughters: Bet (Beth) and Nanny (Nann) (Figures 1 and 2). Assuming the two families were related, they not only represented 30 percent of the 122 slaves on the plantation, but in addition to the relationships already listed, they comprised a network of uncles, aunts, nephews, nieces and cousins. By 1770, extensive kinship lines clearly had developed among North Carolina slaves on large plantations in the east, and probably on such plantations everywhere in the province. Evidence and logic suggest that kinship ties also reached beyond single plantations.[26]

Given the dearth of records, few of the functions performed by these families among colonial North Carolina slaves are known. One documented role was that assumed by some grandparents as effective heads of three-generation families consisting of grandparents, their immediate families, plus those grandchildren who were members of single-headed families. Additionally, older mothers or fathers at times lived with mature children. Grandparents assumed responsibilities for child-rearing, then, at least occasionally, and both parents and children often gave and received support and nurturing throughout their lives.[27]

Equally evocative, again, were slave naming practices. The extended family of Old George and Kate in conjunction with the family of Old Emanuel and Jenny, for example, illustrate that children were named not only after parents but also after grandparents, as well as uncles and aunts separated by two, three or more generations (Figures 1 and 2). These naming patterns

Figure 1

Old George and Kate's Family on the Pollock Plantation, Craven County, Neuse-Pamlico Region, 27 March 1770

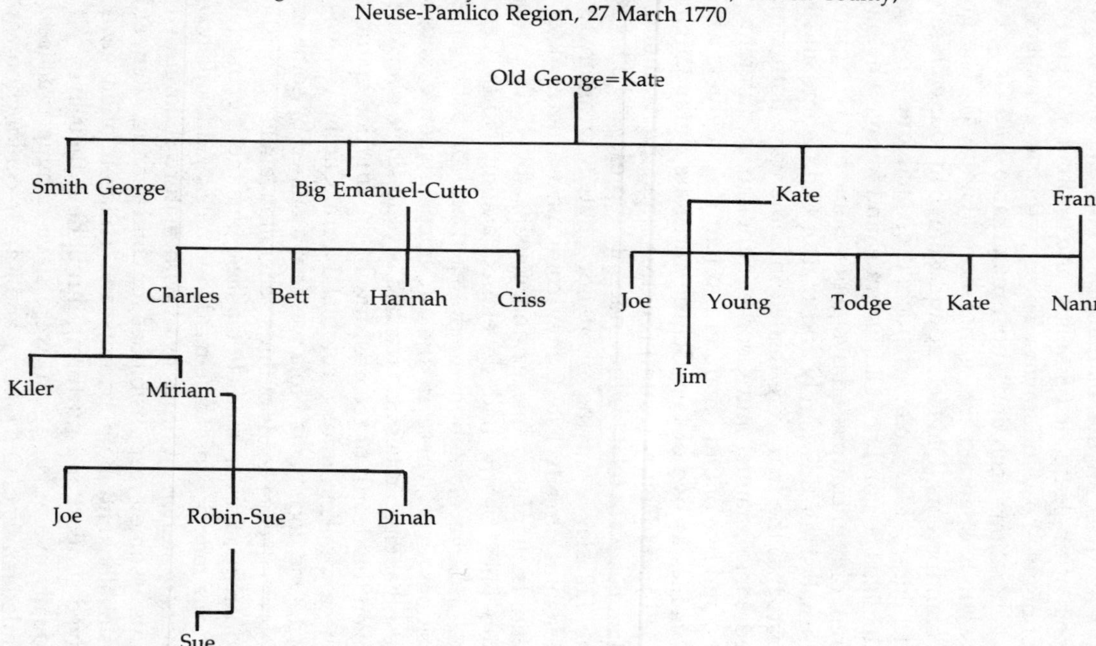

Sources: Lien by Thomas Pollock to Jacob Mitchell, Craven County, Pollock Papers, P.C. 31.1, North Carolina State Archives.

Figure 2

Old Emanuel and Jenny's Family on the Pollock Plantation, Craven County, Neuse-Pamlico Region, 27 March 1770

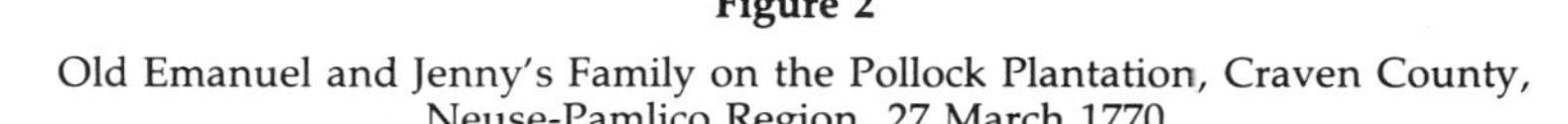

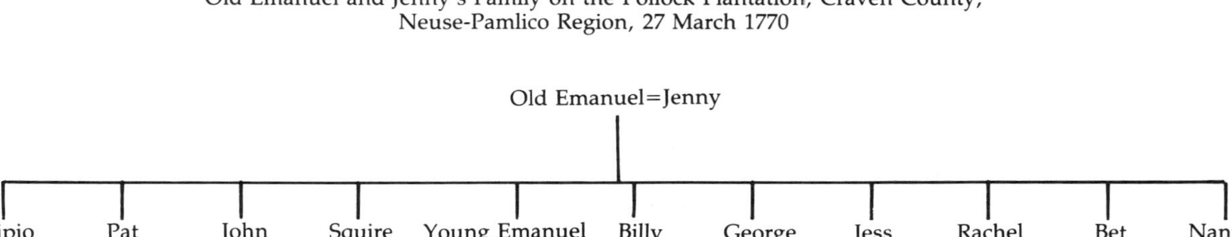

reveal, as Gutman notes, the existence of "self-conscious Afro-American slave kin networks," and suggest the significance of a wide variety of relatives.[28] The paucity of records, unfortunately, conceals the actual roles and functions of such relations and relationships.

Although comparatively fewer slaves in colonial North Carolina had been able to marry and form double-headed households than in the Chesapeake colonies in the years preceding the Revolution, increasing numbers of slaves in North Carolina during the last 25 years of the colonial era drew upon their African pasts to build monogamous marriages and nuclear and extended families. Thus, by the Revolution, perhaps about one-half the colony's slaves constituted double-headed nuclear families on individual plantations. Other African marital and familial characteristics such as bride service, polygyny, lineages and clans never gained a recognizable foothold in the colony. Still others, like bride price, probably had tenuous existences because they remained largely undefined or unaided by the myriad of institutional supports that existed in Africa. A tendency for spouses to accept living in separate households on different plantations, with sufficient visiting privileges, undoubtedly depended more on demographic circumstance than on an African past that somewhat prepared slaves for this eventuality.

Yet, slaves did the best they could under the circumstances, constructing marriages and families that gave them nurture, immense satisfactions and a sense of identity—even well-being—in the midst of forced separations, pain and heartache. In such a context, slaves often could avoid internalizing many of the more nightmarish definitions masters had in store for them. At the same time, they could maintain substantial elements of their traditional values and institutions and sustain the wherewithal to attack the system of bondage so carefully wrought by the slaveowners.

6

Boys' Work on an Eighteenth Century New England Farm[1]

Ross W. Beales, Jr.

On a winter day in 1755, Ebenezer Parkman noted in his diary that his son Breck "(the first time) went to Mill" (22 December 1755).[2] It is clear why Parkman would note his son's first trip to a local grist mill: the event marked a significant step in the boy's maturation as a contributing member of the Parkman household. Not quite seven years old, Breck now had the physical prowess and the sense of responsibility needed to be able to carry grain or corn on horseback to the mill and return with the flour or meal for the family's consumption.

For most boys, even the sons of rural ministers like Parkman, work responsibilities began early and constituted a significant contribution to their parents' households. Eighteenth century children, boys and girls alike, were introduced to work responsibilities at an early age. As children approached adolescence, the significance of their contributions increased with their growing physical statures, their dexterity and their sense of self-direction.

While historians like Edmund S. Morgan and John Demos have sketched the general parameters of childhood in colonial New England,[3] little has been done to trace the *specific* experiences of children as they made the transition from infancy to adolescence. This essay is a test case, or a series of test cases, of the work experiences of boys in Ebenezer Parkman's family. A close examination of their contribution to work on the Parkman farm allows us to describe the relationship between the kinds of work that had to be done on a farm and each boy's growing ability to do that work. At the same time, we can also note the tension that existed between the demands of farm work and the aspirations Parkman had for his sons' education.

Ebenezer Parkman (1703–1782) was minister of Westborough, Massachusetts, from 1724 to 1782.[4] His annual salary was never sufficient to provide for the needs of his large family—twice married, Parkman was father of 16 children (see Appendix A). He was, therefore, like most clergymen, both a farmer and a minister. The two responsibilities often conflicted in terms of his own time, attention and energies. As he noted on one occasion, "So perplexing is it to have the Affairs of the Ministry and of a Farm to manage together" (24 March 1746). When his sons were very young, and after they had grown up and established separate households, Parkman was obliged to hire workers. But for much of his life, he could rely—at least in part—on the labor of his eight sons, all of whom survived the risks of infancy, childhood and adolescence. Fortunately for the historian, Parkman found time among his myriad duties to keep one of the most extensive diaries to survive from colonial New England. The diary provides extensive data on the activities of his household, particularly as they related to farm work and the sphere of male activities.

Like most diarists, Parkman recorded very little about the early years of each child's life. He left some information about the birth, baptism and naming of his children, difficulties his wives experienced in nursing and the decision to wean the children,[5] and the illnesses and accidents of infancy and early childhood. He occasionally referred to birthdays (22 August 1752, 6 January 1769) or to some aspect of early childhood development. Thus, he wrote of one of his daughters, "My little Anna Sophia goes alone across the Room, She being this Day 13 Months old" (18 November 1756). He also noted when "little Suse begins to go alone" at eight and a half months (4 January 1746).

Scattered references suggest that his children had considerable freedom to play. Their activities would not have surprised John Cotton, who had observed in the mid-seventeenth century that it was not idleness for young children to "spend much time in pastime and play, for their bodyes are too weak to labour, and their minds to study are too shallow . . . even the first seven years are spent in pastime, and God looks not much at it."[6] The Parkman children's "pastime and play" seem on occasion to have been unsupervised, at least by adults. Thus, two-year-old

John was "Sav'd from Drowning" when he fell into a hole that his 14-year-old brother Billy had dug to collect rain water. It was not an adult but his brother Samme, then just past his fourth birthday, who "pull'd him out" (16 October 1755). On another occasion, four-year-old Alexander received his just desserts when he taunted a ram. As his father describes the incident:

> In the Morning Alexander struck a Ram that return'd the Blow and knocked him down, and repeated it as often as he endeavour'd to rise—till my Dauter Molly [who was almost 20 years old] running to his relief, was struck down likewise; So that they were both in Some Danger; till I went to their Succour. (19 May 1751)

Life was not all play in the first few years. From time to time Parkman noted the presence of his young children at church services, and these references suggest that their attendance was regular rather than occasional. So, too, we know that he conducted daily religious observances in his home, and at least two sons attended school when they were three years old. Only three weeks after John's third birthday, his father notes, "John goes to School" (11 August 1756). Breck's schooling began at least as early as the age of three years and nine months. In this instance, Parkman noted that Breck was "carry'd home lame from School" with, it was feared, a broken leg (25 October 1752). In neither case does the diary indicate whether or what John and Breck were studying, but Breck's injury to his leg could hardly have resulted from an early encounter with books.

However much Parkman's children may have been inclined to play, the necessities of farm life inclined their father to put them to work. In looking at their early tasks, one is reminded of Anne Bradstreet's meditation: "a wise father will not lay a burden on a child of seven yeares old, which he knows is enough for one of twice his strength. . . ."[7] Some of Parkman's diary entries indicate both the nature of his boys' early tasks and the limitations that their size, strength and dexterity placed on them.

The case of Breck Parkman illustrates the increasingly demanding and independent work that the boys undertook. At the age of six years, seven months, he helped his father rake barley; their joint labor was necessitated, however, by the illness of the older boys, Thomas and Billy (1 August 1755). In the same year, Breck made the trip to the grist mill, as was noted at the beginning of this essay. At age seven, he brought home a load of winter apples—a task probably no more demanding than going to the grist mill (19 October 1756). He still had something to learn about handling tools, for two months later his older half-brother Ebenezer, with whom he was living, brought him home "because," as Parkman noted, "he is Lame, having cut his right Legg with an Ax" (22 December 1756).[8]

When he was eight, Breck helped his brother Alexander, who was two years older, in carting "muck" (manure) (4 May 1757) and carrying ashes out to be spread on the cornfields (3 June 1757). He also hoed corn (8 June 1757), weeded (23 June 1757), raked (6 August 1757), reaped oats (10–11 August 1757) and thrashed oats and rye with Alexander (9 September 1757).

When Breck was just a month over nine years of age, he went to live for nine months with his brother Ebenezer in Brookfield (22 February–16 November 1758), and in the following year he spent another 11 months at his brother's (5 January–28 November 1759). With several other boys living at home, the elder Parkman could easily make Breck's services available to Ebenezer, Jr., whose own children were still too young to contribute much work. After his eleventh birthday, now back at home in Westborough, Breck continued to work regularly with Alexander: thrashing rye (13 February 1760), carting posts from the ministerial wood lot (31 March 1760), plowing in oats (25 April 1760), furrowing a field for planting (8 May 1760), husking at a neighbor's (24 October 1760) and winnowing rye (12 and 29 November 1760).

In each diary entry, Parkman first mentions the older son, indicating his greater responsibility for the task at hand. This would have been especially the case when the two boys worked with a horse or a team of oxen. One can imagine the older boy guiding the plow or furrow with his younger brother leading the animals. Thus, when Billy was 11 years old, Parkman noted that "Mr. Samuel Williams with my Mare, and with Billy to lead, plough'd among my Indian Corn" (10 July 1752).

In addition to references to specific tasks, Parkman's language reveals his pride as his sons advanced in skills and responsibility. Thus, when 19-year-old Ebenezer sowed and plowed in some barley, he was helped by six-year-old Billy, who, according to his father, "begins more manfully to ride to plough" (3 April 1747). On another occasion, Parkman noted that Alexander, age 11, "has been so manly as to hill the Corn in the Orchard" (22 July 1758). A young seamstress came to the Parkman home to make coats for the boys, and Parkman recorded that nine-year-old Elias "goes home with her, very Manfully" (25 August 1770).

While Parkman might take pride in a son's "manful" or "manly" work, there were occasions when he was concerned for their safety. When Alexander and Breck, aged 13 and 11, took a neighbor's oxen and cart to the ministerial lot on a March day to bring in some fence posts, their father was "much concerned for them lest mischief Should befall them," and he "walked to Capt. [Jonathan] Rolfs. However, they returned well, through the Goodness of God" (31 March 1760). On another occasion, 11-year-old Billy "assisted a Drover (one Boardman of Exeter) with a Flock of Sheep and went so far with him as put us in great Consternation." Parkman felt compelled to borrow a horse "to ride after Billy" (30 June 1752).

After his twelfth birthday, Breck continued to work with Alexander, taking corn and rye to a grist mill (30 March 1761), plowing stubble (8 April 1761), repairing fences and looking after the animals (13 April 1761) and mowing bushes (30 May 1761). A gap in his father's diary leaves no information for three years,[9] but when the diary resumes we find 15-year-old Breck working with his younger brother, John, who was then about 11 years old. Breck and John half-hilled the corn in the orchard (7 July 1764), hoed (13 August 1764) and thrashed oats (30 November 1764). Breck was now in the position of supervising some of a younger brother's work and passing on to him some of the skills that he in turn had learned from his older brother Alexander.

By this time, Breck was apparently shouldering nearly full work responsibilities: reaping rye with the help of neighbors, while John hoed (23 July 1764); sometimes working by himself (8–9 August 1764) or for Parkman's neighbors (19–20 July 1764). Two of Parkman's entries point especially to Breck's maturation. In the mid-summer of 1764, Parkman noted that "Breck so commands my mare as to make her plow" (21 July 1764). This task most probably required a combination of patience, physical strength and a commanding voice. Not long afterward, it appears that Breck began an apprenticeship with his older brother, Billy, a housewright by trade, and Parkman's references to his work now occasionally include the wording, "Breck works for me" (30 November 1764).

Thus, in the nine years between Parkman's first reference to Breck's work, at age six, Breck had fully matured—first working with his father or an older brother, then living with an older brother's family in another town, working with a younger brother or by himself, and finally entering an apprenticeship. This gave his master—in this case, his older brother Billy—control of his work. With some variations, largely reflecting the changing composition of the Parkman household, this overall pattern of work socialization was common to all of the Parkman boys.

During their years of work for their father, there is no evidence that the boys received any cash payment for their work. But some diary entries indicate that his children were given animals to raise. By the time John was 12, he was raising his own poultry. Thus, late in 1765, John sent "six Fowl" to market in Boston (31 December 1765). Early the next year, he sent "8 or 9 fowls, and 1 Partridge" to Boston under the care of Deacon Benjamin Tainter (17 January 1766), who, three days later, "returns from his Marketing and pays John for his Fowls, etc." (20 January 1766). John also owned sheep, for his father sold two of them the next year and paid his 14-year-old son four pounds (26 November 1767).[10]

The two years Breck spent in Brookfield when he was nine and ten years of age reveal another dimension to a boy's work. As early as age seven, Breck had lived in his older brother Ebenezer's home after the latter had married and was living in Westborough (20 November, 22 December 1756). Alexander had also lived with Ebenezer, Jr., before the age of six (11 January 1753), and when Alexander was nine, Ebenezer, Jr., spoke with the elder Parkman "about Alexanders living with him till he is 14. But," Parkman noted, "this is not ripened" (30 August 1756). Ebenezer, Jr., had need for even such work as could be performed by a boy of six or seven. His first son, born in 1753, was only three years old when Ebenezer, Jr., sought to secure Alexander's services, and that son was only five when nine-year-old Breck went to live with Ebenezer in Brookfield. At the same time, the elder Parkman's household was large. In 1758, when Breck first went to Brookfield, there were three other sons living at home, aged 11 (Alexander), seven (Samuel), and five (John).

This pattern was repeated, in part, when Parkman's youngest son, nine-year-old Elias, went to Ashburnham to live with his sister, Sarah, and her husband, the Reverend John Cushing, who had been married the previous year.[11] By this time, the Parkman household was considerably smaller.[12] Elias's five-month stay in Ashburnham was probably made easier by the fact that Parkman's 12-year-old grandson, also named Elias, was living with him in Westborough.[13]

The Parkman household was amply supplied with sons in the 1750s, but at other stages Parkman brought boys into his home to perform necessary chores. This was especially the case when the family members were young and again when his children were largely grown. Early in 1726, less than two years after his first marriage, Parkman took John Storey, the son of a sea captain, into his home. Parkman recorded the terms on which Captain Storey placed his son in Parkman's care:

> Take the Lad, Sir, Till about May, when I expect to return from Sea, but if it please God to prevent me, if you like the Boy keep him till he is 15 or 16 years old, when I would have him put to apprentice. All I Desire is that you keep him warm, and feed him Suitably. Instruct him Christianity. My main Expectation and hope is that you'll give him Education proper to such an One. Let him Serve you as he is able, impose not on him those heavy burthens that will either Cripple him or Spoil his Growth. But in all regards I am willing he should Serve you to his Utmost. (20 January 1726)

Gaps in Parkman's diary prevent us from knowing whether Captain Storey survived his voyage or how long young John Storey remained in Westborough. But the understanding between the two men was typical of other agreements that Parkman made with parents: in exchange for clothing, food and some instruction, the boy would perform suitable chores.

Thus, late in his life, Parkman agreed to take William Winchester into his home on the following terms: "I would do what I could conveniently and reasonably in teaching and influencing him in Reading, Writing and Cyphering, according as his Business in taking Care of the Cattle, Cutting the Wood etc. would give opportunity and as his Capacity should admit it" (27 December 1779). A year later, he took 14-year-old Benjamin Wood into his home: "Ben is to live with me for the sake of getting Learning—to Satisfie me, for Instruction, Board, Washing and Lodging, he must tend my Cattle, and cut wood, needful chores, go of Errands etc. and he must tarry with me till next April" (15 November 1780). Other boys were younger than Benjamin Wood. Nathan Knowlton was 11 when Parkman agreed to take him for 12 months, "feeding, Clothing and instructing him" (27 March 1745). His grandson Elias lived with him from age 11 to 13, Benjamin Clark from age 11 to 14, and James Hicks from 11 to 13 (see Appendix B).

The details of these relationships stand in sharp contrast to the practice of "putting out," which Edmund Morgan identifies as a key to understanding the emotional restraints that characterized relations between parents and children in seventeenth century New England. According to Morgan, there were important psychological reasons for placing one's children into other families, even when there was no clear economic advantage to be gained. Morgan hypothesizes that "psychologically this separation of parents and children may have had a sound foundation. The child left home just at the time when parental discipline causes increasing friction, just at the time when a child begins to assert his independence. By allowing a strange master to take over the disciplinary function, the parent could meet the child upon a plane of affection and friendliness. At the same time the child would be taught good behavior by someone who would not forgive him any mischief out of affection for his person."[14]

For the eighteenth century Parkmans, however, there were clear *economic* advantages to placing children in other homes or accepting a child into their household. The availability of sons or the need for labor appears to have been the overriding concern in Parkman's decisions either to place a son in another household or to take a boy into his own home. The timing of these arrangements and the fact that not all his sons went to live with other families strongly suggest that, whatever his emotional ties to his sons, his own needs for workers and the needs of his married children were foremost in his mind. If there were tensions between generations, the only hint appears with reference to Breck when he was living with his older half-brother. As his father noted the news from Brookfield: "Breck is not at rest with living there" (29 January 1759).

Parkman's need for young workers, however, sometimes came into conflict with his desire to educate his sons. More often than not, the economic pressures of a large family compelled him to give a lower priority to education than he might otherwise have chosen. The case of his son Billy illustrates the tension. Billy was attending school by age six (14 January 1747) and began to learn Latin before his eighth birthday. Despite these accomplishments, throughout his boyhood he worked at the full range of farm chores. By the late summer of 1754, when he was 13, matters came to a head. Parkman's oldest son, Ebenezer, was already married, and his next son, 25-year-old Thomas, carried on his trade as a saddler in a shop on the

Parkman property. Much work therefore fell to Billy; the next son, seven-year-old Alexander, was not yet able to assume many responsibilities.

The resolution of this dilemma suggests some level of tension both between Parkman and his son and between Parkman and his second wife, Hannah. Indeed, the tension may have been compounded by the fact that Billy was their first son. Parkman writes:

> I have been in a great deal of Concern about how to dispose of Billy. He Seems not willing to resume his books except I can keep him wholly to 'em—which our present Circumstances forbid. His Mothers Consent to Learning for him, is hard to obtain. It grieves me much to give him up—But as he was yesterday Clearing at the Island Pasture, So there he goes to Day. (4 September 1754)

This marked the end of Billy's schooling, and for the next year and a half, he worked for his father. Parkman began looking for an apprenticeship for Billy just before his fifteenth birthday (12 February 1756), and after several unsuccessful overtures to other men (25 February 1756, 30 December 1756), he persuaded his son-in-law, Jeduthun Baldwin, a housewright, to take Billy (2 March 1757). Billy was then 16 years old.

Parkman's diary contains far more references to his sons' work than to their schooling, and references to schooling—whether at home or in one of the town's schools—appear most often in winter. Thus, in early January 1759, he reports that Alexander, then almost 12 years old, was "a Second Time disgusted with Learning and would throw up, but I now keep him to't, since I have thrown by Business, I designed he should do, and willingly go without it for his sake" (23 January 1759). Later that year, Parkman bought a grammar and a Bible for Alexander (18 July 1759), but his next reference to Alexander's schooling does not appear until December. The entry makes clear the balance that had to be struck between work and study: "Alexander and Breck have been thrashing Rye. They now thrash Oates. They write o'nights" (20 December 1759). Early in January 1760, Joseph Bowman, a Harvard student,[15] began to keep school in Westborough, and Parkman sent "Alex and Breck to learn Latin, and Samuel to read" (2 January 1760). There are two other references to schooling in that month, after which Parkman is silent on the subject—at least with respect to Alexander—until the following January.[16]

The pattern was repeated in Breck's case as well. He began to study Latin before his eighth birthday; as his father noted, "Breck learns in the Accidence" (2 January 1757). He was in school to learn Latin three years later (2 January 1760) and progressed as far the nomenclature (30 January 1760). Ten months later, his father noted, "Breck begins to learn Latin again" (21 November 1760). The struggle was everywhere apparent. April 1761 found "Alexander and Breck about necessary Employments, about the Fences, Creatures, Family Affairs etc. and Nothing about their Books" (13 April 1761).

Only in the case of his last son and youngest child, Elias, did Parkman find the resources of time, money and talent to prepare a son for Harvard College. With most of his children provided for, and with his grandson Elias living in the family for a crucial two and a half years, Parkman could forgo this son's labor. While none of the details of Elias's five-month stay with his brother-in-law, John Cushing, survive, it was probably more than coincidence that Elias was sent to live with a brother-in-law who was also a Harvard-educated minister. Parkman had time to devote to his son's instruction and enough resources to pay to have Elias board with other families to be near the town's school.[17] And, in final preparation for Elias's admission to Harvard, Parkman arranged for Nathan Goddard, a recent Harvard graduate[18] who was teaching in the neighboring town of Shrewsbury, to board and instruct Elias.[19]

This is not to suggest that Parkman's efforts to educate his other sons were in vain or without measurable results. His oldest son, Ebenezer, both farmed and taught school in Brookfield. After losing his farm in 1779, he served in the Revolutionary army and then spent much of the rest of his life as an itinerant teacher. Breck, although trained as a housewright, also taught school for a time and then turned to storekeeping. Samuel became a prominent merchant in Boston. For each of these sons, formal education provided choices that were not available to those who were less well-educated.

Among the Parkmans' sons, Elias was exceptional in that he graduated from Harvard College, but this accomplishment may have resulted as much from family circumstances as from ability. There is no reason to believe that he was any more talented than most of his seven older brothers. His father knew that Elias was his last hope to have a son enter Harvard, and that last hope came when Parkman could more easily afford to devote family resources to education. With fewer mouths to feed, and with a salary that had not yet been devastated by the inflation of the Revolution, Parkman could at last see his fondest hopes realized.

The experiences of Ebenezer Parkman's sons from boyhood to adolescence reveal the stages of their development, as well as the constraints and opportunities that affected them at different stages in the life cycle of the Parkman family. As this case study shows, none of the boys was exempt from hard physical work from the age of six or seven to their early teens. They were put to tasks appropriate to their stages of development. If there were tensions within the family over their work, the tensions stemmed from the conflict between their father's aspirations for them—particularly in the area of formal education—and the relentness economic necessities of providing for a large family. The Parkman family was hardly typical in terms of its status, or probably in terms of Parkman's efforts to provide formal education for his sons. But the kinds of farm work the boys performed, and the increasing range of responsibilities they assumed, were doubtless typical for boys their age throughout New England.

APPENDIX A

Ebenezer Parkman's Family

Ebenezer Parkman	b.	5 September 1703	
	m.	7 July 1724	Mary Champney bapt. 21 May 1699 d. 29 January 1736
	m.	1 September 1737	Hannah Breck b. 10 February 1716 d. 20 August 1801
	d.	9 December 1782	

Children:

Name	*Birth*	*Marriage*	*Death*
Mary	14 Sept. 1725	6 Aug. 1752	16 Jan. 1776
Ebenezer	20 Aug. 1727	21 Sept. 1752	5 July 1811
Thomas	3 July 1729		23 Oct. 1759
Lydia	20 Sept. 1731		in childhood
Lucy	23 Sept. 1734	28 Apr. 1757 (int.) 13 Nov. 1793	
Elizabeth	28 Dec. 1738		14 Jan. 1739
William	19 Feb. 1741	9 Sept. 1766	
Sarah	20 Mar. 1743	28 Sept. 1769	12 Mar. 1825
Susanna	13 Mar. 1745	13 Oct. 1768	30 Nov. 1792
Alexander	17 Feb. 1747	12 Dec. 1768	
Breck	27 Jan. 1749	14 Nov. 1776 (int.)	3 Feb. 1825
Samuel	22 Aug. 1751	11 Feb. 1773	
John	21 July 1753		10 Sept. 1775
Anna Sophia	18 Oct. 1755	21 Sept. 1780	26 Nov. 1783
Hannah	9 Feb. 1758		14 Oct. 1777
Elias	6 Jan. 1761		

Note: In addition to bearing 11 children, Hannah Parkman had two miscarriages (20 February 1738, 25 December 1739).

APPENDIX B

Ebenezer Parkman's Hired Boys Westborough, Massachusetts, 1726–1781

1726–?: Storey, John. *Age*: unknown. *Terms*: [In Boston.] "Captain Storey convers'd with me about his Sons living with me. His words were these about the Conditions of our Discourse. 'Take the Lad, Sir, Till about May, when I expect to return from Sea, but if it please God to prevent me, if you like the Boy keep him till he is 15 or 16 years old, when I would have him put to apprentice. All I Desire is that you keep him warm, and feed him Suitably. Instruct him Christianity. My main Expectation and hope is that you'll give him Education proper to such an One. Let him Serve you as he is able, impose not on him those heavy burthens that will either Cripple him or Spoil his Growth. But in all regards I am willing he should Serve you to his Utmost.' Upon my Consenting to this he said he has no Hatt. Let him have one of yours, and if it should so happen that he doth not remain with you I'll pay for it'" (20 January 1726).

1745: Knowlton, Nathan. *Age*: 11–12. *Terms*: "Proceeded to Mr. Gershom Brighams and din'd at Mr. Joseph Knowltons: with whom I agreed to take his Son Nathan (who is about 11 Years of Age) for a Twelve Month, feeding, Clothing and instructing him" (27 March 1745). "At Eve Nathans Father came and told me they were now somewhat put to it for Boys Help and desir'd me if I could Spare him to release his son, which I did, and he went home with his Father. And may God be gracious to him!" (18 November 1745).

1749: Knowlton, Nathan. *Age*: 15. With his 21-year-old son Ebenezer "being about to go to Harvard," Massachusetts, Parkman sought to obtain one of Mr. Knowlton's sons "to come and live with me" (3 January 1749). Nathan came to the Parkman household on 9 January and appears to have stayed at least until 23 January, after which there is no mention of him. On 24 January, Parkman sought, unsuccessfully, to hire Jacob Knowlton for a year. He then obtained Thomas Chaddock of Hopkinton for a brief time (he is mentioned only on 24 and 26 February). Parkman finally hired Daniel Hastings for three months (21 March, 7 July 1749).

1770–1772: Parkman, Elias (grandson). *Age*: 11–13. Elias came to live with Parkman on 10 January 1770 and returned home "very Contrary to my Expectation, but his Father is unable to go on with his Business and Sends for him" (19 May 1772).

1773–1776: Clark, Benjamin. *Age*: 11–14. *Terms*: "Mr. *David Clark* of *Ashburnham* came with his Son *Benjamin*, to live with me till he shall be fourteen yers old: He, the said Mr. *Clark*, Says his son is in his twelfth year. Will be twelve on the Sixth Day of next January. . . . This Evening I wrote a memorandum of what Mr. *David Clark* promised about his Son, but we were interrupted" (12 November 1773). "Mr. *Clark* in the Morning Signed the Said Memorandum and *Jonathan Maynard* and my Daughter *Sophia* witnessed it. He leaves Benjamin here, and setts out for home" (13 November 1773). Benjamin stayed with Parkman until 18 February 1776. Parkman tried, unsuccessfully, to obtain Benjamin's services for a longer period: "They [Benjamin and Samuel Hicks] bring a Letter from my son *Cushing*, who informs that Mr. *Clarke* of *Ashburnham* does not incline to Send his Son *Ben*" (27 March 1776).

1776–1778: Hicks, James. *Age*: 11–13. *Terms*: "Mrs. *Hicks*, waited on by her son *Zechary*, brings her son *James* to live with me till he shall be 14 Years old. D.V." (11 May 1776). James stayed only until three weeks after his thirteenth birthday (26 May 1778). Parkman learned from his son Breck that "Mrs. *Hicks* of *Cambridge* is not well pleased with what was done for *James*" (27 June 1778).

1778–1779: Bryant, Timothy. *Age*: Unknown. *Terms*: "*Elias Bryant* returns home, and leaves his Brother *Timothy* to live with me a Year, or at least till next March" (1 June 1778). He stayed with Parkman for a year: "N.B. Timothy Bryant's Time being out, he went with Parker, in order to return to his Mother at Stoneham. I gave him eight dollars, which was as much as I could spare. I wrote by him to his Mother. May God be the guardian of his Youth!" (3 June 1779).

1779–1780: Winchester, William. *Age*: unknown. *Terms*: "This evening came William Winchester to live there. Mr. Nehemiah Maynard came with him. N.B. His father Mr. Nathan Maynard sat by and heard. I told Mr. Maynard that I would do what I could conveniently and reasonably in teaching and influencing him in Reading, Writing and Cyphering, according as his Business in taking Care of the Cattle, Cutting the Wood etc. would give opportunity and as his Capacity should admit it. This was in answer to what Mr.

Maynard delivered me as Mrs. Winchesters Errand to me by him" (27 December 1779). Winchester stayed until 8 May 1780.

1780–1781: Wood, Ben. *Age*: 14. *Terms*: "N.B. Ben is to live with me for the sake of getting Learning—to Satisfie me, for Instruction, Board, Washing and Lodging, he must tend my Cattle, and cut wood, needful chores, go of Errands etc. and he must tarry with me till next April" (15 November 1780).

7

The Republican Father
The Family Letters of Charles Nisbet

David W. Robson

The Reverend Charles Nisbet was a Scottish Presbyterian immigrant who came to America just after the Revolution, and he became the first president of Dickinson College in Carlisle, Pennsylvania. His life in America was not a happy one; he made that abundantly clear in a large body of surviving letters that reveal his impressions concerning events taking place in early national Pennsylvania.[1] Nisbet quickly became alienated from American beliefs and behaviors in politics, religion and social affairs.[2] His letters also reveal an ongoing concern for family matters, especially the fortunes of his children as they matured in their new (and, in his view, hostile) environment. In order to understand Nisbet's worldview, it seems necessary to understand his family life. Thus the question arises: what insights might the work of family historians contribute to the research of the political and intellectual historian?

Enough work has been done on the seventeenth and eighteenth century Anglo-American family, from Edmund Morgan's study of the Puritan family to Peter Laslett's work on Tudor-Stuart England,[3] from the early demographic explorations of Massachusetts towns to the more recent explications of middle colony and Chesapeake family life,[4] that syntheses have now appeared. Perhaps the most useful are Philip J. Greven's *The Protestant Temperament* and Lawrence Stone's *The Family, Sex, and Marriage in England, 1500–1800* which are complementary undertakings.[5] The new particularist studies of the 1980s seem aimed at fleshing out their arguments.[6]

We need not reprise the entire synthesis, but three of its arguments are of interest here. First, there appear to have been different types of families from the seventeenth through the eighteenth centuries, each with its own attitudes toward child rearing, family member roles, and intellectual and emotional expression.[7] Second, these family types succeeded one another to a degree; toward the latter part of the eighteenth century, then, familial relations became more affectionate, including kinder conduct by parents toward children, manifested in less restrictive early training and more autonomy for children as they matured into adulthood.[8] Third, there evolved with the different family types a slow change in the roles played in child rearing by mothers and fathers. Among what Greven terms genteel families and Stone calls closed domesticated nuclear families, fathers became less intimately involved with child rearing as they turned more of their attention to a world of work now outside the home, and mothers took over the daily supervision of children, the inculcation of their moral values and even their academic skills.[9]

In this latter process, we know more about the actions of women than men, largely through the work of Mary Beth Norton and others on the Republican Mother.[10] But very recently some scholars, led by John Demos and his students, have turned to the study of the early American father.[11]

These scholars argue that, due to the changing economic role of the family and to the divorce of the workplace from the home, the father's role in the family changed—that his role declined, in fact. Earlier, a father both controlled all the family's property and was home to supervise his realm. He was a patriarch who not only dispensed discipline, but also taught morals, manners, academic skills and practical lessons. He approved marriages and provided for his children's adult lives. He was psychologist, confidante, exemplar of proper conduct, and companion to his children as well.[12] Greven's argument anticipates some of these behaviors, which he associates either with evangelical or moderate temperaments, depending on whether a father tried to break his children's wills and instill a loathing of self or to discipline through shame and withdrawal of affection in order to develop a strong conscience.[13]

By the last third of the eighteenth century, an increasing

number of families turned to fathers as their sole economic supports. Many of these fathers worked outside the home so they could not play the same intimate role in their children's upbringings. A father might still set the standards of morality for his family, might still have the final (but not the most direct) word on discipline, might occasionally play with his children or applaud their actions. But these activities were limited to the time he had left for home—after work. Some of his old roles were disappearing or were already gone—pedagogue, moral overseer, companion—hence the Republican Mother. Oddly, in what became a more emotional, affectionate family, the father became less involved in its emotional life. A father's principal roles became those of provider and of teacher about "the world outside" with all its dangers and corruption.[14] These are characteristics that Greven would attribute to genteel families and Stone to closed nuclear domesticated ones.

Trying to apply the insights from the Greven-Stone models to the family life of Charles Nisbet proves difficult. His "real world" circumstances did not quite match those typical of these models, and his fatherhood was much more complicated than the models suggest it should have been.

Charles Nisbet was nearly 50 years old when he decided to bring his family to America in 1785. He had been born into a modest family, had improved his status through clerical education at the University of Edinburgh, and had been pastor of the church at Montrose, a moderately prosperous town on the northeast coast of Scotland, for nearly 25 years.[15] During the middle of the eighteenth century, the Scottish Church divided into parties over practical issues, such as the provision of ministerial livings by wealthy parishioners, and theological issues, such as the efficacy of good works in the process of salvation. Those who did not support living provisions and salvation through works were known as evangelicals; those who did were moderates. Nisbet was an evangelical and was outspoken in church disputes.[16]

In 1766, Nisbet had married Ann Tweedie, the literate daughter of a well-to-do family, who by 1785 had borne eight children, four of whom had survived infancy. Little is known of the early family life of the Nisbets, but there are suggestions that their relationships were affectionate. Nisbet and his wife could still grieve over the deaths of their infant children some 25 years afterward. They took pains to educate all their children to a high degree of literacy. And they enabled Tom, their eldest, to earn a

Master of Arts degree at Edinburgh in such a way that he could determine his own future.[17]

These few details of the Nisbet's Scottish life prompt the supposition that they were what Stone calls a closed domesticated nuclear family, but that this family was a subtype characteristic of middle to lower-class Puritans and other nonconformists. In these families, the parent-child relationship was affectionate and concerned. Discipline took the form of galvanizing the child's conscience through prayer, moralizing and the threat of damnation rather than the child-centered laissez-faire practices of the rich.[18] If we restate this analysis in Greven's terms, we have in Nisbet a father with some evangelical leanings, but who operated primarily in a moderate mode of child rearing.

Exactly what motivated Nisbet to sacrifice Scottish security for the unknown perils of frontier Pennsylvania is not clear, but he seems to have been partially inspired by a particular view of the American Revolution. He had supported the Americans in their disputes with the British during the 1760s, and he became a partisan of the rebels during the war. When he left Scotland, he wrote to friends that he was pleased to be heading for a land of "Liberty & Plenty," where men's minds were "free from shackles of authority."[19] Once in America, he became rapidly disillusioned with this new land, however. His specific grievances spanned political, religious, social and economic developments, but the underlying theme he repeatedly touched on was a decline of morality from the standard he believed must have existed during the Revolution.[20] Here again, we see characteristics of Greven's evangelicals, gravely disappointed by the failure of the political revolution to effect similar results in moral and spiritual life.[21]

Nisbet, thus, presents a complex picture. He lived during an era and worked at a profession that suggested a moderate family orientation, and some of his conduct indicates that he had that. But he brought what appears to have been both an evangelical and a moderate temperament to his role as father. The roles he assumed toward his young adult children and the ways he tried to influence their conduct once the family was in America confirm the ambiguity and ambivalence of his character.

We know about Nisbet's conduct toward his children through a series of letters he wrote to or about them. Most concern the affairs of two of the children: Tom, the elder boy, and Mary, the elder girl. In 1791, Mary wed William Turnbull, the son of a Philadelphia commercial family. Mary and William went first to Pittsburgh and later to Philadelphia as Turnbull pursued a commercial career.

During these years, Mary seems to have had a pleasant, prosperous, occasionally exciting life. Nisbet kept in close touch with her until his death. Tom, on the other hand, was a black sheep. Full of promise upon his arrival in America, he soon became an alcoholic and a perpetual source of anguish to his parents. He died in his early thirties in a Philadelphia asylum.[22] Charles Nisbet's relationships with Mary and Tom demonstrate the varied and contradictory roles he played as a father in the new republic.

When the family first arrived in America, Nisbet played the genteel father toward Tom by allowing him to select his own profession—the law—by supporting him in his efforts to master it, and by celebrating his early indications of success.[23] When things began to sour for Tom, Nisbet responded by bringing him home, paying his debts and otherwise indulging him, while deluding himself for some time that the boy's affliction was a kind of melancholy.[24] But the father's patience eventually wore thin, and he took an extraordinary course of action. Much as Edmund Morgan has hypothesized the early New England Puritans did with their rebellious children, Nisbet sent the obdurate young man to live with another family. Tom went across the state to live with Judge Alexander Addison, who had become friends with Nisbet on the voyage to America. Tom might disobey his father's wishes, but he was not "so ill-bred, as to oppose a Person in your Station." Nisbet told Tom that he had disowned him, would not communicate with him, nor offer any support until he had mended his ways.[25] No evangelical patriarch could have been more severe.

But Nisbet could not hold to his resolve. Through Addison, he changed tactics, establishing an account for Tom's support (except for drinking debts) and urging the judge to appeal to the boy's conscience:

> Represent to him how mean a Thing it is, for one who was born a Man, to chuse rather to be a Brute, & an object of Scorn and Contempt to every Creature, as he has been by his own Choice for some Years past. Labor to excite in him a lively Idea of the Baseness of Drunkenness and the Destruction it brings to a Man's Health, Life, Character, and Circumstances.

He was sure that Addison had already used the weapon of loss of family affection: "No doubt you have told him, that he is breaking the Hearts of his Parents by his vile Conduct, as well as disgracing his Brother & Sisters, who never mention him, nor suffer any to mention him to them."[26]

Continuing the behavior of a moderate but pushing it to an extreme (as was Nisbet's habit with most things), he soon proposed outlandish appeals to his son's conscience. First, he bid Addison to persuade the young daughter of a mutual friend to visit Tom, "to remonstrate with him on the Indecency of his Conduct" and to obtain a promise of reformation and a return to business. But within a week he had another idea. Recalling that John Bunyan, author of *Pilgrim's Progress,* had begun to muse over the state of his soul when reproved by a woman of unsavory character, Nisbet urged the judge to find a woman of ill-repute and hire her "to abuse [Tom] with all the Rudeness, Contempt and Asperity she can muster. . . . It is necessary that bad People should know what others think of them."[27]

Neither ostracism from his family nor appeals to conscience from any of these sources brought any reformation in Tom. After nearly 18 months, Nisbet brought the young man back home where he lived for some years. Alternating between lucidity and a drunken stupor, Tom read law and worked when he could, but that was not often. Usually he did nothing but bring shame to the family. Nisbet continued to remonstrate with him, but he knew it was a losing battle. He feared that the boy would go insane, and apparently he did, but his lonely death in Philadelphia followed that of his father by a few months. Nisbet found no escape from Tom in this world.[28]

As we have seen, Nisbet's behavior changed with his son's. Tom's early promise, even his initial illness, corresponded with a genteel mode of childrearing on Nisbet's part. Tom's continued degeneration and Nisbet's despair brought out fatherly behaviors that seem to fit the evangelical or moderate mode. Nisbet served as provider, as moral guide, as confidante, as nurse, as companion, but also as patriarch and judge. Charles Nisbet appears to have been confined to no set mode of child rearing; he adapted his behavior as he saw fit to meet each set of circumstances.

Nisbet's conduct toward Mary, part of a much happier relationship, was nonetheless equally complex. He apparently allowed her to choose her own husband, subject to approval, and began to write her shortly after her marriage and removal to Pittsburgh in 1791. He continued the correspondence until ill health overtook him at the end of the decade. A major theme of these letters was advice as to the proper conduct of a wife and mother. From the start, Nisbet counseled Mary about relations with her husband: "you ought to study to make your Husband happy, & to avoid every Thing that may displease him, if you expect that he should promote your Happiness." Mary should "overlook trifles" and "support disagreeable Sensations"; she should "regulate herself entirely by the Taste of her Husband."[29] If Nisbet believed in indulging Mary's wishes at home, he did not think the practice should extend to marriage.

The anxious father concerned himself with other facets of marriage. In a roundabout way, he warned Mary against extramarital sex: "In this licentious Age, even married Women are not out of reach of Temptation, & if a Woman by Levity give Encouragement to it, which she may do with the greatest Innocence . . . she may make herself miserable for Life by her Imprudence and want of Caution." When Mary became pregnant, her father turned medical adviser. He was especially worried by two falls she had and urged her to restrict her movement. Even after Mary's safe delivery of a healthy girl, Nisbet advised caution, "as Women in your Situation require much Care & are exposed to so many Accidents. . . ." She should not even "talk much to those who come to visit you, till you have in good Measure recovered your Strength." When Mary experienced sore breasts while nursing, Nisbet worried about "the Weed," a form of puerperal fever, and he wanted frequent reports of her health.[30]

Only in his advice concerning childbirth did Nisbet indicate that he had conferred with his wife. He passed along pleasantries from mother to daughter, but not advice. If Ann Nisbet ever wrote to Mary, the letters have not survived. Charles and Ann may have had a marital relationship such as the kind he advised for Mary and her husband. Whatever the case, Nisbet felt it his function to counsel Mary on all matters domestic and personal. He continued to do so after the Trumbulls moved to Philadelphia. He was concerned with the occasional outbreaks of disease in the capital, but most of his advice touched on her now elevated social standing. To protect that, he said, she must regulate her conduct, especially conversation. She should not "talk familiarly" with all her visitors, remembering that not all were true friends, "but many come to spy [on] you, & get something to tell to your Disadvantage." He also advised her to repeat no grievances, to make no "Comparisons which are odious," to watch against passions, to "beware of profuse Compliments to Strangers"—the list was endless.[31]

Nisbet's role as intimate adviser to Mary, even on subjects that one would suppose would be in the woman's sphere, again suggests that this post-Revolutionary family's relationships were not all modern. But if the admonitory tone of the correspondence is a patriarchal (evangelical?) throwback, another theme of the letters is equally surprising. Nisbet quite clearly believed that Mary was politically astute. Almost every letter he wrote her contained passages offering his own extremely conservative views of political developments, and occasionally he asked for her own. While Mary lived in Pittsburgh, Nisbet kept her posted on the course of the French Revolution and its effects on England and Scotland. He worried about the actions of the western Indians, asked for her thoughts and observations about them, and noted how both state and national governments treated the issue of frontier defense.[32]

When Mary moved to Philadelphia, Nisbet's observations shifted to state and national party politics. He urged her to be cautious in public: "do not lay yourself open to any Body. . . . You are among a divided People, but it is not necessary that you should take any Part in their Divisions." Mary was to be neutral, but her father was not. His hatred of Republicans was clear. She should "make no Entertainments to Members of Congress or others, altho' Citizen Monroe & the Lyon [Representative Matthew Lyon of Vermont] should inform you that they intend to do you the Honor of dining with you." And by all means, Mary must "abhor French Fashions & Varieties of Dress. Study Neatness & Oeconomy & let any that pleases, imitate the Actresses & Fishwomen of Paris."[33]

The rise of the Republicans in 1798–1799 inflamed Nisbet, who confided his thoughts to his daughter. He informed her of the Carlisle "Democrats" unhappiness at news of a British naval victory over the French and wondered about the reaction in Philadelphia. He also mused on George Logan's reception by the Adams Administration upon Logan's return from his unofficial peace mission to France. In the event of war with France, he wanted to know, what could be expected from the large number of newly arrived Irish immigrants in Pennsylvania? These letters were rife with sarcastic attacks on prominent Republicans: Logan, Albert Gallatin, Monroe, Lyon and Pennsylvania governor Thomas McKean. Mary was presumed to know all about political issues and divisions, even to know enough about her husband's business to understand her father's reflections on how trade would be affected by domestic politics and foreign policy.[34]

The duality of this correspondence is remarkable. In domestic affairs, Mary was treated as a child to be lectured at long distance by a greater moral authority and one with more wisdom and experience. But in the public sphere, Nisbet regarded his daughter as a political sophisticate whom he could address in much the same way as he did his male correspondents. In both these behaviors, Nisbet confounds the standard picture of the early American father.

What to make of all this? With his troubled son Tom, Nisbet played several roles; these ranged along a spectrum from evangelical patriarch to the affectionate but distant genteel father, although he most often acted as a moderate. With Mary, he seems to have been equally contradictory, usurping his wife's role as traditional mother, but at the same time becoming a kind of male analog of the newly emerging "Republican Mother." Nisbet, then, neither adhered to a consistent mode of fatherly conduct, nor even always manifested "fatherly" behavior.

Is it possible that these varied actions add up to a "Republican Father" whose roles were a hitherto unidentified blend of old and new, male and female, evangelical, moderate and genteel roles? I think not, for to hypothesize such a new model would be to create the same kinds of concrete boundaries that would confine others just as the current models confine Nisbet's behavior.

What we can glean from Charles Nisbet's varied roles, however, is that he was caught up in a rapidly changing society, and he recognized the changes and adapted some of his conduct to meet them. He took his family from a culture steeped in tradition to one trying to invent itself, from an aristocratic polity to a highly democratic one, from an established church to one competing for public favor, from a highly stratified society to a nondeferential one, and from an economy still influenced by mercantilism to one beginning to wrestle with the free market and the spirit of individual enterprise. His children, not surprisingly, melded with this new land (for well or ill) more quickly than he did. To maintain his "proper" relationship with them, he tried everything he knew, ranging all over a landscape of behaviors that we—not he—have classified as types.

The "Republican Father," it seems, was a transitional father. What the models tell us is that he fit none of them exactly, but rather drew on modes of conduct that had spanned three centuries in order to meet conditions and circumstances that were both unprecedented and baffling. We can argue, of course, that all eras are characterized by change, but during some of them the pace accelerates and the degree intensifies. By comparing the behavior of individual families to the behavioral models typical of an era, we can gain some appreciation of that family's immersion in the changes that overtook the era and its ability to accommodate them. In the realm of family behavior, as in so many other areas, Charles Nisbet tried to cope with these changes, but ultimately could not.

8

Our Mothers, Our Selves

American Mother-Daughter Relationships, 1880–1920

Linda W. Rosenzweig

In 1917, a contributor to the popular women's magazine, *Good Housekeeping*, made the following assertion:

> In the lifetime of girls even 20 years old, the tradition of what girls should be and do in the world has changed as much as heretofore in a century. It used to be that girls looked forward with confidence to domestic life as their destiny. That is still the destiny of most of them, but it is a destiny that in this generation seems to be modified for all, and avoided by very many. . . .
>
> The mothers of these modern girls are very much like hens that have hatched out ducks. Whether they believe in current feminine aspirations or not makes not very much difference. . . .[1]

These observations highlight the fact that the American family experienced major changes during the late nineteenth and early twentieth centuries and that these changes had a significant impact on the lives of American women. As America evolved into a fully mature industrial society, a number of trends that had emerged during the early decades of industrialization in-

Author's Note: The research for this paper was funded in part by grants from the Radcliffe Research Support Program and the National Endowment for the Humanities Travel to Collections Program. The author wishes to thank Professor Peter N. Stearns for his continuing interest and support and for his comments on an earlier version of the paper, and Professor Jean Hunter for her helpful suggestions and advice.

creased in intensity. The separation of home and workplace was completed, and new forms of both work and leisure developed. The birth rate declined dramatically, and child health improved. New, so-called "scientific" child-rearing advice, directed particularly toward mothers, was promulgated widely. Outside agencies—schools, youth organizations and women's clubs—increasingly intruded into the family.

For girls and young women, these developments resulted in important changes. New kinds of work, such as clerical and department store sales positions, offered more independence. Extended educational experiences, including secondary school and even college for a growing number of girls as well, broadened their horizons, as did the plethora of clubs and women's associations to which they were exposed. At the same time, socialization toward distinctive emotional styles, especially the control of anger, differentiated girls' experiences from those of their brothers; this contrasted with earlier socialization regarding anger, which had not emphasized gender-based distinctions of this type.[2]

In the context of these changes, the perception of an emerging female generation gap, as articulated in the comments quoted from *Good Housekeeping*, is understandable. Certainly during the period from 1880 to 1920, the world of daughters, particularly in middle-class families, differed from the world that their mothers and grandmothers had experienced earlier in the nineteenth century. As Carroll Smith-Rosenberg has pointed out, that earlier world had offered women few viable alternatives to marriage and a traditional role in the family, so that a continuity of expectation and experience linked the female generations and fostered mother-daughter intimacy. Smith-Rosenberg suggests that the disruption of that continuity introduced conflict, estrangement and alienation into a previously harmonious relationship.[3]

It was this disruption and the apparent attendant tension that concerned the author of the *Good Housekeeping* article and many others who wrote for popular periodicals. Throughout the late nineteenth and early twentieth centuries, articles, editorials and advice columns implied that serious problems existed in the area of mother-daughter relationships. Much of this discussion focused on a perceived lack of communication, frequently blaming maternal behaviors and attitudes for daughters' failures to confide in their mothers. In 1884, the first year of its existence, the *Ladies Home Journal* took a firm stand on this matter: "It is the companionable mothers who are the only ones to keep their girls' confidences. The severely critical mothers are not of this clan, nor those who are impatient of a child's many failures and shortcomings."[4] Subsequent issues offered advice along similar lines. For example, mothers were told to avoid sending a daughter to boarding school as it would make her "reticent and disinclined to talk of things nearest her heart," to take an interest in what their daughters were doing, to remember what it was like to be 18, to keep themselves young, and to avoid "sighing" and melancholy moods.[5]

Daughters were urged to do their part to improve communication: "Never be ashamed to tell her, who should be your best friend and confidant, of all you think and feel. It is very strange that so many young girls will tell every person before 'mother' that which is most important she should know," one writer advised.[6] Another suggested, ". . . take as much care to cultivate the friendship of your mother as you would that of a stranger. . . . it's a thousand times more worth having and she'll always put you first."[7]

If communication was defined as the major problem, the discipline and training of young women also generated concern. Late nineteenth century periodicals characterized American daughters as forward and overindulged, and castigated their mothers for the fact that their daughters were not as well-behaved as their European counterparts. Disrespectful daughters were viewed as "vulgar." A mother who was "all she ought to be" would see to it that her daughter would respect her.[8]

Popular magazines continued to emphasize mother-daughter conflict after the turn of the century. Additional communication difficulties were cited during the period 1900–1920: the reluctance of mothers to answer their daughters' biological, intellectual and religious questions; the failure of college-educated daughters and their mothers to respect each others' values and points of view; and the impatience of adult daughters with the whims of aging mothers.[9] While daughters were admonished to do their part to ease the strains in the mother-daughter relationship, they continued to be portrayed as the aggrieved parties. The author of a column for young women began an article entitled "The Mother of My Girl" with a reference to the many letters from readers that caused her to wonder "what the mothers all over the world are doing" regarding their obligations to their daughters. In the same vein, an editorial in *The Independent* in September 1901 observed that:

> The unnatural burden of filial obligations and scruples imposed by some mothers is the prime factor of the secret

> antagonism existing between them [mothers and daughters]. . . . As a matter of fact, there is less need of confidences between the two than is generally supposed,—and much more need of confidence.[10]

The emphasis on mother-daughter conflict in widely read popular periodicals certainly implies that the relationship was in a state of crisis in more than a few families during this period of transition in the lives of American women.[11] Like the periodical literature, the most useful sources for an assessment of the accuracy of this impression—primarily personal documents such as correspondence, diaries and autobiographies—record the experiences of middle- and upper-class white American women.[12] A full examination of mother-daughter relationships would have to consider the possibility that in this area, as in family history more generally, middle-class patterns of behavior defined standards that were applied to the rest of society and presumably had some impact on interactions in other groups, although such standards were not necessarily internalized by those groups.[13] This paper will examine the middle-class experience in a preliminary effort to determine the degree to which the magazines' images of mother-daughter conflict reflected actual family interactions in that segment of society.

An investigation of the sources corroborates the existence of a range of mother-daughter conflicts between 1880 and 1920. But the various personal documents reveal a far more complex picture of relations in two generations of middle-class mothers and daughters than either Smith-Rosenberg's research or the periodical literature acknowledges. Typically, mother-daughter conflict seems to have been balanced—if not outweighed—by powerful support and mutual caring, even in families where daughters' aspirations and experiences differed significantly from those of their mothers. Therefore, interactions were characterized at least as much by understanding as by alienation. Indeed, mothers appear to have played a vital enabling role in the process of daughters' taking advantage of the new options available to them. And daughters seem to have recognized and valued the backing provided by their mothers.

Examples of such relationships span the 40-year period under consideration. Anne Bent Ware Winsor and her daughter, Annie Winsor Allen, offer an interesting first-generation case. A collection of nearly 30 years' worth of letters reveals a demanding, critical mother who complained and nagged incessantly, and a patient daughter who found their relationship stressful, but who loved and understood her mother. When Mrs. Winsor scolded her for looking down while speaking, Annie, aged 21, replied:

> I am so afraid of the criticysm [sic], correction or dissatisfaction that may be in your face and eyes that I do not dare to look up. . . . I am so afraid you will not like my way of doing things, my opinions and my tastes that I seem indifferent and offish . . . it is because I care so much to please you that I despair and grow discouraged.[14]

She not only wanted to please her mother; she was also willing to humor, support and reassure her: "I cannot imagine myself wishing to prevent my mother from showing her full share of interest in me . . . I want you to understand me and not to worry silently," Annie told her mother.[15] Mrs. Winsor took her at her word and continued to express that "full share of interest," feeling free, for example, to ask her daughter, now about 34 years old, "Do you realize that you are habitually stooping a great deal? It's very unbecoming and will soon become so fixed that you can't cure it, unless you set about it at once."[16]

On the surface, this relationship appears to have been a *Ladies Home Journal* classic, but it was more complex. Mrs. Winsor criticized and complained, but she also consistently expressed warm affection for her daughter, encouraged her educational aspirations, and applauded her success as an educator and a contributor (under the pen name Marion Sprague) to the *Ladies Home Journal*. And Annie remained unusually communicative, affectionate, supportive and tolerant of her mother's needs.[17]

Another interesting example is that of M. Carey Thomas, one of Annie's contemporaries and the future president of Bryn Mawr College. She described her relationship with her mother in her journal when she was 22 years old:

> I have just had a talk with Mother and I do believe I shall shoot myself. . . . There is no use living and then Mother would see in the morning that she had been cruel. She says I outrage her every feeling, that it is the greatest living grief to her to have me in the house. . . . that I make the other children unbelieving, that I barely tolerate Father, and that I am utterly and entirely selfish. . . . O heavens what a religion that makes a mother cast her daughter off![18]

This young woman's problems with her mother stemmed from weightier issues than posture and personal appearance. Even as a young girl, M. Carey Thomas had devoted herself to her studies, resisting any notion of traditional female roles and activities. She seriously questioned her family's religious beliefs and eventually rebelled against her strict Quaker upbringing. Her conflict with her mother escalated when she lived at home following two years of study at Cornell. Clearly, as Smith-Rosenberg has also noted, tension was present in this relationship.[19]

Yet it had been her mother who had supported and encouraged the young woman's educational aspirations in the face of her father's religiously based opposition: "Many and dreadful are the talks we have had upon this subject, but Mother, my own splendid mother, helped me in this as she always has in everything and sympathized with me," the daughter had written four years earlier.[20] And it was her mother who borrowed money to send her abroad for graduate study, whose health she worried over while she was in Europe, and with whom she ecstatically shared the triumph of the successful completion of her dissertation and her comprehensive exams, asking on 25 November 1882: "Mother, is it not too splendid to be true?"[21] Here, as with Annie Winsor Allen, mother-daughter conflict, in this case over fundamental value issues, was offset by strong maternal support.

Like Carey Thomas in the previous generation, Hilda Worthington Smith, born in 1888, was committed to her studies. She argued frequently with her mother about her clothes, her interpersonal skills and her sense of responsibility.[22] But her mother—who, like Carey Thomas's mother, had been deprived of higher education herself—understood her daughter's aspirations. She encouraged Hilda's college activities, providing both laundry service and moral support for Hilda at Bryn Mawr: "I was sure your speech *would* be a success. Did you add anything to it? Write me any more said about it! When does the next one come?" she wrote enthusiastically on one occasion.[23]

In this instance, maternal support was somewhat ambivalent, as Mrs. Smith often objected vigorously to any plans proposed by her children that would result in their living away from her. Her ambivalence seems to be more reflective of the fact that she was widowed at an early age than of any fundamental disapproval of her daughter's activities, but in her journal, Hilda complained about her mother's attitude on more than one occasion.[24] Yet with her mother's blessing, she became a successful social worker, labor educator and an administrator at Bryn Mawr, where her mother eventually lived with her. Some

20 pages of Hilda's journal record her grief and her sense of loss following her mother's illness and death from pneumonia on Christmas morning, 1917: "I cannot *bear* to have her gone. I think I was more of a companion to her than the others [her siblings], we had read so much & done so many things together. . . .," she wrote.[25]

Among the letters of condolence she received is one of particular interest, written by M. Carey Thomas (whom she knew from Bryn Mawr) on 20 January 1918:

> Ever since I heard of your Mother's death I have been wishing to write to tell you how deeply I sympathized with you, but I hesitated because I remember as if it were yesterday—and it is thirty years ago—how hard it was for me to get letters about my Mother after she died. There is nothing in the world quite like one's Mother's death and I think one never ceases to miss her however long one survives her.[26]

Neither M. Carey Thomas nor Hilda Smith was a "traditional" daughter. Neither ever married. Both were outstandingly successful, independent, professional people. Annie Winsor Allen followed a more traditional path in that she married and had three children of her own, but she also continued to pursue her career. All three women experienced conflict with their mothers, but all relied on maternal support as they fulfilled their aspirations.

The sources document many other intriguing instances of maternal support for daughters' untraditional activities. For example, Vida Scudder's widowed mother took her sewing and went with her daughter to tutorial sessions at Oxford because the tutor preferred not to meet alone with female students; she had previously accompanied Vida to Northampton at the beginning of her freshman year at Smith, where she walked a mile and a half to the dormitory at 6:30 every morning for several weeks to help her daughter, who had never "'done'" her own hair.[27] Mary Simkhovitch's mother also traveled with her daughter when she went abroad for graduate study: "Girls were not free then to take trips by themselves, and in any case, it was a great adventure for us both . . .," Mary explained in her autobiography.[28]

While few mothers would have had the freedom or the inclination to accompany daughters to European universities, three final examples attest to the fact that such types of unqualified support were certainly not rare. The mother of Louise

Marion Bosworth offered enthusiastic encouragement to her daughter at Wellesley. "Oh Louise, I believe you have a future before you . . . I am so glad you could go to college . . . I feel sorry for these girls who have a mother so narrow, that they have to wait until they are married before they can do the things that young people love to do . . .," she wrote in 1902. Her support continued as Louise pursued her career in social work: "I enjoyed reading the clipping you sent. It certainly seems that your work is greatly appreciated. I feel proud that I have a child who can do so much good."[29]

Marion Talbot's mother's support extended beyond the sort of moral support provided by Mrs. Bosworth; she organized the Association of Collegiate Alumnae, the predecessor of the American Association of University Women, expressly to build a community for women college graduates when more conventional childhood friends ostracized her daughter following her graduation from Boston University.[30] Finally, Ethel Sturges Dummer provided unequivocal support for all four of her daughters in diverse ways—for example, accompanying the oldest daughter and her fiancé when they eloped without his parents' knowledge, and assuring another daughter: ". . . if any plan comes up that really tempts you, you and your life and work, that which you have to offer to the world, must be considered as of most importance . . . Your life must not be stunted by us . . . Our love can make any leaps of time and distance."[31]

The foregoing examples, and others too numerous for inclusion in the present discussion, suggest that the emphasis on mother-daughter conflict in the late nineteenth and early twentieth century periodical literature does not necessarily reflect actual middle-class family experience. Conflict certainly existed, but middle-class mothers apparently were far more tolerant of their daughters' untraditional choices and activities than the literature would indicate. Indeed, they appear to have provided essential support in more than a few cases. Thus, despite Smith-Rosenberg's contention that the "new" young women of the late nineteenth and early twentieth centuries repudiated the world of their mothers, it seems clear that their mothers did not repudiate the daughters or their world.[32] The explanation for this discrepancy between the periodical literature and the personal documents must be sought in the trend toward "scientific" motherhood, the nature of the popular periodicals, the particular experiences of individual mothers and daughters, and the collective social and psychological experiences of women.

The sense of crisis conveyed by the periodical literature may actually reflect the "professionalization" of motherhood in the second half of the nineteenth century and the development of formal public concern over adolescence at the beginning of the twentieth century, rather than any generalized growth of mother-daughter conflict.[33] The growing emphasis on the importance of so-called expert advice as essential for proper child rearing, which is also exemplified in the proliferation of advice books for mothers, may account for the number of magazine articles that blamed mothers for intergenerational difficulties and offered guidance for solving such problems. Indeed, articles of this sort may have been responsible for identifying occurrences formerly viewed as normal parts of family life as serious problems—moody daughters or impatient mothers, for example.

On the other hand, the impression that earlier nineteenth century mother-daughter relationships were untroubled and harmonious may be erroneous. While Smith-Rosenberg found no evidence of tension in her study of the female world during the first two-thirds of the nineteenth century, other sources document the presence of mother-daughter conflict during this period.[34] It is possible that conservative editorial writers and columnists were personally uncomfortable with the changes in the world of women; therefore, they might have exaggerated the newness of the tensions between mothers and daughters as well as the extent of the conflict. The *Ladies Home Journal*, for example, may reflect the point of view of its male editor, Edward Bok, who was not known for his liberal views, rather than any major increase in intergenerational discord.[35]

With regard to periodical literature generally, and certainly in the present case, it is relevant to note that articles about controversial topics help to sell magazines. Some mothers and daughters who were troubled by tension and conflict undoubtedly turned to magazine articles for help. But others who did not personally identify with the discussions may also have enjoyed reading the articles and congratulating themselves on avoiding such problems. Thus, if reader response suggested that the focus on troubled relationships between female family members helped to boost circulation, magazines would have found it profitable to publish articles on this topic.

Several aspects of women's individual and collective experiences suggest additional explanations. First, and perhaps most obviously, individual personality differences must be taken into account. Not all mothers nagged and complained as Annie Winsor Allen's mother did; not all daughters were as patient and tolerant as Annie was. Similarly, very few mothers were as sophisticated and open as Ethel Sturges Dummer was. Certainly conflict in the relationship—or its absence—was at least in part a function of the specific characteristics of individuals.

Similar, specific experiences may help to explain the lack of conflict in particular instances. Certain widowed mothers may have felt that it was essential to remain in their daughters' good graces since they were otherwise alone in the world. They may have accepted what, in some sense, was unacceptable to them in the interests of preserving a relationship that they needed for their own security. Such women may also have been able to fill the void left in their own lives by the loss of a spouse through their involvement in their daughters' lives. While this situation would seem more typical in the case of a mother's relationship with a married daughter with children, it may also describe mothers whose daughters chose less conventional options—for example, the mothers of Vida Scudder and Hilda Worthington Smith. Likewise, mothers whose own educational aspirations had not been fulfilled may have lived out those desires vicariously through the act of assisting their daughters to achieve their goals.[36]

Although domestic roles still dominated the lives of middle-class women in the period under consideration, their lives were not as narrowly circumscribed as might be expected. During most of the nineteenth century, women were active in various religious and social organizations and causes outside the home. Involvement in external activities was not a new idea to late nineteenth and early twentieth century mothers, nor was secondary education, which had been available earlier in the century in the form of private female academies and seminaries and even in a public high school for girls founded in Worcester, Massachusetts in 1824. Thus while their daughters' aspirations extended beyond the boundaries of the mothers' own experiences to encompass college and career goals, their own socialization did include the concept that women's "sphere" reached beyond the home.[37] In this sense, the modification of women's destiny referred to in the introduction to this paper may represent a development along a continuum rather than a significant disruption.

Throughout the nineteenth and early twentieth centuries, women's socialization also encouraged the suppression of anger. This fact probably explains the general absence of overt expressions of anger between mothers and daughters. Failure to express anger, however, certainly does not indicate that women did not feel this emotion throughout the nineteenth century and during the period 1880–1920.[38] Recent research has suggested that for some middle-class young women in the past, unexpressed family conflict—particularly mother-daughter tension—was manifested through serious illnesses, specifically anorexia nervosa and related eating disorders.[39] While relatively few daughters suffered these illnesses, the possible connection between these disorders and the repression of mother-daughter conflict encourages further consideration of the role of psychological issues in the historical interpretation of the mother-daughter relationship.

Feminist theorists have stressed the relevance of object-relations theory in explaining the dynamics of mother-daughter interactions. This theory emphasizes the importance of the child's social relational experience from earliest infancy. It argues that the experiences of girls are unique because they share the gender of the primary caretaker, the mother. Mothers tend to identify with infant daughters; they do not experience them as separate entities as they do infant sons, but rather seem to view them as extensions of themselves. Girls remain attached to their mothers for a longer period of time and therefore experience difficulty in separating from them. Eventually girls may alternate between total rejection of the mother who represents infantile dependence, and identification of themselves as the mother's double.[40]

Object-relations theory has been used in analyses of contemporary mother-daughter relationships.[41] It is ahistorical in that it does not take into account social and cultural conditions and changes in the family over time. Because it posits a nuclear family structure characterized by role divisions like those found in the late nineteenth and early twentieth century middle-class American family, however, it may offer a useful supplementary perspective for our analysis of the mother-daughter relationship during this period.[42] The application of the theory to 1880–1920 data suggests that the characteristic combination of conflict and caring might in some sense mirror the ambivalence and fear of separation attributed to both mother and daughter by object-relations theory. This also raises interesting questions regarding the nature of mother-daughter relationships in the preindustrial family, when women did not yet concentrate so intensely and exclusively on mothering.

While this brief survey of the mother-daughter relationship indicates that actual family experiences differed from the impressions conveyed by popular magazines, it also reveals that mother-daughter relationships were viewed as profoundly important by individual women and by the wider society during the period 1880–1920. Probably the sentiment expressed by one outspoken mother in a letter written in 1910 would have been applauded by more than a few of her contemporaries: "Daughters are wonderful luxuries; they are well worth a bad husband in my opinion: at least mine are."[43] Further study should illuminate the subtleties of mother-daughter interactions in the past and help to establish a historical context for the evaluation of the sense of tension in the relationship that has been articulated, both formally and informally, by so many contemporary American women—women who, in turn, should also help us to better understand our mothers, our daughters and ourselves.

9

Medicine and the Health Crisis of the Urban Black American Family, 1910–1945

David McBride

Historians of modern American medicine have commonly identified the early twentieth century as a period of profound change in both the provision and consumption of health care. Physicians strove to increase their scientific expertise, professionalism and social authority while limiting the number of poorly trained medical practitioners.[1] Hospitals pressed forward in expanding their patient care functions, clinical teaching programs and clinical research.[2] Public health physicians, administrators and nurses assumed wider roles in applying new epidemiological advances in the community and in undertaking campaigns among the poor sponsored by the large philanthropies. The era also saw increased roles for government health agencies in their enforcement of the growing number of health regulations.[3]

This expansion of the medical establishment was intertwined with the growing industrialization and urbanization of early twentieth century American society. Among the millions who were drawn to American cities during the first three decades of the twentieth century were 2.25 million rural blacks who left the depressed farming regions of the South to settle in the nation's large cities.[4] This rural-to-urban shift left many blacks and their families concentrated in crowded, impoverished neighborhoods where widespread health problems existed. As accurate statistics on health conditions became available, health professionals became aware of serious discrepancies between black and white mortality rates. Statistics from Birmingham, Alabama, were typical of the situation. There, infectious diseases such as tuberculosis caused an annual death rate between 1905–1915 that averaged 80 (per 100,000) for white residents but 390 for blacks. Blacks comprised 39 percent of Birmingham's total population in 1915, but 76 percent of the tuberculosis deaths.[5]

The census returns for 1900 and 1910, though incomplete, provided medical and government authorities with enough information to create alarm about the extraordinarily high death rates for blacks in most of the major infectious-related disease categories. In 1910, mortality rates for whites and blacks in the cities were approximately 14.6 and 25.5, respectively. In both the urban North and the urban South, black death rates tended to be double those of whites.[6] This substantial gap in general mortality rates between the nation's black and white populations was largely the result of high black death rates from infectious diseases and childhood illnesses. For instance, in 1914, the *excess* mortality figures for blacks from tuberculosis, influenza-pneumonia, and heart disease—the three leading causes of death—were 260, 101 and 97 (per 100,000) respectively.[7]

Infant mortality rates were also consistently higher for blacks. In 1915, for example, the number of deaths of black infants one-year old and younger per 1,000 live births was double that of whites.[8] Data for specific cities was even more discouraging. The 1910 census reports for New York City revealed death rates for black infants of 333 per 1,000, compared to 144 per 1,000 for whites, an egregious descrepancy even assuming that enumeration mistakes and the tendency for health authorities to inflate black mortality were common during this decade.[9] The 1920 census reported equally glum patterns. In three cities—Cincinnati, Kansas City and Louisville—the black infant death rate was nearly triple that of whites, while in Baltimore, Indianapolis, Los Angeles, Norfolk, Richmond and Washington, black infant mortality rates were about twice as high as those of the babies of white families.[10]

Thus, throughout the first half of the century, the expanding medical establishment viewed the problem of black-white health discrepancy in American cities as an ongoing crisis. This study investigates the changing understanding of this crisis on the part of both the medical establishment and the public. Initially, most medical authorities interpreted the black health crisis as a question of "racialism"—a form of biological determinism that stressed racial traits as the key determinants of the disproportionate illness rates of blacks.[11] However, several changes both within and outside of the medical fields eroded the popularity of such racial explanations for the higher disease mortality rates for blacks. During the interwar period, racial explanations were replaced by a growing body of clinical findings and epidemiology which focused on the healthiness of the family and on the environment of blacks.

Two health-related changes eroded the dominance of this racial conceptualization of the black health crisis. One was the growing effectiveness of public health surveys and preventive medicine; these stripped away illusions that blacks and their families under similar sanitary, household and work conditions still would not reach the health levels of whites. The second was the development of the national ethos of Depression-era social welfarism that stressed the family, the child and the mother as the chief vehicles for health and social rehabilitation. This impulse resulted in policies by government and philanthropies that increased community health services as well as maternal and infant care for poor blacks and whites. By World War II, the nation's medical community had discovered that the roots of improved health for American blacks lay not in traditional racial theories, but in greater access to medical care for families, especially maternal and child populations.

The racial interpretation of high mortality among urban blacks had emerged primarily from medical professionals of the pre-World War I South. Throughout the slavery era, southern physicians had been intimately involved in the health care of black populations. Since nine-tenths of the nation's blacks still lived in the South at the turn of the century, the nation's health care authorities logically looked to the southern medical community to explain the extraordinarily high death rates for blacks. The nation's leading medical publications regularly featured articles by southern physicians focusing on the physical and mental health of blacks.[12] Themes of biological determinism and Negrophobia pervaded these discourses.[13] For example, at the convention of the American Public Health Association in 1915, a Baltimore physician derided estimates of an assistant surgeon general which suggested that tuberculosis death rates among blacks appeared to be declining substantially. "[T]he Negro, particularly under urban conditions, . . . will continue for generations to suffer a higher mortality than the whites in spite of all that will be done for them in the way of social and economic amelioration," he insisted.[14] So prominent were racial interpretations of black health problems that some authorities like

F. L. Hoffman, Edward Eggleston and Raymond Pearl predicted that the extinction of the black race was all but inevitable.[15] One Virginia state health official suggested in 1915 that if the exceedingly high mortality rates for the state's urban black population were accurate, ". . . then on December 9, in the year 2058, the last Negro left in those cities would die."[16]

Yet even southern medical experts who believed that black susceptibility to disease was an inborn racial trait recognized that the high mortality rates of urban blacks were a serious public health problem, if only because "disinclination to recognize the Negro as a potent factor in the transmission of disease" was "evidence of our neglect to safeguard the white race." The Savannah physician who provided this motive for improving the health of blacks recognized the role that environment played in encouraging disease in the black community. He called for better sanitation laws to improve the physical environment and thus deal with the high rates of infectious diseases and the high infant death rates.[17]

The dominance of racial reductionism in American medical thought did not decline in one fell swoop. Rather, it was peeled away, layer by layer, as different clusters of medical specialists—in pediatrics, obstetrics, infectious diseases and public health—sharpened new findings on the connection between social conditions and health patterns. The area of maternal and infant care was an early arena of reform activity. The movement to provide effective prenatal services began in Boston in 1912, the same year that the federal government established the Children's Bureau.[18] Six years later, the Maternity Center Association of New York City initiated a prenatal health movement that became the model for many other communities around the nation.[19] Beginning in 1919, the American Child Health Association began to publish its Statistical Report on Infant Mortality, which provided a growing pool of data for local and national health authorities, who in turn became increasingly convinced that social and economic factors were the key determinants of infant mortality rates.[20] The efficacy of prenatal care centers and infant health programs in reducing infant mortality led obstetricians to advocate and participate in such programs.[21]

The resulting new knowledge of the complex links between social factors and the health problems of women and children—black and white—led, in the twenties, to research that directly attacked the notion that blacks and whites, under similar circumstances and with equal access to medical care, would experience different illness rates. A pioneer in this effort was J. H. Mason Knox, a public health physician and professor, who stressed the need for epidemiological analysis of the black child's health problems "if the forward march of public health . . . is not to be retarded."[22] Knox studied three aspects of the health problems of black children. First, he examined the deaths of infants due to the then major infectious diseases: tuberculosis, syphilis and pneumonia. Second, he investigated the prevalence of infant illness such as ophthalmia neonatorum (severe conjunctivitis in the newborn) stemming from infections carried by the mother. Third, he underlined the correlation between higher infant mortality and illness rates, and unhealthy environmental factors or "living conditions." His approach demonstrated the continued importance of communicable diseases as factors in the higher black American death rates.

But Knox also enhanced the understanding that was growing in the medical community that the health problems of blacks were not universal or racially induced, but rather resulted from the general standard of living in the black community. The health differential between blacks and whites could not be reduced to inherited traits, Knox and his co-researcher Paul Zentai insisted in 1926: "The excessive morbidity and mortality rates among Negro infants are due to [social and environmental] conditions which are a menace to the whole population, white and black alike."[23]

The latter twenties and thirties saw the final demise of the traditional notion that racial weakness caused the high black death rates. A steady stream of health experts demonstrated that poor socioeconomic conditions increased death rates and that blacks were more frequently the victims of such material deprivation. The attention of the public health community and the health reformers turned to improving the conditions under which blacks lived, with attention to the community and especially to the family.

A clear turning point in the debate over the causes of poor black health came with President Hoover's White House Conference on Child Health and Protection that convened in November 1930. The participants made direct reference to the need to solve the particular health and social problems of the nation's blacks in their introductory statement:

> The whole problem of Negro health is still a difficult one to solve and much study is being given to it by many

> groups. . . . It is to be hoped definite information may be secured, for it must be remembered that the health of the Negro population . . . concerns nearly ten percent of our total population, and the health of the Negro has a direct influence on the general health of the community.[24]

An important innovation at the White House Conference was the inclusion of black health experts on the agenda. Before the thirties, most black doctors and health professionals had been relegated to a small network of about 100 all-black hospitals and "group practices."[25] The appearance of a number of prominent blacks at the conference foretold closer interracial cooperation between government and philanthropic health sectors, on the one hand, and the black community's traditional health and welfare professionals, on the other, in developing and implementing the family and household-oriented policies that would attack the health problems of black children in particular and the black community in general. Thomas Parran, the health commissioner for New York state, believed that the most significant thrust of the Conference was demonstrating "the desirability of integrating any program for maternity and child hygiene with the basic health organization of the community."[26]

The black speakers who discussed the problems of black children asserted that the social and economic situation of blacks was largely the cause of their health problems. Eugene Kinckle Jones of the National Urban League stressed three factors: first, the Great Migration to the cities which overtaxed the welfare resources of the municipalities; second, the "constitution of the Negro family" in large cities, which often produced a substantial population of children who lacked sufficient parental supervision; third, inadequate housing that was frequently in disrepair and lacked proper sanitation systems. Jones advocated increased aid to mothers and children to alleviate the effects of these social conditions. He also urged that all social welfare organizations serving blacks have "Negro representation in administration and support of these agencies."[27]

Sally Stewart, the president of the National Association of Colored Women, placed particular emphasis on the need to strengthen the black family in order to improve the conditions facing impoverished children. Citing her 34 years of social work with black children, Stewart emphasized that improved lives for the black child to be "built in the Negro home, and [with] intelligent motherhood [to] protect the child in the primitive and formative years of his life."[28] One apparent result of the White House Conference was the full involvement of the U.S. Public Health Service in coordinating the National Negro Health Movement—public relations campaigns conducted throughout the nation's black communities to promote preventive health and sanitation measures.[29] In 1936, it was estimated that this program reached more than one million black families in 2,000 communities through its local "health education week" campaigns, bulletins, posters and radio shows.[30]

There were other indications that blanket racial explanations for high black mortality rates had passed from the scene. At a conference of the National Tuberculosis Association (NTA), the nation's most influential antituberculosis philanthropy and public research network, a Tennesee state welfare official specializing in Negro affairs asserted that the causes of high TB rates among blacks were to be found in living conditions, not genes: "[Y]ou will find (the Negro) living near the railroad yards, the river bottoms, the dump pile, the back streets and alleys, the slums; he lives in tenements that are literally nothing but hovels, with an insufficient supply of light, fresh air, and decent accomodations."[31]

M. O. Bousfield, the nationally prominent physician and specialist on black health affairs for the prestigious Julius Rosenwald Fund, dismissed the emphasis on racial factors as the explanation for poor black health in an address to the National Conference of Social Work in 1933. He said, "It is gratifying that the more investigators worthy [of] the name, get into the field, the matter of biological differences becomes less specific, while environmental and economic causes gain in importance. . . . A failure to recognize [this] has prevented public health measures [from] being made more available to Negroes, because of a preconceived opinion that [even if] such unusual methods are necessary that little can be gained."[32]

In the mid-thirties, a major wave of sociologically oriented health research that supported preventive health care for black families emanated from the government and philanthropic sectors. This research proved and re-proved the strong association between the high mortality of black citydwellers and the specific inadequacies they confronted in housing, sanitation and medical care. Further, this research galvanized the creation of supportive links between the medical researchers and experts, and black community organizations and institutions. This new triangular alliance—between public health researchers, the mainstream medical profession within the large hospitals and sanatoriums, and health advocates from black communities—in turn developed priorities within the federal government, national nonprofit health organizations and philanthropies emphasizing increased medical care for black families. Elizabeth C. Tandy of the Children's Bureau conducted extensive studies of infant mortality among blacks. She reflected the new perspective when she concluded that "[t]he excess in the [mortality] rates in urban areas for Negro infants . . . emphasizes the great need of child-health activities for Negroes [especially] in southern cities."[33]

Two federal initiatives had a fundamental impact on the health of black families and communities. The first was the Social Security Act of 1935. Social Security funds, administered primarily by the U.S. Public Health Service and the Children's Bureau, enabled state health boards to increase maternal and child health, occupational hygiene and community sanitation programs. The result was the establishment of public health projects in poorer black communities.[34] The second initiative was the Public Health Service's National Health Survey during the winter of 1935–36. Drawing on 20 years of experience with using family canvassing as a method to study illness and disability, this survey was the agency's most comprehensive mass investigation since its inception. The survey involved some 700,000 households comprising 2.5 million people in 83 cities.[35] Advocates of increased medical resources targeted to urban and rural black families used the data from this survey to buttress their arguments for the next decade.[36]

The widening focus of the public health community on family health and household sanitation as the means of dealing with the health problems of black families had a pervasive impact on health officials on the state level. One result was to encourage greater emphasis on providing more services for their urban black citizens and using black medical personnel to serve the black community. By 1937, for instance, the West Virginia state health department was coordinating county health departments and public school systems in such a way as "to give the Negro the same attention for health services as they give to other citizens of the state," according to the state superintendent of public schools, W. W. Trent. In response to a survey by M. J. Bent of Meharry Medical College on public health education programs for blacks, Trent noted that in Kanawha County, which encompassed Charleston, the overall effort was to reach more black infants, preschoolers and expectant mothers. "In preschool conferences, well-baby clinics, and school work, again their is no distinction made as to race. All are eligible to attend, and do attend, the same clinic or conference and are received the same way." The school system also employed blacks as part-time school physicians, dental hygienists and public health nurses. Trent saw no alternative to opening up health resources to blacks, since "[t]he purpose of our health department is to promote the health of citizens, regardless of race."[37]

Other southern health officials, while not completely abandoning the racial arguments, increasingly stressed that the immediate living environment and access to medical care were probably the *chief* causes for the racial discrepancy in infectious disease-related deaths. When a North Carolina health official discussed a recent TB survey of 130,000 blacks and whites throughout the state, he noted that the skin test revealed about an equal proportion of positive reactors (individuals exposed to the tubercule bacilli), while X-ray data showed that blacks were twice as likely to have developed the disease. He did suggest that such findings might indicate that whites had stronger "racial resistance" to tuberculosis. But he further remarked that "living conditions of most Negroes in cities are such as to make a high mortality rate for almost any infectious disease almost inevitable, regardless of racial resistance or anything else."[38] The health community had clearly embraced the conclusion that black health problems were connected with their low social and economic status and the resultant environment.

The health problems of the urban black family did not decline simply because of this new recognition of its basic causes. Indeed, figures at the end of the thirties suggested that this health crisis remained as severe as in the past. While there were clear indications that major infectious diseases were declining in the general population, they remained discouragingly high among urban blacks.[39] What *had* changed was the response of the medical community to this ongoing crisis. The decline of the racialist explanation for black health problems and two decades of public health experience in managing infectious diseases and maternity and infant health problems led to a new, activist approach. Federal and state agencies, voluntary health organization and foundations—especially the NTA, the American Social Hygiene Association and the Rockefeller Foundation—were among the most active in developing new policies to direct preventive and curative care toward the urban black family and community.[40]

An additional factor that intensified the push for family-centered medical services was the concern during World War II for the health and nutritional status of all Americans, both in the military and the civilian populations.[41]

Much of the effort to improve the health of black community was directed at the basic unit of the family—the mother and the child. The Children's Bureau was especially aggressive in stepping up its sponsorship of state and local programs for maternity and child health efforts in southern cities. This agency allocated funds to hospital and maternity services for families living below the poverty level, a large percentage of whom were black. For example, the Bureau found that in Jefferson County, Alabama, the site of Birmingham, in 1942 about 70 percent of the blacks and 20 percent of the white's "were unable to provide for themselves even a minimum of preventive medical and nursing care." Thus, the Bureau became involved in a special project at the Slossfield Health Center, a black facility in Birmingham, to increase medical supervision of childbirth and to improve infant care for the city's blacks. A Bureau report in 1943 described this mix of specialized medical care for expectant and new mothers who were unable to obtain services in larger hospitals:

> Three maternity clinics weekly are held at the Slossfield Health Center. Home deliveries are attended by practicing physicians and supervised by the junior obstetrician. Home delivery, medical and nursing services, and postpartum care are given. Bedside care is given by graduate nurses for acutely ill postpartum patients in the home. One building at the Slossfield Negro Community Center has been converted into a ten-bed maternity hospital providing medical care at delivery.[42]

It must be stressed that the Bureau's maternity and child health funding programs throughout the South were implemented in conformance with local patterns of harsh segregation of medical facilities. What is important for the purposes of this family medicine study is that even *within* these segregated arrangements, black and white physicians stressed the need to work in conjunction with the patient's family unit and home.

The benefits of adequate hospitalization for maternal and child care was exemplified in the development of the premature infant care unit at Harlem Hospital in New York, located in one of the largest and most impoverished black communities in the country. During the early thirties the yearly neonatal survival rate for premature and full-term infants delivered at the hospital was very low. At this time, premature babies in the hospital were placed in the hospital's general nursery under crude heat lamps, in makeshift miniature cribs. However, beginning in 1938, the hospital eliminated this potentially infectious environment by organizing a premature infant unit in accordance with standards set by the New York City health department's division of maternity and newborn. The unit was divided into subnurseries of two to six beds equipped with incubators and resuscitators and staffed by specially trained nurses. The results of these improvements were pronounced: between 1938 and 1950, the annual survival rate for premature babies more than doubled.[43]

The emphasis on improving black health in conjunction with the black family was nowhere clearer than in the treatment of chronically ill children hospitalized for long periods of time. Social Security funds enabled segregated black hospitals in southern cities not only to provide some in-patient care for these children, but also to involve the family and community networks in their care as well. In 1940, sixteen states began using such funds to provide services for children with rheumatic fever and heart disease. In Virginia, the state's only long-term care facility for such black children was developed as an additional unit of the all-black Richmond Community Hospital. The staff at Community found the most effective therapeutic arrangement involved bringing into the hospital the child's family as well as rehabilitative and educational workers. A 1943 report by the Children's Bureau described the measures used at Richmond Community to achieve this goal: "Close contact is maintained with the children's family" who visited the hospital frequently. Moreover, "[c]ommunity groups are encouraged to help occupy the children's time and to satisfy their varied interests. Sunday school classes are conducted at the hospital under the supervision of the First African Baptist Church and other local churches." In addition, a teacher came to the hospital to instruct children several times each week, and an occupational therapist and a nutritionist also visited regularly to provide services.[44]

By the end of World War II, the medical needs of urban black families had become a national policy issue. The Urban League, supported by the NTA, the National Organization of Public Health Nursing and the National Recreation Association and funded by the General Education Fund, undertook a survey of the health needs of the black populations in five cities. The widely respected preventive disease physician, Paul B. Cornely, was one of the principal investigators. Cornely cited case after case of discrimination and improper treatment of black children and mothers in urban hospitals, particularly in southern institutions protected by legal segregation. There were also large gaps in care for blacks in northern cities: "The lack of maternity beds is well shown in one of the northern cities where 98 percent of the white mothers were delivered in hospitals, as compared to only 60 percent of the Negro mothers. Negro mothers in this industrial city would have gladly gone to hospitals if such facilities had been available." Cornely also decried the insufficient supply of hospital beds for victims of tuberculosis. In one southern city with a population of 120,000 blacks, only 24 beds were available for blacks suffering from TB when several hundred were needed.[45] Following the survey, the Urban League convened local councils of social welfare agencies to design and implement a plan to fill the gaps in health services for needy blacks in these cities.[46]

Clearly, the first five decades of the twentieth century saw a major shift in the understanding of and approach to the health crisis of the urban black family. This crisis, exemplified by high infant and maternal mortality rates and a high death rate from infectious diseases, was not solved during these years. What changed was the medical community's perception of the causes of this crisis. The racialist explanations that blamed the poor health of blacks primarily on their inferior genetic makeup discouraged positive efforts to deal with the crisis. The overturning of this racialist position and its replacement by the knowledge that the poor health of blacks resulted from their environmental conditions and lack of access to medical care, which in turn was the outcome of their poor economic status, offered the medical and social welfare communities an agenda for change. The social welfarism of the New Deal, bolstered by such new explanations of the black health crisis, began to attack the problem. Many of its programs and policies were directed to the needs of the black family, and especially to mothers and children. Perhaps the capstone of the reforming effort was the Hill-Burton Hospital Survey and Construction Act of 1946 which, by providing for an expansion of hospital facilities, greatly improved the health conditions of the urban poor.[47] Indeed, against the backdrop of the half century of racialist medical thought and care policies that preceded the Hill-Burton program, the post-World War II federal health initiatives marked a fundamental reformulation of the relationship between medicine, government and needy minority families throughout urban America.

10

Urban Immigrant Families

A Comparative Study of Italians and Mexicans[1]

Richard J. Altenbaugh

It has been estimated that some ten million Mexicans, the largest and most prominent of the Hispanic groups, now reside in this country. "By the year 2000, in key areas of this nation, the majority population will be Hispanic."[2] Given the historical experience of immigrants in this country, what will be the fate of Mexicans and their children? How will they perceive education? How will they respond to the assimilation process?

These questions remain largely unanswered. The past two decades have witnessed a "renaissance" of studies in social history that focus on the relationship between ethnic minorities and education. However, a paucity of literature is available that concentrates on the educational past of Hispanics. The little that does exist may be relegated to two basic categories: institutional based and minority group activities themselves. The former covers public school policies, including long-term discrimination, chronic underachievement, and assimilationist curricula while the latter stresses the Hispanic quest for educational equality, namely efforts to curb school discrimination and campaigns for the linguistic and academic needs of their children. Yet one overriding question remains: How unique is their experience? There appear to be some similarities in the educational experiences of Mexican Americans and other language minority groups of European descent. But, as San Miguel observes, "new studies comparing and contrasting the educational experiences of Mexican Americans with other minority and immigrant groups are needed."[3]

Therefore, one manner of addressing such questions is to analyze the historical experience of a similar immigrant group, namely the Italians. Why study Italian immigrants in order to gain insights into the Mexican experience? From 1880 to 1920, 4.5 million Italians sailed for the United States. Like present day Mexican immigrants, Italians settled largely in urban areas; emigrated from an environment of poverty; maintained their steadfast allegiance to Roman Catholicism; viewed schooling with suspicion; saw themselves as temporary immigrants (hoping to eventually return to their home country); and, finally, cultivated a strong sense of community through a vital and enduring commitment to the family. Both groups presented the existing North American culture with a profound challenge: principally, how to educate, and ultimately assimilate, this massive body of non-Americans. For, as Dinnerstein and Reimers posit, "members of groups whose economic and educational aspirations were low and who therefore lacked mobility were least likely to be assimilated."[4] Many Italians and Mexicans certainly would be included in this category.

Three concepts—ethnicity, education and community—are important for understanding this study. These concepts are not mutually exclusive, but are, in fact, interrelated. Thus, working definitions are necessary. Ethnicity encompasses the whole cultural milieu of an individual or group: "To understand ethnicity it is important to remember that each ethnic group brought with it a unique life style. Roles of family members, expectations of spouses and children, and attitudes toward education and religion often determined how quickly and how well minorities have been absorbed into American society."[5] Further, ethnicity is a matter of "cultural transmission" from family to child. Likewise, historians have perceived education as a cultural experience that encompasses a host of institutions. Lawrence Cremin broadly defines education "as the deliberate, systematic, and sustained effort to transmit, evoke, or acquire knowledge, values, skills, or sensibilities, as well as any learning that results from the effort, direct, or indirect, intended or unintended." [6] Cremin's perspective of education encompasses the pedagogical role of the family, religion, schooling, the workplace, printed and nonprinted materials as well as the impact of various political, social, economic, and military events and activities. Therefore, if ethnicity reflects a cultural transmission and education functions as a cultural phenomenon, then ethnicity is the product of an educational experience. To this end, the ethnic community plays a key role. Thomas Bender sees community as a dynamic force: "Community, which has taken many structured forms in the past is best defined as a network of social relations marked by mutuality and emotional bonds. . . . A community involves a limited number of people in a somewhat restricted social space or network held together by shared understandings and a sense of obligation."[7] Community, therefore, can be characterized better as an experience than as a place.

The public schools, by socializing immigrant children into a different perception of community—i.e., American nationalism—have been viewed with reserved antipathy at best and outright hostility at worst by immigrants. They have usually responded by transplanting or creating their own educational institutions, specifically the family, the church, mutual aid societies and socioeconomic organizations, such as unions, to protect their interests and needs and to preserve their traditions and values.[8] And the family has represented the most formidable social institution in preserving immigrant traditions.

As Virginia Yans-McLaughlin points out, historians and sociologists have grappled with many different interpretations of the immigrant family experience. Oscar Handlin saw disorganization and "alienation" as the consequences of the transition from a peasant village to an industrial nation. Rudolph Vecoli challenged Handlin's model, arguing that immigrants transplanted their Old World culture to America, that past experiences determined subsequent behavior. Talcott Parsons shifted the focus from the cultural disorganization or cultural continuity dichotomy to a perspective that stressed the emergence of a new "functional" family form, replacing the outmoded, preindustrial extended pattern.[9] "The transition from the old country to the new molded the Old World family into a mobile, detached, nuclear form whose roles and relationships fit the demands of a more 'rationale' industrial economy."[10] This was simply not the case.[11] In sum, the first view paints a pathological picture of the immigrant experience; the second provides a linear approach; the third makes a false assumption.

Virginia Yans-McLaughlin borrows from Clifford Geertz to offer a fourth, more dynamic model that accounts for family change and continuity:

> Social change . . . does not necessarily imply the dissolution of traditional family forms or a systematic fit of institutions,

> but rather the adaptation of one institution to another. The relationship between modernity and tradition, then, is neither dichotomous nor linear but dialectical. From this perspective the family is a flexible organization, which, while adapting to new social conditions, may continue to rely upon traditional forms and ways of relating.[12]

It is through this prism that we must examine the Italian and Mexican immigrant family experiences and their responses to the acculturation process.

The immigrant family has represented a vital and resilient social institution, as well as a conserving force. On the one hand, it did not wither when it encountered American capitalism, relying on a mediating process with the new and alien, and often hostile, society. As Bodnar asserts:

> Immigrant kinship associations not only continued to perform indispensable functions in the industrial society, such as helping to organize the movement of workers into the economy, but actually flourished. At times the relationship between the industrial economy and immigrant families could almost be described as symbiotic, as kinship groups proved very responsive to demands of workplace, the city, and the individual.[13]

On the other hand, the family never lost sight of its deep and rich cultural heritage: "The maintenance of ethnic identification and solidarity ultimately rests on the ability of the family to socialize its members into the ethnic culture and thus to channel and control, perhaps program, future behavior."[14] Therefore, the assurance of economic subsistence and progress, as well as the maintenance of ethnic identification and solidarity, began with the family.

In a concrete sense, the key function that the family performed both in the homeland and in the United States was its central and enduring attachment to the value of cooperation. This served as a means to accomplish one major goal: survival. Bodnar generalizes this to all immigrant groups, no matter where and when they have settled in this country: "While not every ethnic group or family behaved in identical terms or pursued exactly the same objectives, an overwhelming majority lived their lives and pursued their goals through familial and household arrangements which often functioned in a similar manner."[15] Family goals superseded individual aspirations, and parents and children both worked vigorously to contribute to the family's welfare. This often became manifested through parents' direction of their children's career paths, resulting in the parents, not the children, deciding the amount of schooling children would receive. This strong sense of cooperation is best seen through an examination of the kin network, the cultural role of the family, and the family economy.

KIN NETWORK

Networks of immigration began in immigrant homelands, providing vital information about settlement locations and jobs in the United States as well as crucial assistance in securing lodging and employment. Bodnar writes:

> Whether immigrants were recruited directly for their abilities or followed existing networks into unskilled jobs, they inevitably moved within groups of friends and relatives and worked and lived in clusters. Friends and relatives functioned so effectively, in fact, that they invariably superseded labor agents and "middlemen" in influencing the entry of newcomers into the industrial economy and were usually able to create occupational beachheads for those that followed.[16]

The traditional family structure in southern Italy represented a unique concept, unlike any of its European counterparts, functioning as "an inclusive social world in and of itself." The Italian family system perpetuated a set of beliefs and values that "affected all areas of social life, including work, education, and definitions of social status."[17] In this context, family obligations took precedence over individual needs and desires.

Southern Italian migration began in 1880, and by the turn of the century, a chain of migration had begun. As Yans-McLaughlin notes about the Italian experience in Buffalo, "people facing a crisis like migration often seek to ascribe some familiar meaning to the world around them. In this case, immigrants put their Old World family ties to novel uses in America." In southern Italy, the nuclear family prevailed, with the extended family performing social and ritual obligations, e.g., godparents. These informal links expanded during migration to assume formal kinds of assistance. "The original religious basis of a godparenthood, for example, expands to secular areas—to enhance relationships between parents and godparents, to provide economic aid, and to ensure social controls."[18] In the New World, community networks involved relatives, friends and neighbors, functioning in interdependent relationships. This experience frequently permeated entire Italo-American neighborhoods. Moreover, by 1905, at least 26 percent of over 2,000 Italian households in Buffalo had adopted complex structures.

Settlement in this country encouraged new and long-term commitments to kin, assuming many manifestations. These encompassed economic, emotional and cultural forms. First, families combined meager incomes to share apartments, purchase houses or finance businesses. Second, parents shared their households with newly married sons and daughters. Third, Italians opened their homes to Italian-immigrant boarders, helping them until the new arrivals became permanently settled. These male lodgers usually saved their money in order to send for their wives and children. Fourth, newly arrived families often found themselves welcomed in a kin household, easing their transition to this country. "The fact that so many could bypass rooming houses again indicates how strongly personal ties between adults used in novel ways cemented this community together. In 1905 these Italians had established a personal, familial community."[19] Italians used their families to insulate themselves from the unwholesome American culture.

In fact, family migration represented common practice, amounting to 50 percent in the Buffalo sample. Whole families felt secure in migrating since friends and relatives would welcome and support them in the United States. Of the husbands and fathers who had preceded their families, clearly 81 percent had established or sent for their families by 1905.[20]

Mexicans, like Italians, maintained a strong allegiance to kin, with the family's needs taking precedence over individual interests. The extended family represented an important institution among Mexican Americans during the nineteenth century, but it evolved gradually and steadily to a nuclear one. Griswold del Castillo's study of urban southwestern families focuses on San Antonio, Santa Fe, Tucson and Los Angeles. It reveals that in 1850 extended families comprised 75 percent of Mexican households, but by 1880 this figure had dropped to 50 percent. This still represented a significant figure, with little deviation between native-born Mexican Americans and immigrant Mexicans.[21]

The familial migration network appears to have been common.

After one family situated itself, it would attract relatives and friends from the original home in Mexico. Prior to 1916, immigrants came in equal numbers from the central and northern states in Mexico; during the later migration, the majority claimed roots in northern Mexico, especially Durango, Sonora and Chihuahua. A Mexican resident, who had arrived in Santa Barbara in 1916, vividly recounted the migration pattern:

> One family comes from Durango and establishes itself here. From here it writes and says come! come! come over it is good here. It brings others and others. Well, one was here . . . Juan Esparza—he brought 28 families from Durango.[22]

Once in the American urban environment, Mexican immigrants retained strong ties to their families and kin back home.

Cultural factors superseded economic necessity and emotional dependence, but all three still played key roles in the formation and maintenance of Mexican-American extended households. "The evidence surrounding family solidarity among Mexican Americans suggests that the kinship network functioned primarily as a support system during times of crisis." For example, a family would assume responsibility for a relative's children during a time of economic hardship. But these children usually did not contribute economically to the host family. Furthermore, the nuclear household did not necessarily take in aged parents and relatives. "Contrary to the contemporary ideal conceptualizations of the Chicano family, there were very few aged *abuelos* and *abuelitas* (grandfathers and grandmothers) who lived with nuclear families." Therefore, extended households among the Spanish speaking served as an important "emotional support system." As Griswold del Castillo adds: "The existence of extended households which had little economic support from resident kin was evidence that cultural ideals of familism continued to provide strategies for survival during hard times."[23] This resulted, as Camarillo observes in the barrioization process in Santa Barbara during the early decades of this century; the barrio essentially became a "Mexican city within a city."[24] This represented a rational choice:

> For Mexican Americans, particularly those of lower status, the family is often the primary source of refuge from what is often seen as a hostile world. In fact, a historical function of the Mexican-American family structure has been to protect individuals from the dominant Anglo white society.[25]

Cultural Resistance

The immigrant family also stressed cultural homogeneity and shaped social roles. Marriage patterns indicate that immigrants, if not already married, would find mates from their own ethnic group, often from their same village or religion.[26] The family also established family roles, based on gender and age, that followed traditional practice and, at the same time, adapted to new demands. In these ways, the immigrant family represented a social institution that confronted American cultural values.

Italians maintained one of the highest rates of endogamy among immigrant groups. In 1900, 97.9 percent of Italian marriages in Buffalo were strictly endogamous. And the rate remained significantly high for subsequent generations, with 76.7 percent in 1950. Except for Jewish immigrants, "Italians had the highest in-group marriage rates of seven ethnic groups." As recently as 1973, Italians still retained a high propensity for endogamy: "Sixty-six percent of the Italian Catholics were endogamous compared to 50 percent or less for Polish, Lithuanian, eastern European, German, Irish and English. The only groups with higher rates of in-group marriage were the Spanish-speaking Catholics and French Canadians."[27] This strong pattern of endogamy, coupled with kin networks, fostered a deep sense of order in the Italian community:

> Layer upon layer of interaction among relatives, compari, and paesani provided a security or insurance system for families; bonds between them created a personal sense of community. . . . Members of the close-knit, homogeneous community shared values and ideologies that were reinforced by frequent interaction; and the Italian-American institutions, especially the Catholic church, added to the pressure for homogeneity. This consensus in social values acted as an effective means of social control.[28]

The family thus operated as the "primary socializing agent," establishing gender and age roles. Italian patriarchy represented a complex experience, not the stereotypical view of the male-dominated family. This reflected premigration behavior. The cultural heritage of southern Italy ensured an unusually high level of prestige for peasant women. In many cases, they inherited ancient Roman patterns, including matrilineal descent and female property rights. Nevertheless, women assumed the appearance of traditional roles. The mother and her female relatives, for instance, supervised the nurturing of the children. Yet, this was an important role: "the mother was the center of the family in a society where nonfamilial relationships were secondary. In a world where the family status was judged not by the occupation of the father but by the signs of family well-being which emanated from the household, the mother played an important role in securing the status."[29]

Italian parents seldom relinquished economic and familial control over their young. While Italian parents distrusted public schooling, they perpetuated *ben educato* among their children. This connoted education in the broadest sense, that is, imbuing children with proper behavior, values and attitudes, habits and skills. In this context, work, which served as a matter of pride among adults, functioned as moral training for the young: "To work is to show evidence that one has become a man or a woman, a full member of the family."[30] Work, unlike schooling, represented a concrete symbol of accomplishment and directly benefited the family, as we shall see.

Intermarriage between Mexican Americans and Anglo Americans remained quite low for all generational groups throughout the nineteenth century. Mexicans, like Italians, insulated themselves from American society. In Santa Barbara during the 1880s and 1890s, Mexicans responded to Americanization pressures through social and ethnic persistence. Since 1945, exogamy has gradually increased, but the number of these marriages still remains modest. In 1980, the southwestern male intermarriage rate reached 13.5 percent, while the figure for females amounted to 11.9 percent. Outside of the Southwest, the figures leap to 36.9 and 39.4 percent, respectively. "Even these rates, however, demonstrate that Mexican Americans are a long way from complete assimilation into the larger society."[31]

The Mexican family, like its Italian counterpart, has been stereotyped as a strong and static patriarchy. Griswold del Castillo analyzes this phenomenon and asserts that a far more dynamic and complex experience unfolded over time. As early as the colonial period, a woman's position in central Mexico varied according to the socioeconomic status of her family, with wealthy women having relatively more freedom than poorer women. This tradition traced its roots to the Spanish legal system: "Women could inherit property and titles, testify in court, and sign contracts. Spanish laws gave married women the right to limit their husband's control of the dowry, and single women, especially widows, had a great deal of economic independence which was supported by law."[32] Thus, throughout the colonial era, women established households, owned property and managed their spouse's entrepreneurial activities. Although nineteenth century Mexican legislators adopted the Napoleonic codes, which restricted women's rights and institutionalized patriarchy, many women deviated from this submissive ideal, producing a variegated pattern. On the Spanish and Mexican frontiers, men and women worked and fought together to survive. The Mexican War of Independence and the chaotic years of the Mexican Republic (1821–1848) challenged older patriarchal values. Notions of egalitarianism, seeping in from the revolutions in North America and France, also weakened patriarchal authority.

As part of American society, especially between 1850 and 1880, economic conditions influenced household structure, and a general increase in female-headed families resulted. A lack of steady work forced male family members to seek employment as teamsters, cartmen, wagon drivers, drovers, miners, vaqueros and farmworkers, which often took them away from home for various periods of time. Consequently, Mexican-American women were far from trapped within the rigid confines of a male-dominated family. "As heads of their own households, they were relatively independent of male supervision, even if their husbands were temporarily absent."[33] In addition to temporary departures, women faced permanent abandonment through the deaths of spouses, heading more than 25 percent of all Spanish-surnamed households in the urban Southwest in 1880.

Griswold del Castillo points to the emergence of four different kinds of family experiences since 1910. First, a small—but socially and politically influential—portion of Mexican immigrant families came from the middle and upper classes in Mexico, transplanting their cultural ideals of class with them. They generally accommodated themselves more easily to American society than did the working-class immigrants. Second, the upper-class native-born families similarly represented a well-acculturated segment. The Hispanic aristocracy of New Mexico symbolized this experience; they considered themselves to be "set apart by their Spanish heritage," seldom identifying with Mexican immigrants or even native-born Mexican-Americans. This aristocracy probably felt "more a part of American society than any other group."[34]

The third and fourth categories consisted of working-class Mexican Americans, immigrants and native-born, and comprised the overwhelming majority of Mexicans living in this country. The former generally resided in cities and were monolingual Spanish-speaking. This represented the most disadvantaged portion of Mexican-American society. In 1939, about half of the Mexican workers in San Antonio received public assistance. In order to subsist, everyone in the family over the age of 12 worked. Regardless of location, the conditions surrounding urban Mexican-immigrant family life were oppressive. Overcrowding, high infant mortality rates, substandard housing, malnutrition, juvenile crime and economic insecurity plagued both immigrant and native-born working-class Mexicans.[35]

Native-born working-class families usually spoke both Spanish and English but lived in rural areas. In 1930, only 41 percent lived in cities. They often owned homes, but usually of low value, "which suggests that the native families were not necessarily better off than the immigrants." They maintained smaller families, employed fewer adults per household, and hosted a lower proportion of lodgers than did immigrant families. "Overall, however, the differences in living conditions were not as great as the similarities." Employment opportunities generated by war production during World War II lured rural Hispanos to the cities. Still, because of low wages, they usually had to resort to a migratory strategy, seeking other jobs during the off-season or during bouts of unemployment. Generally, native-born Mexican Americans experienced little more social mobility than their immigrant counterparts because of Anglo prejudice. And, although some differences and occasional conflicts arose between immigrants and the native-born Mexicans, "Mexican immigrants as well as Hispanos felt the same kind of racial and cultural prejudice by Anglos."[36]

With the progressive secularization of Latin American society in general, and with Mexico's independence from Spain in particular in 1821, the family rather than the church assumed increasing responsibility for the child's education. However, during the American period, and especially after the 1880s, the public schools, through compulsory attendance laws, began to encroach on the prerogative of the family and the church. This tended to fragment authority. The schools directly assaulted Mexican culture, a culture that subordinated the child's needs to the family's requirements and expected the utmost respect from the child. "Increasingly Mexican Americans were presented with models of proper behavior which conflicted with their traditional culture."[37] Mexican-American families responded to this dilemma by either withdrawing their children from school or protesting the curricula and methods of instruction. In 1931, for instance, Mexican parents challenged the policies of the Lemon Grove schools near San Diego. They objected to their children being assigned to a separate school in order to facilitate learning English. Not only did the parents and children boycott the school, but they filed a suit and won it.

ECONOMIC SURVIVAL

In addition to the premigration patterns that affected American experiences and the cultural homogeneity that reinforced a collective nature, economic conditions in the United States also shaped the immigrant response. American industrial and agricultural wages may have appeared attractive to these immigrants, but from all indications most of their families could not survive on the income of one wage earner. An 1893 analysis of skilled workers in the coal, iron and steel industries revealed that the "husband's" earnings, on the average, only accounted for 85 percent of the total income needed to support the typical working-class household.[38] Since skilled workers constituted the highest paid workers, unskilled and semi-skilled industrial and agricultural working class families faced an even greater fiscal shortfall.

The family relied on a variety of strategies to compensate for this serious deficit, becoming "a working productive unit." First, immigrants sometimes opened their homes to lodgers. Boarders could not be accommodated, however, unless the family rented a larger apartment or purchased a house. In either case, such an arrangement produced a speculative financial situation. The money collected from the lodgers had to defray the increased costs in rent or mortgage payments. If a boarder suddenly moved out, the family had to immediately find another lodger or had to assume the debt out of its already meager income. Moreover, boarders often disrupted the household routine, further crowding already cramped living quarters and causing considerably more work for the female family members. Taking boarders did not prove to be a widely used strategy. Working-class immigrant families appeared to be similar to their middle-class counterparts in that they guarded their privacy, relying on a nuclear structure.[39]

Working women represented a second alternative, but they had to overcome numerous cultural restrictions and economic barriers. Women usually maintained traditional domestic roles, centering on child nurturing and home care. Further, towns dominated by heavy industry offered few job opportunities for women.[40] Yet, economic reality sometimes dictated that married immigrant women find work. They developed ingenious ways to combine their dual roles as mother and worker. Domestic work, such as caring for lodgers, basting and sewing clothes, or making artificial flowers, became common tactics.

Other households depended on a third option, that is, working children, in order to supplement their income. Both sons and daughters worked. At the turn of the century, some two million children below the age of 16 were working. A 1916 government study on the conditions of child and women wage earners determined the value of this strategy. The report encompassed the cotton, clothing, glass and silk industries, and discovered that working children, aged 14 and 15, accounted for 18.3 percent of the family income.[41]

The fact that the immigrant family depended on working children to supplement the household income meant that these children were simply not in school. In 1914, for example, approximately 65 percent of the children enrolled in the public schools dropped out by the end of the fifth or sixth grade. Therefore, because of their dire economic situation, immigrant families circumvented, or at least minimized, the acculturation process of the public school system by withdrawing their children from this institution as soon as legally possible.

In Italy, a fluctuating and often geographically dispersed agricultural demand for workers had caused entire families to migrate to find work. "Wheat growing areas demanded a heavy concentration of labor for June and July harvest; the olive season extended from September through January; fruits claimed the fall, and almonds August through October." These rhythms created some work throughout the year. Women provided labor in many of these cases, but not as individual wage earners; rather, they functioned as members of a family group. Boys began work at 12 years of age, laboring in the fields or training as apprentices. Girls, like their mothers, rarely worked outside of the home, except in specific, family-monitored situations.

The Italian family employed a variety of strategies to survive in the United States. Italian women and girls rarely left home to work either as domestics or factory laborers. In 1905, only 13 percent of Italian wives in Buffalo, 28 percent in Chicago, and 34 percent in Rochester found employment outside of the home.

Wives often contributed to family income by taking roomers and boarders into their households. Italian women appeared more likely than any other ethnic group in Buffalo to supplement family income in this manner. Married and single women also remained at home basting and stitching. By the twenties, however, unmarried girls began to enter the labor market.

Boys usually worked in street trades, as newsboys or shoeshiners, for instance. In Buffalo, whole families toiled in the canneries from April through November. The unique division of labor among each member of the family attested to southern Italian adaptation. If the fathers did not already have a job outside the cannery, then they worked apart from the women and children. The women and children labored together weeding, harvesting, husking, or snipping beans, "so that the tasks of disciplining the children and of directing the work stayed in the mother's hands." Economic conditions shaped these decisions, of course. But, as Yans-McLaughlin points out: "South Italian values influenced these decisions concerning family work patterns."[42]

As we have seen, the family represented the single most important obligation. Individual success was sacrificed for the family's well-being. Schooling offered long-term, intangible promises while work ensured immediate concrete relief. Thus, in 1905, 79 percent of Italian sons and 82 percent of the daughters, 15 to 19 years of age, left the Buffalo schools. "Boys withdrawn from school had to pay the price of restricted job mobility, which helps to explain the Italian's slow rise up the occupational ladder. It may also explain why upwardly mobile second generation Italians so often became printers and electricians, not doctors and lawyers."[43]

Although the opportunities for occupational mobility appeared slim, Italians became notorious for saving money to invest in property. "The desire to own a home can be seen as the wish of former peasants to possess—even at great sacrifice—something which had been denied to so many for generations." Extended family cohesion involved some cooperative home buying efforts, as noted above. In the nuclear household, wives generated income by collecting boarders' fees or finding occasional part-time work. Italians also sacrificed a higher standard of living in order to save money; they delayed gratification. This thriftiness often bordered on outright deprivation. Finally, children played a key role in subsidizing a house. It remained a simple fact that most Italian families could not afford a home until the children grew up and went to work. "Italian children took their obligations seriously."[44] Thus, in many cases, Italian sons contributed to house payments more out of a sense of family loyalty and less out of a concern over economic necessity. More importantly, parents must not be perceived as selfishly neglecting their children's interests or futures. Property—a tangible asset—could be proudly bequeathed to children, serving as a mode of upward mobility.

The Mexican-American family also adapted to economic conditions in this country. Male heads of households, beginning in the nineteenth century, faced persistent unemployment and migrated frequently to secure seasonal work. A deteriorating family status during the 1880s in Santa Barbara dictated a break in the traditional roles of women and children. Until that time, Chicanas seldom worked outside of the home, but they now began to enter the labor market in order to contribute to the family's economic survival. "In these instances the Chicana assumed the triple responsibilities of head of household, mother, and wage earner." Women and children found jobs in domestic services and agriculture-related work. Women worked as launderers, needle workers, dressmakers and domestics, and both women and children labored in canneries. Chicanas and their children also found employment as seasonal agricultural workers on the developing fruit and nut ranches in the Santa Barbara region. During the early summer season, the entire family would migrate from the city to pick fruit. The "family seasonal harvest" maintained a clear division of labor, that is, women and girls worked in the packing house while the men and boys picked the fruit. Camarillo makes a compelling conclusion: "Thus, with the last two decades of the nineteenth century, Chicanos—especially women and children—originated an enduring pattern of employment that characterized future generations of the Chicano working class in Santa Barbara."[45] He finds similar patterns in the histories of San Diego and Los Angeles.

During the 1920s, migration to northern cities brought little relief. As Acuña notes, "Salaries were much higher than those in the Southwest; most important was that they worked year-round. However, even with higher pay, two-thirds of Mexicans in Chicago earned less than $100 a month which was below the poverty line."[46] As the end of the twentieth century approaches, this burden of poverty still persists. In 1975, 24 percent of Mexican-American—contrasted with nine percent of Anglo—families fell below the poverty line.

As a result, the female's dual role as mother and wage earner has persisted throughout the twentieth century. Chicanas have faced three types of prejudice: racial, social class and sexist. In 1919, the Texas Industrial Welfare Commission reported that in El Paso, Mexican women suffered severe discrimination and received the lowest pay in the city. For instance, in that city's department stores, Anglo women worked on the main floor while Chicanas toiled in the rear or basement. "Anglos earned as high as $40.00 a week compared to Mexican clerks who were paid $10.00 to $20.00."[47] Throughout southern California, Mexican women found themselves restricted to work in domestic services, food processing, the textile industry and agricultural pursuits. Most of this work appeared to be relegated to part-time or seasonal unskilled labor. To exacerbate matters, Chicanas encountered wage differentials and unequal treatment because of gender. By the mid-seventies, nearly 40 percent of Chicanas aged 16 or older worked, earning three-quarters of what African-American and Anglo women made.

Conclusions

Striking parallels exist among Italian- and Mexican-American families. As Griswold del Castillo cogently notes:

> Like the Mexican Americans, the Italian immigrants and their children sustained a strong ideal of family solidarity, valued extended kinship relations, socialized children to be *ben educato*, or well educated, in showing respect for their elders and family, maintained their native language in the home, lived in ethnic enclaves, and had a low rate of intermarriage with non–Italian-heritage populations.[48]

First- and second-generation Italian families resembled their Mexican counterparts in key affective and structural ways. Further, although third-generation Italians experienced upward mobility more frequently than Mexican Americans, some traditional patterns persisted among Italian families. Likewise, a sense of continuity has existed among Mexican-American families. Of course, this has been constantly renewed with new infusions of Mexican immigrants. Therefore, while Mexican families adapt to their new environment, they, like the Italians, have retained many of their cultural values and traditions. Their distrust of American schooling, because of cultural conflict, and their inability to send children to school since economic pressures require the children's labor, will probably persist. Blame does not fall on the Mexican-American family. Instead, only fundamental cultural sensitivity and economic changes on the part of American society will resolve this historical dilemma.

11

Courtship by Mail

The World War II Letters of Barbara Woodall Taylor and Charles E. Taylor

Judy Barrett Litoff and David C. Smith

Camp Wheeler, Georgia 27 August 1941

Dearest Barbara:

I had not forgotten you, just haven't had time to do a thing on my own hook. . . .

I am in hopes that you are holding a few words and actions sacred; they should mean as much to you as they mean to me. I know you are wondering just what last weekend meant to me—(Well)—last weekend was one of my happiest since I have been in this man's army. . . .

In this letter I have to sort of feel you out to see whether or not you were only infatuated or whether you are in love with me. Frankly (real Frank?), I am not infatuated. I am definitely in love with you. In fact, you have been constantly on my mind ever since I left you on Sunday. I am hoping you and I can keep the flame burning from now on. . . . You know it takes the two of us to make this affair

---

Permission to use the correspondence of Barbara Wooddall Taylor and Charles E. Taylor in the preparation of this paper has been granted by the letter writers.

This article is adapted from chapter one of *Miss You: The World War II Letters of Barbara Wooddall Taylor and Charles E. Taylor* by Judy Barrett Litoff, David C. Smith, Barbara Wooddall Taylor and Charles E. Taylor (Athens: University of Georgia Press, 1990) and is reprinted by permission of the authors and the publisher.

beautiful—so if you will only meet me halfway, we will have something that no one can tear up or change.

All my love,
Charlie

P.S. Write soon what I want to hear.[1]

When 21-year-old Private Charles E. Taylor of Gainesville, Florida wrote this letter, he could not possibly have known that it would mark the first of approximately 800 letters that he would write to Barbara Wooddall over the course of the next four years. Nor could he have known that, as a recently enlisted man or later as a lieutenant in the United States Army, he would travel thousands of miles within the United States while he trained for combat. It would also have been difficult for him to predict that he would eventually be called upon to fight in a war that was then raging in Europe but which the United States had not yet officially entered. What he did know in August 1941, however, was that he was "definitely in love," with an 18-year-old brown-eyed, blond-haired beauty from the small town of Fairburn, Georgia, whom he had only recently met.[2]

Barbara Wooddall was equally in love with Charles Taylor. In a 16 July 1942 letter to Private Taylor, in which she described her impressions of their first date, she recalled:

> About the night we met—I'll never forget how you looked when you walked in the living room. You were smiling and I knew from the start that I had loved you all my life. I wanted to go out with you, but I was almost afraid to. I knew that if you told me to jump I would do so and quick too! Then the next thing I liked about you was the fact that you liked good hot swing bands. Then out at Jennings, I'll never forget how your eyes looked right through me—I felt as if you could tell me what color underwear I had on. . . . I didn't want to go home—I wanted to stay with you all my life because I knew that night without you I would never be completely happy.[3]

Like thousands of other young couples caught up in the exigencies of World War II, Charles Taylor and Barbara Wooddall experienced a whirlwind romance followed by marriage. Although their courtship spanned an eight-month period from their first date in August 1941 until their secret marriage on 5 April 1942, they were rarely able to be together. As long as Private Taylor was stationed at Camp Wheeler in Macon, Georgia, he could arrange for occasional weekend visits to Fairburn.

When he was transferred to Fort Leonard Wood, Missouri, in October 1941, however, such trips to Fairburn became much more problematic. In fact, the young couple saw each other only one additional time between October 1941 and their marriage the following April. In total, they spent no more than four weekends and a brief furlough in each other's company prior to their marriage. Because the opportunities to be together were so limited, Charles Taylor and Barbara Wooddall relied upon their letters to answer fundamental questions regarding their ages and the names of each other's parents, sisters and brothers. Most importantly, they used their letters to develop and nurture their love.

Surprisingly, historians know more about the personal meaning of courtship in earlier times than in this century. As Ellen K. Rothman succinctly points out in her recent book, *Hands and Hearts: A History of Courtship in America*, letter writing between courting couples had, until the twentieth century, been a "mainstay of courtship" and provided the chief means of learning about each other. Telephones and ease of travel after 1920 made letter writing less necessary, and, consequently, historians have been forced to rely on published material on dating and sexual behavior when studying recent courtship practices. However, the period of World War II provides an exception; sweethearts and lovers, separated by the wartime emergency, took to pen and paper once again. Unfortunately, the millions of wartime letters that were written remain hidden away in attics or closets, or, in many instances, have been destroyed.[4] Charles and Barbara's wonderfully detailed letters, which total more than 4,000 double-spaced, typewritten pages for the 1941–1945 period, now give us a needed intimate look into modern courtship and marriage.[5]

Both Charles and Barbara repeatedly acknowledged the importance of each other's letters in the growth of their love. For example, in a 6 January 1942 letter, Barbara recounted a humorous incident that clearly underscored the importance she placed on Charles's letters:

> Sunday Daddy got the mail for me and there was a letter from *you*. I was right in the midst of it in the Sunday School class when my teacher asked me to read something for her. I got so frustrated that I dropped my pocket book one way, gloves the other, and almost started reading the letter out loud. Boy, did my face get red.[6]

But, on a more serious note, she confessed:

> Your letters mean a great deal to me and my outlook on life. They make my day happy or sad. If I don't hear from you I'm *bad*! All inside I mean. I suppose you've just spoiled me in that respect.[7]

Charles concurred. On 9 January 1942, he declared:

> Dear, there is doubt (*a very little doubt*) in my mind *only* when I do not get a letter from you. Please let us both be true and keep each other happy. The only way we can keep each other happy is by letters. I feel nearer to you every time I get a letter from you. I feel so warm inside and so very happy and contented when I read lines that *you* wrote.[8]

While both Charles Taylor and Barbara Wooddall knew that their deep attraction for each other represented much more than a frivolous wartime romance, their courtship did have its difficult moments. When they first began dating, Charles was involved in a rather serious relationship with another young woman. In a letter written on 16 July 1942, Barbara poignantly reminded Charles of the pain and heartache she had suffered upon learning of this earlier liaison:

> Then that awful weekend that you brought, er, I don't know her name (not much!!) to Fairburn. I knew that there was too much competition for me, so I made up my mind to forget you. I wouldn't answer your letters, and I burned yours up as fast as I could read them.[9]

Charles's early letters to Barbara are interspersed with his disavowals of love for this "other woman." On one occasion he stated, "I am in your hands and you know it. I would not trade a hair off of your head for two [of her] complete." A week later, he reiterated, "[She] is completely out of my life as far as I am concerned. You have completely taken her place and built yourself up in my mind and my heart, and no other woman will have a chance at me. . . ."[10]

On the other hand, Charles had his own concerns about Barbara's social life, and Barbara found it necessary to reassure him that the many young men whom she was seeing meant little to her. In a letter written 4 February 1942, she stated, "Remember what you said about my having dates? You know it's funny—in a mild sort of way! When I'm out on a date, I feel as if something definite in my life is missing. It's you, Charlie."[11] One week later, she announced: "Our YWA [Young Women's Auxiliary] leader is planning a social for us. She wants to invite some *selected* men from Fort McPherson. Of course, I think it's *nice* to be *nice* to *nice* boys in the Army, but what do you think? In case she does this, honest I won't give a *'soldier a break!'*"[12]

"Dating," the modern practice of young people of the opposite sex pairing off, had emerged in the newer social mores of the post World War I era. Throughout much of the nineteenth century, the formal act of "calling" was one way that couples were able to meet. In addition, group activities, such as contra and square dances, box socials and sleighing parties, had offered young people the opportunity to pair off, but not in a regular or formal way. By the 1920s, however, changes in dating practices were occurring very rapidly. As informal get-togethers became "dates," another casualty was the chaperon. Now the extent of activities was determined by the peer group rather than by fixed rules of an outdated system. The differences in mores can be seen in the successive editions of Emily Post's standard work on etiquette, as chaperons diminish in importance, decline in discussion and then disappear entirely, along with such matters as group dating.[13]

Changes in dating practices continued to take place in the 1930s. Movies, dance halls, restaurants, the radio, wider and better education, shorter working days, increased leisure time, and especially the automobile had all appeared in the twenties, but they expanded throughout small towns and rural America and well beyond the social elite in the next decade. Charles and Barbara came from more conservative backgrounds than the persons discussed by such well-known observers of the day as Frederick Lewis Allen and Willard Waller. Nevertheless, the circumstances of their courtship mirrored these societal changes.[14]

In the case of Barbara Wooddall, group activities continued to be more important than paired dating, but Charles was still bothered by the frequency with which she chose to go along on these outings. The exasperation he felt was reflected in a 25 February 1942 letter:

> . . . you tell me how much you love me, but everytime you write, you just came in from a date or you went someplace with someone. You don't have to make me jealous, 'cause I

> already am. But where I come from a girl that is *in love* with someone does not run around as much as you claim to be doing. Yes, I realize that you are there and I am away up here, but I don't go out like that, I sit.[15]

After their secret marriage on 5 April 1942, the question of whether or not Barbara should date took on new significance. In a letter written on 12 April, Barbara pinpointed one of the special problems she encountered when she announced to a girlfriend that she was no longer dating:

> . . . Evie called, and she couldn't believe that I didn't have a date tonite. I told her that I wasn't dating anymore and she just laughed and laughed. Finally, I made her believe me in a mild sort of way, and she said that if I really didn't date anymore she would know I was married. Dopey, huh?[16]

A similar announcement to her parents brought forth the comment that for once "We'll know what it is like to have a daughter."[17]

Even after Charles and Barbara became "officially" engaged in June 1942, the question of Barbara's going out with other men still occasionally arose. The following passage from a July letter demonstrates that Barbara even experienced brief pangs of regret at having to turn down dates.

> I'm going to tell you someting I know that I shouldn't but it's so very seldom that I just give-away to my feelings that I feel that you should know. This afternoon about 5:00 I was dressing to go have something to eat before I went to BTU [Baptist Training Union]. A guy called me and wanted me to go to the show tonight. He said he knew that I shouldn't go out and furthermore he shouldn't call me, but if I'd go he'd be very glad and be good to me. Well, I didn't accept his invitation, of course, but it made me want to go somewhere terribly. Well, I . . . saw him riding with one of my girlfriends and they were laughing and seemingly having such a good time. I know you understand what an empty feeling I had. I went in . . . and cried for about twenty minutes. . . .[18]

Although Barbara may have let her feelings "give-away" on this one occasion, her letters reveal that she usually was able to keep her emotions in check. One week later she offered:

> Charlie, now you listen to me, it is *not* hard for me to stay

> home when my girlfriends are all going out. Why I feel sorry for them, yes, they have my deepest sympathy, because they do not have a beautiful love like ours, and they do not have a darling Charlie like I have. So there![19]

One of the ways that Barbara managed to endure the long periods of separation from Charles was by continuing her busy routine. In addition to maintaining a full-time job as a secretary at Twentieth Century Fox Film Corporation in nearby Atlanta, she took a leadership role in the local Cotillion Club and was an active member of the Fairburn Baptist Church where she sang in the church choir, taught Sunday School and served as President of the Young Women's Auxiliary. What leisure time she had was spent roller skating, biking, bowling, swimming and playing tennis. She was determined, in her own words, to keep her "chin up." On 20 February 1942, she wrote:

> Yes darling, I'm keeping my chin up. You wanta' know why? Why because I have the finest man in the world! He's backing me in what I do and I'm backing him in what he does, rite or wrong, good or bad! He's true to the good 'ole USA and what it stands for, and I love him, yes, I love every part of him.[20]

Both Charles and Barbara recognized that the times required that they make quick decisions about their future together. In her first letter to Charles after Pearl Harbor, Barbara exclaimed:

> Well, what about this WAR business! Oh, Charlie, will you still get your Christmas leave? You must get it because I'm counting big on being with you again. . . . What's going to happen to us? There is no doubt in my mind as to whom shall win the war, but how long will it take us? It makes you feel like getting the best of everything before it's all gone. Now I know that isn't the right way to feel, is it Charlie?!?!?!?[21]

Charles, too, recognized that war had sped up the pace at which time was passing for them. In discussing his upcoming Christmas furlough of 1941, he remarked:

> Barbara, I want to impress you with the fact: I have but seven days off—four of them on the road to Florida from Missouri and back. Things will have to happen fast. Remember that—.[22]

At the same time, however, both Charles and Barbara went to

considerable lengths to explain that their love for each other was *not* to be regarded as a casual wartime romance. Early in 1942, when the topic of marriage began to be discussed seriously, Charles made it clear that they were not rushing into a wartime marriage. In a letter of early March, he emphasized this point:

> I am not afraid of war and you (if you were afraid) are over your war fright. Therefore, this would not be considered as a *war* marriage. Too, we have had quite a test *of our love*. I believe if we were married that it would be a *lasting* one.[23]

One week later, he noted: "I am well aware of this war, but it has not made this love of mine any different. I would have loved you just as much had there been no war."[24] Barbara also worried that others might think that their love was nothing more than a wartime fling. On 2 June 1942, she expressed her concern:

> Some people criticize "war loves and marriages" but as for me, I would do the same thing again. As a matter of fact, I don't know but what this war is going to reform this whole world. It's teaching us the importance of real, true love.[25]

An almost continuous discussion of wartime marriage took place in the United States during this period. The speed of the changes brought on by the war, especially in the length of engagements or the formality of the wedding ceremony, worried some. Others felt that marriages might provide stability and add an ethical edge to wartime relationships and counseled that marriages were all right, with the provision that true love be the force in speeding up events, not casual encounters or sexual hungers.[26] Special counseling was often available at United Service Organizations for prospective couples, and wartime fashions that would maintain traditional aspects of weddings were featured in the popular press. *LIFE* magazine gave its approval to war marriages in 1942 when it featured on its 22 June cover a war bride carrying a Victory-stamp bridal bouquet.[27] The fiction of popular magazines added a further dimension to the discussion as plots described every possible controversy.[28]

An equally significant discussion of the pros and cons of war marriages took place in the serious press. Sociologists took note of the fact that war had the immediate effect of accelerating the marriage rate, which was then followed by a decline as more and more men went off to war. In actuality, there were one million more marriages from 1940 to 1943 than would have been expected at prewar rates. Concern was expressed that "hasty marriages" followed by long separations could mean that family life was "more fictitious than real. . . ." One sociologist went so far as to claim that "there was a greater dispersion of family members and families as groups between 1936 and 1942 than in any other six-year period in the history of the world."[29]

Family and marriage counselors, as well as home economists, focused on the important roles they could play in helping young people to make up their minds about marriage. With proper counseling, these professionals were optimistic that war marriages would last. As one home economist concluded: "Generals and armies may win the war, but they can never win the peace. A lasting peace will have to be won on the home front by the kind of family which we evolve during the present crisis."[30]

Charles and Barbara were undaunted by the vociferous public debate on wartime marriages. They undoubtedly discussed the possibility of matrimony during their brief 1941 Christmas holiday together. In a 4 January 1942 letter, written just three days after they had parted, Charles left little room for anyone to question his intentions on this matter:

> I intend to marry you on my next trip or furlough, even if it is not the best thing. You said you did not want to marry me when I was there because you did not want to tie me down. Can't you see, just as you said you wanted me to boss you, I want to be tied down by you.[31]

Barbara, however, displayed a bit more restraint when she discussed the prospective marriage. On 29 January, she replied to his comments:

> You know that I want to be Mrs. C. E. Taylor worse than anything in the whole wide world, now, don't you? But it seems to me as I just couldn't marry you in Feb. Now don't get the idea that I am letting us down but you said to help plan and that's just what I'm doing. I have quite a few small bills that I would like to get paid up first. And also, if you get a short leave, your Mother will want you to come right home. You know, you've never told me how she feels about me. But, darling, we will continue planning. Maybe there will be some light on the subject soon.[32]

During the first three months of 1942, both Charles and Barbara grappled with the financial and logistical problems of arranging their marriage. Hoping that he might be stationed in Fort Benning, Georgia, Charles applied to Officer Candidate School. When his application was turned down in late February, his spirits reached a low point.[33] For the next two weeks, Charles's letters reverberated with bitterness toward the Army as he attempted to reconcile himself to the fact that he would not be going to Officer Candidate School. The prospects of receiving some time off at Easter, however, helped to raise his spirits. On 12 March 1942, he wrote that he had "high hopes of being on furlough."[34]

Barbara was equally excited about the possibility of their being together again. Upon learning that Charles had been granted a two-week leave, she exclaimed, "Darling, I am actually too excited even to write! I love you so very, very much and just the thought of being with you again seems entirely too good to be true. I can hardly wait!!!" When Barbara asked for time off from her job at Twentieth Century Fox so she could be with Charles, her understanding and patriotic boss replied, "I'd do anything for the boys in the service!"[35]

Marriage was now a realistic possibility. After spending most of the Easter furlough together, Charles and Barbara were secretly married on 5 April 1942. After their marriage, the couple immediately returned to Charles's home in Gainesville and retired to separate bedrooms. Because of the stress of the war, they felt the need to be officially married, but they were satisfied with just the ceremony for the time being.[36]

The decision to keep their marriage secret was a mutual one. As the following excerpt from an April letter from Barbara and Charles suggests, however, the young couple did not understand the full implications of this decision until after they were married:

> I'm not ashamed of you and I don't think it would be a sin for people to find out about us—BUT—it was our agreement not to tell for more reasons than one. In the first place, it would hinder us both—you in the Army and me at home and especially at the office. In the second place, our parents would lose all trust in us. . . . Now, if you'll apply a little common sense to the whole affair you'll understand it perfectly. Charlie, we've got to keep it a secret for a while anyway! I mean it!![37]

On more than one occasion, Barbara expressed regret that she had not been able to be open and honest with her parents about the marriage. When she learned that Charles had given the Army her name as his wife so that she could receive an allotment check, she became extremely upset. In an uncharacteristically curt note, dated 22 June, she stated:

> Received your letter this morning and I certainly think you were foolish to turn my name in as your wife. Mercenary, aren't you? If you have to give them my address, have them send it to the P.O. in Atlanta-General Delivery!! Please don't get that messed up![38]

Later that day, after giving the situation a bit more thought, she wrote Charles a much longer letter, urging him to "ignore the note of this morning!" Still, though, she was far from happy about the situation, writing that she was "petrified" at the thought "of getting a letter addressed to Mrs. Charles E. Taylor. . . . If we positively *have* to tell everyone we're married I certainly don't want it to leak out." What Barbara did not understand was that Charles had acted under orders when he submitted her name for an allotment. Failure to comply might have mean court martial.[39]

Shortly after Charles and Barbara's secret marriage, they began to make plans for a public ceremony. In June 1942, Charles's parents purchased and mailed him an engagement ring which he quickly sent to Barbara. In a flourish of excitement, she wrote that it was the "prettiest, loveliest, and everything goodiest ring that I've ever seen."[40]

The following month Charles wrote to Mr. Wooddall, formally asking him for his daughter's hand in marriage. Before he could send the letter, however, he had to find out the full name of his future father-in-law. On 10 July, he told Barbara that he was "ashamed to say" that he did not know her father's initials and requested that she provide them.[41] Even in these rapidly changing times, however, some formalities could not be forgotten. The letter Charles wrote is a significant expression of the efforts of this young couple to retain a sense of propriety in their new world.

> 14 July 1942
>
> Dear Mr. Wooddall:
>
> Perhaps this letter from me will come as a surprise to you, but it seems to me that even in these extraordinary circumstances in which we find ourselves today, formalities should still be observed.

I realize that you are completely aware that Barbara and I have plans for marriage upon her arrival in St. Louis, but before we go any further in our plans, I would like to have your consent. I already have the consent of my family, they are very proud to add such a wonderful person as Barbara to their family.

Sir, I am sorry that we are in War, which does not afford Barbara and I time, under the circumstances, to have the luxury of a normal peace-time wedding. However, there could be nothing about a big formal wedding that could have any effect upon the life and beauty of Barbara's and my life as husband and wife. . . .

Needless to say, I am looking forward to the day when I shall become a member of your happy family.

Respectfully yours,
Charles E. Taylor

Barbara, who had arranged for vacation time from her job in Atlanta, now made preparations to travel by train to St. Louis, Missouri, where she and Charles would be married in early August. The July letters of Barbara and Charles teem with excitement as they look forward to their forthcoming public marriage. Barbara's last letter to Charles before leaving for St. Louis reveals just how much significance she placed upon this public ceremony:

> As I told you, I wrote to the Clerk of Superior Court and a Mr. McAtier in St. Louis answered my letter. I have to be 19—you have to be 21. No waiting, no physical exam, no witnesses, no *nothing* required. . . . We can find a Baptist preacher and get married in his study and then we can wire our folks and everything will be nice and clean and good in the sight of God and man.[42]

The wedding occurred as planned on Sunday, 2 August 1942. However, in a letter to her parents, Barbara gave the date as 1 August, the date of her arrival. Later that week, Charles and Barbara had a candle burning ceremony in which they took the first marriage certificate from 5 April and burned it. They then changed the date on their second certificate from 2 August to 1 August to match the date Barbara had written to her parents.

After their weekend in St. Louis, the "newly married" couple headed to Waynesville, Missouri, and Fort Leonard Wood, where Charles was required to report for duty on Monday morning. After enjoying 18 days together—the longest single amount of time they had ever spent with each other—Barbara returned to Georgia. It would be more than three years, however, before Barbara and Charles would have the opportunity to lead a normal life together as husband and wife.

12

Adapting to Changing Familial Roles

25 Years of "Can This Marriage be Saved?"

Jean E. Hunter

In 1952, *Ladies Home Journal* staff writer Dorothy Cameron Disney was assigned to do a series of stories on the relatively new and somewhat controversial practice of marriage counseling. To complete her assignment, Disney headed west to Los Angeles to the American Family Institute, headed by Dr. Carl Popenoe, the recognized dean of American marriage counselors. Disney decided that the best way to bring the realities of marriage counseling home to her readers was to recount actual cases. She chose four cases from the files of the Institute and then proceeded to interview both spouses and the counselor about the problems the couple faced and their resolution. She presented the material by telling each spouse's side of the conflict. The counselor then offered his/her analysis of the case and described how the couple had worked out their differences.[1] The first installment of "Can This Marriage Be Saved?" appeared in January 1953.

Thirty-seven years later, this feature continues in the pages of the *Journal*, still following the format Disney developed and still offering hope to the reader that indeed, marriages can be saved.[2] Despite innumerable changes in the magazine over the years, "Can This Marriage Be Saved?" remains, having become the longest running feature in this or any other women's magazine.[3]

The popular appeal of "Can This Marriage Be Saved?" is obvious. It allows readers into the intimate lives of ordinary individuals who have ordinary problems with which readers can identify. And it offers hope. To a clearly unrealistic extent, these problem marriages *are* saved. Husband and wife see the error of their ways, and with determination and good will, plus counseling, they effect the necessary changes that will allow, if not "happily ever after," at least a modicum of peace and satisfaction.[4]

The appeal of "Can This Marriage Be Saved?" to the historian is equally obvious. Here is a column read by millions of women (and not a few men) every month for nearly four decades that provides detailed descriptions of the problems Americans were facing in their marriages and family lives. For the historian who is trying to understand the changes that were occurring during this period in American society in general and in the American family in particular, "Can This Marriage Be Saved?" is a fascinating resource. Yet it must be approached with care. The families described in the *Journal*'s pages cannot be assumed to be "average." There can obviously be no statistical correlation between the marriages described here and the rest of the American population. Thus, no conclusions can be drawn about the incidence of a particular problem in the general population from its incidence in the column.

Despite these caveats, there is much to learn from "Can This Marriage Be Saved?" Clearly, the authors and the editors chose subjects that they thought would interest and appeal to their readers. The purpose of the feature was also didactic; it was designed to provide examples of solutions for those who might be facing similar problems. Indeed, the difficulties faced by the subjects of the feature were rarely exotic, but rather tended to the pedestrian: money problems, in-law troubles, role conflicts, sexual incompatibility, etc.[5] The women and men described were likewise reassuringly typical. They represented the solid white American middle class. The men were salesmen, engineers, mechanics, factory workers, small businessmen, teachers, technicians, with an occasional executive, doctor or lawyer. The women were secretaries, clerks, teachers, nurses and, of course, homemakers, with an occasional overachiever who had made her way into the middle ranks of executives. The vast majority had children and almost all of them lived in detached houses in the suburbs. Most of the women were between the ages of 25 and 35, and most of the men were three to five years older. Most had married in their early twenties and only about 15 percent had been married before.[6] If not "statistically average," these women and men certainly reflected the then current image of the "average American couple." They also reflected the readership of the *Journal*.

Thus, the problems described in the 232 "Can This Marriage Be Saved?" features between 1953 and 1977 undoubtedly resembled the problems faced by many American couples, and they can provide additional information about the changing shape of American marriage during this 25-year period as well. Likewise, the analyses and solutions offered by the counselors and the introductory comments that were often provided by Dr. Popenoe provide insight into the view of marriage that was current among the professional "experts" in the field of marriage counseling. Finally, the prescriptive power of the feature should not be ignored, although it must not be overstated either. Readers who perused the column regularly could learn much about what marriage should be like and receive suggestions about how they themselves could bring their own relationships closer to the ideal.

"Can This Marriage Be Saved?" began at a time when American marriages were undergoing rapid change. Elaine May has chronicled these changes in her recent book, *Homeward Bound*. Rather than adhering to the current myth that the fifties family was the last incarnation of the "traditional" family, May and other historians have concluded that the family that emerged in the wake of World War II was markedly different from its predecessors. Long established demographic trends toward smaller families, later marriages and increased divorces were actually reversed during the fifties as young men and women, seeking comfort and security within the confines of the home, established families at an unprecedented rate. Old living patterns disappeared as millions of young people flocked to the suburbs to create new communities awash with children. Young women sought their identities as homemakers, ignoring—or indeed, rejecting—the promises of equality that had moved earlier generations of women. Young men, facing an increasingly bureaucratized world, sought their identities in a newly defined role as husband and father. Whatever this was, it was not the "traditional" family.[7]

Change continued into the sixties and the seventies. Married women entered the workplace in increasing numbers, though most of them had jobs rather than careers. Betty Friedan's *The*

Feminine Mystique challenged the fifties' belief that women could find fulfillment at home, while the introduction of the pill made the sexual revolution of the late sixties possible. The birth rate began to fall and the divorce rate began to rise. The National Organization of Women (NOW) was established, women's rights became the goal of significant numbers of women again, and a band of militant feminists seized the offices of the *Ladies Home Journal*, demanding a new editor and a new editorial policy for the magazine.[8] Historians are ever loathe to claim that one era or another saw the most change, but in the history of the family, the quarter century between 1953 and 1977 must rank high on the list of periods of rapid and destabilizing shifts in the ways families were supposed to operate.

The impact of these changes was well illustrated in the pages of "Can This Marriage Be Saved?" Here were women and men wrestling with the changing expectations of marriage and family life and the realities they faced in their daily existence. That these changes caused conflict is clear—of all the kinds of problems that were described in the column, the most frequent had to do with disagreements over role responsibilities. Indeed, in nearly three-fourths of the cases, the wife complained that the husband was not in fact fulfilling his role. In particular, the complaints had to do with the failure of husbands to provide adequately for their families (19 cases), the propensity of husbands to overwork and ignore their families' emotional needs (42 cases), the failure of husbands to provide any help around the house (40 cases), and the husbands' inadequacy as modern fathers (50 cases). In another 23 cases, the wives complained that their husbands controlled the finances and either kept them in the dark or kept them short of money—or both. In an additional 32 cases, wives complained that their husbands were domineering and failed to take their wishes and needs into account. Finally, the failure to show the wife love and affection was a complaint in 31 cases. Thus, in 72 percent of the cases described in "Can This Marriage Be Saved?" between 1953 and 1977, wives complained that their husbands were not living up to the prevailing expectations.[9]

The question arises as to whether there were noticeable changes in the incidence of these complaints over time. An investigation of the percentage of the features in which these problems occurred leads to some interesting conclusions (Table 1).

First, the complaints about problems with the husband's role responsibilities were the highest in five of the seven categories

Table 1: WIVES' COMPLAINTS CONCERNING HUSBANDS

	Percentage of Cases				
	1953–57	*1958–62*	*1963–67*	*1968–72*	*1973–77*
Inadequate Provider	2	13	10	7	7
Overworks	14	27	21	15.5	16
No Help at Home	17	30	12	17	12
Inadequate Father	26	24	17	17	19
Controls Finances	14	27	17	17	12
Domineering	26	22	21	22	24.5
Lack of Affection	14	15	14	10	14

and were high in the other two during the late fifties and early sixties. The new ideology of family life had had time to become widely accepted, but individuals might well not have had time to adjust. Second, the one complaint that increased substantially was that the husband was not an adequate provider. This change may reflect the higher expectations of families in the latter years. With the exception of this five-year anomaly, what is notable is the lack of change in the percentages. For example, during the first five years, 26 percent of the women claimed that their husbands were domineering. Twenty years later, 24.5 percent of the wives were making the same complaint.

What did the marriage counselors say about these complaints? How did they respond to men who sought to dominate their wives, who exclusively controlled the money, or who failed to live up to their responsibilities as husbands and fathers? The counselors in "Can This Marriage Be Saved?" provided no support for these husbands. The wives were told that they were equal partners in marriage, that they had rights as individuals, that they did not have to accept these behaviors from their husbands.

One of the earliest articles, entitled "Fred Was Too Masterful," offered a clear delineation of the problem of the domineering husband. Fred was a tax accountant in his mid-forties while Ivy, ten years younger, had her own public stenography business. Ivy's complaint was simple. "Fred talks incessantly of the duties of wives and the privileges of husbands and insists on being the absolute master. I almost hate him." Briefly put, Fred was money hungry, tyrannical, had a power complex and believed that all the problems of modern civilization were caused by women "telling men what to do and robbing them of their manhood." His wife's position was simple, too. "Either he is to consider me as a partner in our marriage and as a human being, or we will have no marriage." Few other tyrannical husbands were quite so blunt as Fred who baldly stated, "It is my right to make all family decisions. I cannot grant my love to Ivy unless she acknowledges my full authority as a husband."[10]

The counselors were unanimous in their responses to Fred and to other domineering husbands. Marriage was a partnership, not an absolute monarchy, and it was the counselor's job "to work out an equitable division of rights, duties, privileges and obligations. . . ."[11] The diagnosis was always the same as well: the husband was a tyrant because of his basic and deep-seated insecurity and lack of self-esteem. One prescription was for the wife to learn to show her love and appreciation. The other was for the husband to learn to respect and trust his wife.[12]

Regarding the issue of control of the family finances, the experts responded that it was unfair of husbands to keep their wives uninformed about the state of the family finances and then, as was often the case, to complain about wives' spending habits. Wives had every right to know what was in the family exchequer and to share equally in determining how family resources were to be used. Again, the partnership nature of marriage was stressed, and the experts insisted on the need for good communication in this as in every aspect of family life.[13]

"Can This Marriage Be Saved?" also had much to say about the responsibilities of the husband to his wife and family. There was no doubt that a husband was to provide for his family, but as the figures suggest, relatively few of the marriages described in the *Journal* faced problems because of the husbands' economic failure. In the expanding postwar economy, most white American men could support their families.[14] Both the wives and the counselors insisted, however, that financial support was not enough. There was more to being a husband and father than bringing home the bacon.

The case of Deborah and John in 1971 was a perfect example of a man who, while a good provider, was a bad husband. As the introduction noted, "John was married to his computer. He seemed to love it more than Deborah and their four children." In fact, John was a compendium of unacceptable husbandly traits. A computer scientist, he gave all his time and energy to working out the bugs in a new computer system he had recommended to his employer. He was never home; he neglected his children; he failed to show his wife any affection, and he presented to her a cold, remote facade. John had even stopped having sex with his wife since the new computer had been installed. He was worried and upset because he felt responsible for the new system, but he never told Deborah what was on his mind. They no longer shared any common interests and hadn't done anything together for over a year.

As Popenoe noted, John was one of those men who thought that if he provided enough money for his family, he had done all he needed to do. John was wrong, as his counselor quickly and definitely pointed out to him. Once John was convinced that his personality and behavior were the problems, he made up his mind to change. He started working less; he spent more time with his family and got acquainted with his sons. He and Deborah began doing things together, and he began to open up about his own private concerns. He learned how to show affection, and their sex life improved as he took Deborah's needs into account. John became the epitome of the perfect husband and, according to his counselor, a much happier person.[15]

The *Journal* sent an unambiguous message to its women readers through the columns of "Can This Marriage Be Saved?" Wives had a right to expect more of their husbands than a weekly paycheck. They had a right to expect respect, trust, companionship, help with household tasks, shared parenting and signs of affection. The frequency with which cases describing a husband's failure to meet these changing role expectations occurred throughout the period suggests the difficulty that American men had in adapting to these new definitions of husband and father.

The role responsibilities of wives were also changing during this period, but rather than requiring women to alter their behavior *within* the family, the new roles for women were chiefly *outside* its confines. Perhaps this is the reason that the wife's failure to fulfill her role responsibilities was an issue in about half as many cases as the husband's role failure. Still, in 38 percent of the cases cited, problems with the woman's roles emerged as important issues troubling the family. The complaints about wives and their roles form an interesting oppositional pattern. On the one hand, there were complaints that the wife was an inadequate homemaker or mother in 40 cases. On the other, there were complaints that she was *too good* a homemaker in ten cases. Likewise, in 39 cases the problems centered on the wife's activities outside the home, generally with work, but sometimes with volunteer activities; but in 23 cases, the

Table 2: HUSBANDS' COMPLAINTS CONCERNING WIVES

	Percentage of Cases				
	1953–57	*1958–62*	*1963–67*	*1968–72*	*1972–77*
Inadequate Homemaker	17	27	19	15.5	12
Overly Meticulous	9	6	2	3	2
Activities Conflict	24	12	12	26	9
Housebound Problem	14	24	2	5	7

difficulty lay in the wife's *lack* of activities outside the home. The frequency of complaints about women's role responsibilities can also be charted to demonstrate differences over time (Table 2).

The first and simplest conclusion from the figures in Table 2 is that overmeticulous housewives had become much rarer by the sixties and seventies. Likewise, after peaking between 1958–62, complaints about wives being housebound declined markedly. It is interesting that the editors and authors consistently featured the problems of the wife, the one who had no access to the world beyond the home, so prominently during the years that spanned the publication of *The Feminine Mystique*. Clearly, the issue was in the air before Friedan loosed her bombshell. Finally, it is suggestive that problems arising from the wife's activities outside the home were most prominent between 1953 and 1957 and between 1968 and 1972. Nearly 90 percent of these cases dealt with the wife's employment. During the first period, married women had just begun their march into the workplace, so it is not surprising that adjustment to this new role caused marital problems. The second period covers the years of the reemergence of the modern feminist movement when women's access to employment opportunities had become a primary demand of the reformers. That the *Journal* should feature the potential problems that women's employment could cause for a marriage made good editorial sense.

The treatment given to the issue of the legitimacy of women's nonfamilial activities provides the clearest statement of the emerging norms regarding the wife's roles within marriage. A review of the 39 "Can This Marriage Be Saved?" features where this was an issue yields not a single suggestion that a wife should get all her satisfaction from her family and ignore her own needs. In case after case, counselors advised wives to find or maintain interests outside the home, often in volunteer work, but often in the workplace. There was a real appreciation of the fact that women needed and deserved more than home and family to make them full and contented human beings.

A striking but typical example dealing with this issue was the 1966 case of Beth, 39, the wife of an engineer and mother of three daughters. Married for 18 years, Beth and her husband Jack had come to the Institute because she was suffering from terrible moods and depression that were threatening the marriage. It turned out that Beth was an extremely talented artist who believed she was being self-indulgent when she painted for her own satisfaction. Her domineering mother had imbued her with the sense that family needs must always come before personal preferences, so Beth could paint only when it had some family-related purpose, like decorating the school classroom or doing posters for the Girl Scouts.

Counseling helped Beth to accept that she too had needs and that chief among these was the development and use of her talents. Beth began painting regularly, setting up a studio in the house and setting aside undisturbed time when her family could intrude only in the event of a serious emergency. Within a year, she had a show in a local gallery and began selling paintings. Her moods and depression disappeared, and her marriage became more solid than ever. Popenoe's comments on this case were telling:

> The wife who enriches her own life wisely is improving her home and strengthening her family at the same time. She need never feel guilty, so long as she keeps her eye on the home as the center of her existence—though not the totality of it. . . . When she [Beth] began to express her whole personality, instead of crippling a vital part of it, she not merely improved her health but became a much better wife and mother. A million wives could profitably follow her example.[16]

Beth's painting could be considered a career, though it was undertaken within the confines of the home. But millions of women had entered the workforce and were pursuing careers outside the home. The potential for role conflict was much greater for women who had made this kind of commitment. Nowhere was this better illustrated than in a 1955 feature entitled "If a Wife Values Career above Husband." Patrice, 36, was copy chief for a large advertising firm—a very responsible, demanding and remunerative position. Her husband Gid was a real estate salesman. They had a four-year-old daughter, Ruthie.

Patrice had always been career-oriented and had married late, fearful of her ability to handle both marriage and career. At first all had been well, but recently the marriage had deteriorated and the husband was demanding that she quit her job.

After talking to both spouses, the counselor concluded that "Patrice's career obviously wasn't the basic cause of the trouble in this marriage. The way she handled her career, her husband and her child did the damage." Even Gid recognized that "For Pat to quit work would be no solution." What Pat had to do was to put her career in perspective and make time for her husband and child. She stopped working overtime; she didn't work at home when Gid was there; she stopped praising her boss and started praising and appreciating her husband; she learned to laugh at his jokes; she saw more of Ruthie and learned to love her. Patrice and Gid started doing things together and began to associate with his friends and business associates. In turn, Gid recognized and supported Pat's "emotional need to hold a job outside the home."[17]

In many other similar cases between 1953 and 1977, the denouement was the same. The committed career woman kept her job and the necessary adjustments were made. Sometimes, as in the case of Patrice, the wife made the adjustment by insuring that her work responsibilities did not interfere with her family responsibilities. Other times, the husband changed his attitudes and habits, accepting the right of the wife to work outside the home and shouldering a larger share of the family duties. It appeared that the message to the wife was the same as to the husband: work was fine, but marriage and family should and could come first.

But the message was actually more ambiguous, at least in the years before 1970. In ten of the 22 cases where there existed a conflict over the wife's work, the process of saving the marriage included the wife either giving up her job or going from full-time to part-time work. When 35-year-old Beth, a busy accountant, and Tim, her electronics engineer husband, sought counseling in 1961, they were at an impasse over her career. She had worked hard to put him through college and to help him meet extensive financial obligations to his family. When their money problems passed, Tim wanted Beth to quit and enjoy the leisure she so richly deserved, only to discover that she wanted to keep on working. Tim complained:

> I then found out that her job meant more to her than being a wife and mother. She flatly refused to quit. She made it

> clear that her work, routine accountancy, was more important to her than anything on earth. When she reminded me that she earned a handsome salary, I could tell that she had no more faith than my father in my earning ability and scientific talents.

The counselor in this case felt that the husband needed the most help, especially regarding his tendency to see everything as an attack on his competence. As the counselor reported, "There was no reality to his belief that Beth worked outside the home because, like his father, she mistrusted him as a breadwinner. Beth preferred a job to housework because she was made that way." To make Tim happy, however, Beth cut her assignments to the bone. She only worked as an accountant a couple of days a month and directed her desire to be active into very impressive volunteer work. Tim was reassured, and this marriage was saved.[18]

For most of the years under study here, then, the message of "Can This Marriage Be Saved?" about women's role responsibilities within marriage was clear. Women could and should have a life outside of home and family. They could work outside the home. But they were to sacrifice their careers and outside activities if these threatened the marriage, even if, like Beth, they were "made that way." The preservation of the family and the bolstering of the husband's ego were more important than the wife's needs and desires. The counselor in a case where the husband had become interested in another woman put the matter succinctly: "She [the wife] did not reflect that a man of Leonard's personality and background, handicapped by his emotional insecurity, could hardly be expected to tolerate a career wife."[19] Popenoe warned of the dangers that a wife's career could pose to a marriage if she did not have her priorities established:

> . . . if the wife has an outside job, she is more likely to find . . . [that] competition develops to a disturbing degree. She may easily give home (and husband) second place in her time and thoughts, may cultivate friends who can be useful to her in her own work and refuse to entertain her husband's friends, may even neglect her own children, under the spur of a strong desire for self-assertion.[20]

In 1961, Popenoe insisted on the need for counselors to help men to become men and women to become women. Gail and

Guy's 12-year marriage was threatened by her take-charge attitude and her general competence. She was instructed to fit herself more closely to society's version of womanhood to save her marriage by changing her "self-willed, assertive, highly independent manner."[21] In 1957, Eve was warned "to guard against the signs of masculinity within herself that lowered Ron's [her husband's] masculinity and, of course, her respect for him."[22] As late as 1969, Christine was reported to have "found out the way to win a man's heart is not to be aggressive, competitive and argumentative. She used her intelligence to curb these unfeminine tendencies"—and she saved her marriage.[23]

The seventies saw a change in editorial direction at the *Ladies Home Journal*, in the wake of the March 1970 Women's rights demonstration. The editors became much more sympathetic to the renewed feminist movement and more supportive of the working wife. It is noteworthy that comments about the need for women to "curb . . . unfeminine tendencies" like independence, assertiveness and self-confidence disappeared from "Can This Marriage Be Saved?" after 1970. There was also a change in the attitude toward working wives. More than half of the wives in the cases described in "Can This Marriage Be Saved?" between 1970 and 1977 were employed.[24] Before 1970, the cases in which there was a conflict over the wife's job resulted in the wife either quitting or reducing her commitment by taking part-time work in 45 percent of the cases. After 1970, this was the result in only 33 percent of the columns.

In one such case, the wife had been working weekends, and her husband felt trapped in her absence. She quit that position but reserved the right to take a more convenient job.[25] In another, a chronically fatigued wife left her very demanding job, but she took on extensive part-time assignments and regained her health.[26] Another wife gave up her job as an executive secretary because her insecure husband was jealous of her boss. She took another position.[27] Finally, in 1975, a registered nurse reduced her hours to boost her husband's ego and to help him with his drinking problem.[28] It should be noted that in none of the counselors' analyses of these marriages were any negative comments made about working wives. In fact, in five cases during the same period, the solution to the problems in the marriage included the wives' *going* to work.[29] Rather, comments by Popenoe noted that if both partners worked, it was the responsibility of the counselor to work out a suitable division of labor, with the children doing their share.[30] In one case, the husband objected vociferously to his wife's becoming a lawyer; the counselor was proud to report that Buddy had finally been brought to see the error of his ways.[31]

The roles of wife and husband certainly changed during the 25 years under study here, and the columns of "Can This Marriage Be Saved?" reflected the problems in adjusting to these changes. The evidence from this study suggests that this adjustment was more difficult for men. It also demonstrates that women had the support of the experts and the media when they insisted that men fulfill newly defined role responsibilities as husbands and fathers. Men were to view and treat their wives as equal partners, respect their opinions, support their interests and trust their capacities. Men were to be good providers, but place their marriages and families first. They were to share in the duties of the household, provide their wives with affection and be caring, involved fathers. They were to accept the entrance of their wives into the workplace, at least by the seventies, and adjust to the changes this created in their lives.

Women had always been told that they should place their marriages and families first. Now men were being given much the same message. Women were being encouraged to find more of their identity outside the home, to broaden their horizons. Men were being encouraged to find more of their identity within the home, and perhaps to limit their autonomy. Elaine May suggests that during the fifties, as these new definitions of the husband's role were emerging, many American men concluded that home and family could provide much desired security and real concrete rewards.[32] Barbara Ehrenreich suggests that during the sixties and the seventies, American men increasingly fled from the demands and commitments of family life.[33] This study suggests that by the mid-seventies, changing role responsibilities had provided wives with more options, but husbands' adjustments to their new roles still created a number of problems in marriages. Thus, the *Journal* tried to show its readers how these modern marriages could be saved.

Notes

Notes to Essay 1/Bielinski

1. Outstanding examples of the anecdotal genre of historical writing on the Dutch are Ellis L. Raesly, *Portrait of New Netherland* (New York, 1945); Henri and Barbara Van Der Zee, *A Sweet and Alien Land: The Story of Dutch New York* (New York, 1978); and the work of Alice P. Kenney, in particular in *Stubborn for Liberty: The Dutch in New York* (Syracuse, 1975). In *Holland on the Hudson: An Economic and Social History of Dutch New York* (Ithaca, 1987), Oliver A. Rink has combined a synthesis of more disciplined scholarship with original research in both Dutch and printed sources. His chapter entitled "The People of New Netherland," represents a more accountable demographic profile, 139–171. Most responsible for the resurgence in New Netherlandic studies is the "New Netherland Project" at the New York State Library, which translates and presents Dutch language source material and provides a broad umbrella for scholarly and cultural activities. The newest scholarship on the Dutch is embodied in a forthcoming collection of 26 articles entitled "Selected Rensselaerswyck Papers." A comprehensive review of recent literature appears in Joyce D. Goodfriend's "The Historiography of the Dutch in Colonial America," in *Colonial Dutch Studies: An Interdisciplinary Approach*, edited by Patricia U. Bonomi and Eric Nooter (New York, 1988), 6–32.

2. The history, organization and resources of the Colonial Albany Project (CAP) and the elements of its research, programming and service operations are described comprehensively in "The People of Colonial Albany: A Community History Project" (annually since 1984). The current edition of this working document is available for inspection from the CASHP, 3093 Cultural Education Center, Albany, New York 12230.

In general, the Colonial Albany Project studies the lives of the people who lived in the community during its preindustrial age—functionally defined as before 1800. Research is guided by a belief that individual life stories constitute basic building blocks and that early Albany's story is most authentically represented through the lives of individuals and how they functioned in groups. The family represents the most basic and most essential identity unit for the study of life in early America.

Like all Colonial Albany Project programming, this article represents the cooperative efforts of a large number of past and present project associates. In particular, the author is grateful for the support of

Thomas Burke, Thomas Topolski and Nancy Zeller.

3. The charter text is printed in *Colonial Laws of New York from the Year 1664 to the Revolution* (Albany, 1894) I, 195–214. Its impact on the people of the community is assessed in Stefan Bielinski, *Government By the People: The Story of the Dongan Charter and the Birth of Participatory Democracy in the City of Albany* (Albany, 1986), 47–58.

4. Each of more than 50 surveys is described in detail on pages 38–46 of the CAP "Guide" (1988 edition). A major purpose of the "Guide" is to chronicle research activities. See also, *Sources on the People of Colonial Albany: Narrative Sources* (Albany, 1988 edition).

5. The goal of this reconstitution program is complete origins (background), birth, death and marriage information for each early Albany person. The plan to reconstruct the families of colonial Albany and to recover marginal people from the historical record is described in the "Guide," 47ff.

6. The principal features of the life course biography provide demographics, chart activities and achievements throughout an individual's life and also evaluate attitudes and beliefs. These components are explained further in the "Life Course Biographies" section of the "Guide." By the end of 1988, more than 9,000 biographical cases were established on a mainframe data management system.

7. The participatory nature of city government is discussed in Bielinski, *Government By the People*, 47–57. Distinct record sets were generated for municipal (city) government (complete common council minutes from 1686); county government (chiefly legal and registry); at the provincial level (revenue, regulatory and administrative); military (relating to the garrison, city militia units, and the four wars against the French); Commissioners of Indian Affairs (diplomatic but involving accounts for Indian gifts, interpreters, and meetings such as the Albany Congress of 1754); extra-legal (de facto local bodies established to cope with Leisler's Rebellion and the Revolutionary struggle); missionary (the SPG records, for example, are rich in Albany-related material); and Albany churches (aside from registering the equivalent of vital statistics, the Dutch Reformed Church in particular filled a number of socioeconomic vacuums in the emerging community). Copies of these record sets are held at the CAP office.

8. We acknowledge with thanks the support of Robert R. Dykstra and John F. Reynolds for helping focus our research design. "List of the Heads of Families . . . June 1697," New York Colonial Manuscripts, New York State Archives, XLII, 34.

9. Copies of maps drawn by Reverend John Miller (chaplain at the fort) in 1695 and by Colonel Wolfgang Roemer (a military engineer) in 1698 from the British Public Records Office are part of the CAP "Graphics Archive." These resources detail community geographical features. Survey resources include assessment rolls for 1689, 1702 and 1709; oaths and petitions for 1699, 1700 and 1701; subscription lists for 1683 and 1699; and a freeholder list for 1720. Copies of these lists and of records of city government, court minutes, real estate records and estate information are described in the "Guide" and are available at the CAP office.

10. Both Schuyler brothers were Albany residents from the 1650s

until their deaths. However, both were able to acquire extensive rural lands which diluted the focus of their commitment to the emerging community. Both were counted among the community's elite as principal fur traders as early as 1660.

Citations refer to the computerized CAP biographical case numbers. Each fact in these is documented by information referenced and filed at the CAP office. Philip Pieterse Schuyler (1628–1683), case no. 1742; David Pieterse Schuyler (1636–1690), 1262. For Margarita Van Slichtenhorst Schuyler (1628–1711), see 96. Her marriage to Philip Pieterse in 1650 provided the carpenter with fur export connections and enabled him to gain land under the Dutch and to enhance his holdings under the English. For Catharina Verplanck Schuyler (1639–1708), see 1108. Alida Van Slichtenhorst Schuyler (c1655–1747), 5877, widow of Gerrit Van Schaick, lost a second husband in 1696. For Pieter Schuyler (1657–1724), see 61. Few individuals were able to touch all the bases of opportunity so well. Johannes Schuyler (1668–1747), 100, married widow Elsie Staats Wendell (c1654–1737), 99, who was 14 years his senior—the only marriage encountered during this time period involving a substantial age disparity. David D. Schuyler (1669–1715), 1263, married the daughter of a prominent New York City family (Rutgers). He was appointed mayor of Albany in 1706. Myndert Schuyler (1672–1755), 101, was mayor from 1719–1721 and 1723–1725, was elected to the provincial Assembly and was active in Indian diplomacy, a family constant throughout the colonial period. Jacobus Schuyler (1675–1707), 1326, a merchant, died prematurely. Abraham D. Schuyler (1663–1726), 921, shipped out produce and forest products on his own sloop. The politics of marriage and of relocation are discussed in Stefan Bielinski, "Coming and Going in Early America: The People of Colonial Albany and Outmigration," *De Halve Maen* LX: 2 (October 1987), 12–18.

11. For Alida Schuyler Van Rensselaer Livingston (1656–1727), see case no. 95. The frustrations of her marriage and business career are related in Linda Biemer, "Business Letters of Alida Schuyler Livingston, 1680–1726," *New York History* LXIII: 2 (April 1982), 183–207. For Robert Livingston (1654–1728), see case 94. The career of this Scot, representing an extraordinary American success story, is portrayed masterfully in Lawrence H. Leder, *Robert Livingston, 1654–1728, and the Politics of Colonial New York* (Chapel Hill, 1962). For Geertruy Schuyler Groesbeck (1661–1747), see 1737.

12. For Evert Janse Wendell (1615–1702), see 2655. The retailing/officeholding/landowning sons identified as Albany householders in 1697 were Evert, Jr. (c1660–1702), 2656, and Abraham (c1670–1755), 2653. Philip Wendell (1657–1743), 2701, married a Visscher women, fathered ten children and followed the leather trade in his modest hillside home. For Johannes Wendell (1649–1692), a once-prominent fur trader, see 2942. His second wife, Elsie Staats (1654–1737), is profiled in case 99. For Evert Janse's grandchildren, see Bielinski, "Coming and Going in Early America," 15.

13. For Dirck Wesselse Ten Broeck (1638–1717), see Stefan Bielinski, "Becoming American: An Essay on Leadership in An Early American Community" (graduate thesis, SUNY Albany, 1986). This biography of the founder of the Ten Broeck family is based on data consolidated in

case 32. For his children, see "Becoming American," 26, 32n. For Wessel Ten Broeck (1664–1747), see case 83. Particularly useful for family information is Emma Ten Broeck Runk, *The Ten Broeck Genealogy* (New York, 1897).

14. For Jan Janse Bleecker (1642–1732), who began in America as a shoemaker, see case 2. One of the youngest of the New Netherland-era settlers, he had been a community magistrate during the early 1680s and was extremely active in city-based civic and social affairs until he moved west to Guilderland after 1713. For his son, Johannes Bleecker, Jr. (1668–1732), see 199. This young man's ambitions were frustrated by the vitality of his father—whose career still was on the ascent. In 1686, a desperate Johannes, Jr. was with the Albany men apprehended by the French for trading in their territory. Later, he was among those disgruntled Albanians who supported Jacob Leisler. On the prospects and frustrations of sons of original settlers, see Bielinski, "Becoming American," chapter 6, and the sources cited in notes 1–7. By 1756, the census taker was able to count eight Bleecker-named households in the city.

15. For Hendrick Hansen (c1660–1724), who married the sister of Rip Van Dam in 1692, see 4939. For his father, Hans Hendrickse (c1620–1694)—the original emigré, see 4937. For Eva De Meyer Hansen (c1620–1705), see 6504. For Johannes Hansen (c1675–1748), see 4940. Like the Ten Broecks and Bleeckers, the Hansens were able to maintain leadership status until the end of the colonial era.

16. For Hendrick Van Rensselaer (1667–1740), see 5053. He married the daughter of Pieter Van Brugh, an Albany insider. For Albert Janse Ryckman (c1650–1737), see 1905. Ryckman's brewery was separate from his house and employed several helpers including his sons. He received substantial patronage business from city government, the Indian Commissioners and the fort. His descendants continued the family brewing tradition. For Albert Janse's daughter, Catharina (c1670–1740), who married high constable Anthony Bries, see 1911. She succeeded Bries (c1670–1704) in the Indian trade when his life ended prematurely, see 6333.

17. For Johannes Becker, Jr. (c1662–1738), see 6031. For Van Brugh (1666–1740), see 5300. A former smith, Appel left no descendants in Albany; see 6283. For Teller (1659–1725), a younger son of a prominent fur trading family that left Albany for New York and Schenectady, and who himself relocated to Schenectady, see 5337. For Pieter Bogardus (1645–1714), a precharter magistrate and the son of a Dutch minister and Anneke Jans, see 6381. For Martin Creiger (c1650–1702), son of a noted Dutch soldier, see 5312. For Van Buren (c1640–1704), see 6505. For Van Allen (c1670–c1740), an outmigrant tailor's son and marginal trader who prospered as a Hudson River slooper, see 5637.

18. For Harman Bastiaense Visscher (1619–c1696), the original settler, see 4064. For his widow, Hester Dircks (died after 1709), see 6455. For their daughter Ariaantie (c1655–after 1709), the widow of a shoemaker/trader who headed a household of four in 1697, see 4100. Johannes Harmanse (1669–1749), married the daughter of an Ulster County (New York) Englishman, lived in a landmark house on Pearl Street, and sat as an alderman on the city council; see 4141. His householding sons were: Frederick Harmanse (c1665–after 1715), who ran a sawmill on the Beaverkill, 4069; Dirck Harmanse (1652–1725),

another sawyer who owned income property near his third ward home, 4067; Nanning Harmanse (c1660–1730), a riverman and occasional trader, 4160; and Bastiaen Harmanse (c1655–1737), a brewer, 4102.

19. For Hendrick Janse Roseboom (c1640–1703), see case no. 622. His householding sons were Johannes (1661–1745), 1671; Hendrick, Jr. (c1670–after 1734), 1655; Gerrit (c1665–1739), 1609; and Myndert (c1675–1722), who was active in church and local government service, 1950. Barent Bradt and his sons are the subjects of two of my unpublished manuscripts entitled "The Bradt Family and Ethnic Identity in a Pre-Urban Community," (1983) and "Barent Bradt's Sons and the Character of an Early American City," (1987). Both are filed at the CAP office. These articles on the descendants of a Norwegian woodcutter describe the transition and assimiliation of a non-Dutch, New Netherland-era family, and rely on the following CAP life course biographies of Bradt family householders in 1697: Barent Albertse Bradt (1633–after 1712), 4182; Anthony Bradt (1657–c1722), soon to be city treasurer and sexton of the Dutch Reformed Church—a graphic representation of the adaptability of these one-time Lutherans, 4197; Daniel (c1677–1722), who, as an Albany insider, was able to relocate his family on a farm he obtained from the city at Schaghticoke, 4340; Dirck (c1666–after 1720), 4344; and Johannes Barentse Bradt (c1673–1711), a moderately successful trader, 4253. Wouter Vanderzee (born c1670), the son of Barent Bradt's late brother, Storm Vanderzee, later moved to the country with his large family, 5584. Maria Post (2221), was listed as a householder with five children in 1697 and identified as "Jan Bradt's widow." Jan Bradt was another of Barent's younger brothers. In 1699, she married Edward Corbet, a native of Brazil like herself.

20. For Gerrit Frederickse (dead by the 1670s), the original emigré and Lansing family patriarch, see 3060. For Elizabeth Hendricks (c1610–c1694), his widow, see 3061. All of her children probably were born in Europe. Wouter Albertse Vandenuythof (c1610–1699), a prominent baker and long-time Albany resident, had taken a third wife by 1697; see 5669. For Gerrit Lansing (c1635–1708), a baker/trader and church officer, see 3698. For Johannes (c1635–1728), see 3440. For Hendrick (c1635–1709), a butcher/shipper of meats, see 3350. For Abraham (1663–1745), son of Gerrit the baker, who married Magdalena Van Tricht in 1703, see 3062.

21. For Claes Ripse (c1630–c1710), who was appointed alderman by Jacob Leisler in 1689, see 6352. His son, Rip Van Dam (1660–1749), built his later career on his association with Robert Story, a Manhattan-based merchant who had an Albany trading house in the 1670s. Rip Van Dam was the first of several Albany boys who found spectacular success elsewhere; see 6343. For Paulus Van Benthuysen, see 5338. For Debora Van Dam Hansen (c1670–1742), see 6351. For Leendert Philipsen Conyn (c1630–c1704), see 3769.

Other householders in 1697 whose descendants did not appear on subsequent community surveys were Pieter Van Olinda, Pieter Van Woggulum, Benomi Van Curler, Jan Verbeeck, Pieter Mingael and Jan Vinhagen. The descendants of Jacob Lookerman, Anthony Coster, Isaac Ouderkirk, Jacobus Turck and Jan Nack were able to persist in Albany for part of another generation.

22. By the 1730s, the Ketelhuyns had left Albany for the countryside. In 1697, four Ketelhuyn-named households were described on the census: Willem (c1655–1746), owned several residences in Albany and then relocated to Schaghticoke, case 4652; David (c1675–1711), a frustrated illegal trader, was killed by Indians at Schaghticoke, 4634; Daniel (c1670–1731), a merchant and landholder, was active in city government service activities and participated in the Canadian expedition during Queen Anne's War, 4633; and Anna Willems (c1640–c1700), the widow of Jochim Ketel—the original emigré—cared for three children in her third ward home, 4626. The family saga of some drama is related in Arthur J. Weise, *The Ketelhuyn Chronicles* (New York, 1899).

In 1697, Marselis France (or Janse) (c1620–1700), the original Marselis family member, see 731; his brother or cousin, Hendrick Marselis (died 1697), the city porter, 722; Marselis Janse's sons, Gysbert (c1660–1740), a shoemaker/merchant, 716; and Ahasueres (c1675–1730s), a shoemaker who moved to Schenectady by 1700, 623. His daughters married Albany householders Joseph Yates, Joseph Janse Van Zandt and Lucas Lucase Hooghkerke. For Huybertje Marselis Yates, see 726; for Zytje Marselis Van Zandt, see 853; for Judith Marselis Hooghkerke, see 741.

Van Ness family householders were Gerrit (1645–1715), a wheelwright and long-time city resident, 899; and Jan (968) and Cornelis (886), both of whom later relocated in the Mohawk Valley.

The Groesbecks included Willem Claese (1659–1722), a carpenter who married a Schuyler, 3381; his father, Claes Groesbeck (1624–1712), an original settler who lived across the street, 3369; and Stephanus (1662–1744), a prosperous trader, city official and pillar of the Dutch church, 3377.

The so-called "Van Iverens," were Myndert Frederickse (c1630–1706), who came from Europe and formerly was a blacksmith, 2465; Tryntje Carstens (1624–1703), widow of the other original settler, 6498; and Warner Carstens (1674–after 1742), a newlywed tailor, 2500.

The Van Deusens included the widow Catharina Van Eslant Van Deusen (1645–c1710), who boarded lodgers, 6506; Willem Jacobse (c1670–1731), a trader, 5574; Harpert Jacobse (1665–1742), another merchant, 5529, and Abraham Tewisse (1671–after 1700), a shoemaker, 3892.

23. Smaller, but mainline "Dutch" families were represented on the 1697 census by: Philip De Foreest (1652–1727), a cooper, 4706; Jan Fonda (1655–1737), who moved to the country, 3766, and Jellis Fonda (1670–1738), a gunsmith, 3767; Harman Gansevoort (1635–1708), patriarch of the Albany family and a brewer, 4653; Hendrick Oothout (c1660–1740), a trader and landholder, 428, and Johannes Oothout (c1665–1745), the son of a brewer, 4284; Jan (2139) and Wouter Quackenbush, Jr., 2323; Cornelis (c1660–1753) 4515, who moved to Schenectady, and Albert Slingerland (c1670–c1731) 5408; a newlywed; Juriaen Van Hoesen (c1630–c1717), a glazier/trader and eldest son of an original settler, 6053; and Volkert Van Hoesen (c1660–1725), 6417; Anthony Van Schaick (1655–1737), a trader, 3934; Jacob Winne (c1676–1706) 2935, a newlywed, and Frans Winne (c1659–after 1715), a trader and alderman, 2913; the Witbeck householders were Jan Thomase, the original emigré and a long-time regional land trader, 1820; and Johannes Janse, who later moved to the country, 1822.

24. Regardless of actual ethnicity, all New Netherland-era householders listed on the census have been considered with the Dutch majority. Chief among the non-Dutch, "Dutch" residents were Scots (Glen, Sanders), Scandinavians (Bradt, Douw) and Germans (most of Albany's one-time Lutherans). The eight Britons among the 15, post-New Netherland, non-Dutch householders all married daughters of local "Dutch" era families. The other seven, chiefly of French and Spanish ancestry, typically found spouses from outside the Albany community. The non-Dutch householders in 1697 were Jean Rosie (1654–1737), a Frenchman, Indian interpreter and long-time Albany resident who managed to acquire real estate and to maintain status despite a suspect background, case no. 6456; William Hogan (c1670–c1739), an Irishman who married a local woman and ran a popular inn, 4396; Joseph Yates (c1640–1730), a soldier, blacksmith and contractor at the fort—in 1697 six of his children were living in his house, 4419. Thomas Williams (c1670–c1752) came from New York, married successive Albany women (a Gansevoort and a Bronck), prospered in import/exports, owned city real estate, was elected alderman and later was appointed sheriff, 6285; Pierre Villeroy (aka Pieter De Garmo)(c1660–1741), a French Catholic who despite marrying a Vanderheyden, was excluded from trading and left to sell his services as a laborer, 947; John Finn (Fyne) from Ireland, also married local women and practiced the cooper's trade, 6028; John Carr (Jean Kerr) (1663–after 1702), another Irishman, 6051; James Parker (1660–c1717), the son of a soldier and long-time city marshall, 5308; Joseph Janse Van Zandt (c1660–1753), a long-time Albany resident identified on the census as of Spanish origin. However, he married Zytie Marselis, supported the Dutch Reformed Church and enjoyed modest success in transportation-related enterprises, 291. Jonathan Broadhurst (c1660–after 1705), an Englishman who married the widow of Dominie Gideon Schaets, later was appointed sheriff, 5334; Omie La Grange, Jr. (1672–1722), from a Lutheran family, was a newlywed who moved to the countryside, 5928; William Hollie (d.1712), was a city retainer who had been in the community since the 1670s, 6048; Frans Janse Pruyn (c1640–1712), a tailor and Catholic founder of a regular early Albany family, 3535; and John Gilbert (c1640–1707), an Englishman and baker/trader, married a Vandenbergh and made the other compromises necessary for success. He had lived in Albany since the 1670s, 5155. Two others, Rachel Van Valkenburgh Radcliffe (1399) and Elizabeth Beek Salisbury Bradshaw (6029) were the widows of former English soldiers.

25. For Dellius (c1650–1710), whose notorious land grabbing was nipped by the Earl of Bellomont, see 5319. These "fringe" families can be identified with the Albany Lutheran Church. However, with few surviving church records, the strength of their commitment remains unconfirmed. However, these families did not prosper in Albany trade and did not achieve leadership recognition.

26. Barent Ten Eyck (1679–1710), married in 1700, fathered eight children, but died prematurely at age 31, see 4811; Hendrick (1680–1772), was a baker whose long Albany life was marked by frequent community and church service, 4818. These brothers alone were acknowledged as co-heads of households on the census. Their

mother, Gerritje Coeymans Ten Eyck (1654–1736), lost her husband about 1693 yet was able to maintain the house until the 1730s, 241. For Coenradt Jacobse Ten Eyck (1678–1753), the silversmith, see 4812. For Jacob Ten Eyck, the first family member in Albany, see 4807.

For Abraham Cuyler (c1665–1747), a successful trader who married the daughter of Jan Janse Bleecker, see 358. For Johannes Beekman (c1660–1732), see 3858.

27. For Staats (c1655–1735), see 4595; for Van Dyck (c1660–1707), see 830.

28. For Ryer Schermerhorn (1652–1719), the eldest son of a New Netherlander, a prominent Schenectady proprietor and a member of the first provincial Assembly in 1683, see 5490. He had maintained a dual residence for almost two decades—a stretch of propriety that he and a few others were afforded. His Albany was a convenient refuge for his family after the Schenectady Massacre of 1690. Like most Schenectady refugees, he returned to the Mohawk Valley. His younger brother Cornelis (c1668–1730), was a more regular Albany trader, although he also maintained country residences. See 5455.

Notes to Essay 2/Kierner

1. This work was supported in part by funds from the Foundation of The University of North Carolina at Charlotte and from the State of North Carolina.

2. For a general overview of the family's economic activities, see Patricia Joan Gordon, "The Livingstons of New York, 1675–1860: Kinship and Class," (Ph.D. dissertation, Columbia University, 1959), pp. 65–66, 82, 142–88; Sung Bok Kim, *Landlord and Tenant in Colonial New York: Manorial Society, 1664–1775* (Chapel Hill, 1978), esp. chs. 4–5; Irene D. Neu, "The Iron Plantations of Colonial New York," *New York History*, 33 (1952): 3–24.

3. For the development of elite culture, in general, see Richard M. Bushman, "American High-Style and Vernacular Cultures," in Jack P. Greene and J. R. Pole, eds., *Colonial British America: Essays in the New History of the Early Modern Era* (Baltimore, 1984), pp. 349–67.

4. See Lawrence H. Leder, *Robert Livingston, 1654–1728, and the Politics of Colonial New York* (Chapel Hill, 1961), esp. chs. 2–3.

5. Estimates based on letters exchanged by Robert and Alida Livingston, Livingston-Redmond MSS., Franklin D. Roosevelt Library, Hyde Park, NY, reels 4 and 6. Livingston was abroad in 1694–1696 and 1703–1706. See Leder, *Robert Livingston*, ch. 5, pp. 187–97.

6. See, for instance, the letters in Linda Briggs Biemer, ed., "Business Letters of Alida Schuyler Livingston, 1680–1728," *New York History* 63 (1982): 183–207, as well as Biemer's biographical sketch of Alida Livingston in *Women and Property in Colonial New York: The Transition from Dutch to English Law, 1643–1727* (Ann Arbor, 1983), ch. 5.

7. The concept of the "deputy husband" is taken from Laurel Thatcher Ulrich, *Good Wives: Image and Reality in the Lives of Women in Northern New England, 1650–1750* (New York, 1980), ch. 2.

8. Henry Douglas to Philip Livingston, 27 May, 27 Dec. 1709,

Livingston-Redmond MSS., reel 6; Joanna Livingston Van Horne to Robert Livingston, 8 July 1725, reel 4; Henry Livingston to Robert Livingston, 11 Oct. 1742, reel 7. Jean P. Jordan, "Women Merchants in Colonial New York," *New York History*, 58 (1977): 420.

9. Philip Livingston to Robert Livingston, 30 Jan. 1745, Livingston-Redmond MSS., reel 7.

10. Arthur W. Calhoun, *A Social History of the American Family from Colonial Times to the Present*, 3 vols. (Cleveland, 1917), 1: 166–67, 183; Biemer, *Women and Property*, esp. pp. x–xiii. On coverture and *femes covert* in colonial and Revolutionary America, see Linda K. Kerber, *Women of the Republic: Intellect and Ideology in Revolutionary America* (Chapel Hill, 1980), chs. 4–5.

11. Livingston gave his wife power of attorney when he went to England in 1694 and 1703, and again in 1711 when the fulfillment of a provisioning contract necessitated that Alida be given full authority over the Manor and all its resources (Powers of attorney to Alida Livingston, 12 Oct. 1694, 30 Apr. 1703, Livingston-Redmond MSS., reels 1 and 2; Robert Livingston to Alida Livingston, 11 Apr. 1711, reel 3). For Alida's activities as a victualer, see, for example, Robert Livingston to Alida Livingston, 9 Apr. 1692, Livingston-Redmond MSS., reel 1; James Weems to Alida Livingston, 23 Oct., 21 and 30 Nov. 1700, Livingston-Redmond MSS., reel 6. Entrepreneurial wives, though fewer in number, continued to use these strategies down to the Revolutionary era. See, for instance, Jordan, "Women Merchants," esp. pp. 414–15, 436–39; Mary P. Ryan, *Womanhood in America: From Colonial Times to the Present* (New York, 1975), pp. 21–81.

12. Lois Green Carr and Lorena S. Walsh, "The Planter's Wife: The Experience of White Women in Seventeenth-Century Maryland," *William and Mary Quarterly*, 3rd ser., 34 (1977): 542–71; Joan R. Gunderson and Gwen Victor Gampel, "Married Women's Legal Status in Eighteenth-Century New York and Virginia," *William and Mary Quarterly*, 39 (1982): 133–34.

13. Leder, *Robert Livingston*, ch. 13; Philip Livingston to Jacob Wendell, 21 Apr. 1739, Livingston Papers, Museum of the City of New York, box 2 (hereafter cited as MCNY); Philip Livingston to John DeWitt, 5 Mar. 1741; Livingston-Redmond MSS., reel 9; Robert Livingston to Gulian Verplanck, 20 Dec. 1749, Robert R. Livingston Papers, New-York Historical Society, reel 1 (hereafter cited as NYHS). Philip built a second gristmill—and probably a sawmill—at Ancram in the 1740s. See John Waddell to Robert Livingston, 24 Mar. 1752, Livingston-Redmond MSS., reel 7.

14. Philip Livingston to Robert Livingston, 20 May 1724, Livingston-Redmond MSS., reel 7; Passes issued to Robert Livingston, 8 Mar. 1727, 6 Aug. 1730, *Calendar of Historical Manuscripts in the Office of the Secretary of State, Albany, NY*, 2 vols., ed. E. B. O'Callaghan (Albany, 1865–1866), 2: 498, 512; *Early Records of the City and County of Albany and Colony of Rensselaerswyck*, 4 vols., ed. A. J. F. Van Laer (Albany, 1916–1919), 4: 176; Joel Munsell, ed., *The Annals of Albany*, 10 vols. (Albany, 1850–1859), 10: 120, 132.

15. Philip Livingston to Samuel Storke, 20 Nov. 1734, 2 June 1735, Livingston Family Letters, American Antiquarian Society, Worcester,

Mass. (hereafter cited as AAS); Philip Livingston to Jacob Wendell, 23 May, 9 Nov. 1738, 21 Apr. 1739, Livingston Papers, MCNY, box 2; Peter Van Brugh Livingston to Robert Livingston, 26 Feb. 1735, Livingston-Redmond MSS., reel 7; Jacob Lansing, Jr. to Robert Livingston, 9 June 1739, Livingston-Redmond MSS., reel 7; Joseph Mico to Robert and Peter Van Brugh Livingston, 3 May 1740, Livingston-Redmond MSS., reel 7. See also, William I. Roberts III, "Samuel Storke: An Eighteenth-Century London Merchant Trading to the American Colonies," *Business History Review*, 39 (1965): 147–70.

16. Henry Livingston to Henry Van Rensselaer, 21 June 1736, Misc. MSS., Henry Livingston, NYHS; Philip Livingston to Storke and Gainsborough, 12 June 1738, Livingston Family Letters, AAS; Philip Livingston to Jacob Wendell, 7 Mar. 1738, 13 Mar. 1739, 29 May 1742, Livingston Papers, MCNY, box 2; Henry Livingston's invoice for sugar and molasses, 18 Aug. 1752, Livingston Papers, MCNY, box 1; Henry Livingston to Robert Livingston, 5 Mar. 1774, Livingston-Redmond MSS., reel 7; Philip Livingston to Jacob Wendell, 5 Jan. 1745, Misc. MSS., Philip Livingston, NYHS; William Walton and Co. to James Beekman, 30 Nov. 1751, in Philip L. White, ed., *The Beekman Mercantile Papers*, 3 vols. (New York, 1956), 2: 552; Virginia D. Harrington, *The New York Merchant on the Eve of the Revolution* (New York, 1935), pp. 194–95; Milton M. Klein, "The American Whig: William Livingston of New York," (Ph.D. dissertation, Columbia University, 1954), pp. 71–72.

17. Thomas Elliot Norton, *The Fur Trade in Colonial New York* (Madison, Wisc., 1974), pp. 149–50; Roberts, "Samuel Storke," pp. 166–68.

18. Philip Livingston to Storke and Gainsborough, 25 Apr. 1738, Livingston Family Letters, AAS; A Book of Trade for the Sloope *Rhode Island*, Dec. 1748–July 1749, Misc. MSS., B.V. *Rhode Island*, NYHS; James G. Lydon, "New York and the Slave Trade, 1700 to 1774," *William and Mary Quarterly*, 3rd ser., 35 (1978): 375–94.

19. Philip Livingston to Storke and Gainsborough, 7 June, 20 Nov., 28 Nov. 1734, Livingston Family Letters, AAS; Philip Livingston to Robert Livingston, 12 Sept., 3 Dec. 1740, Livingston-Redmond MSS., reel 7; Roberts, "Samuel Storke," pp. 160–61.

20. David Arthur Armour, "The Merchants of Albany, New York, 1686–1760," (Ph.D. dissertation, Northwestern University, 1965), p. 215; Harrington, *New York Merchant*, pp. 200–01. On the growing importance of the coastal and southern European trades, in general, see John J. McCusker and Russell R. Menard, *The Economy of British America, 1607–1789* (Chapel Hill, 1985), pp. 79–80, 89–98.

21. Robert Livingston's accounts with Manor store, 20 May 1735, 16 Apr. 1737, 13 Feb. 1741, Livingston-Redmond MSS., reel 7; Philip Livingston to Robert Livingston, 24 Mar. 1739, Livingston-Redmond MSS., reel 7; John DeWitt to Robert Livingston, 17 Aug. 1739, Livingston-Redmond MSS., reel 7; Henry Van Rensselaer, Jr.'s account with Robert & Peter Livingston & Co., 28 May 1735–8 Sept. 1737, Misc. MSS., Robert & Peter Livingston & Co., NYHS.

22. Peter Van Brugh Livingston to Storke and Gainsborough, 28 Sept. 1736, Livingston Family Letters, AAS. Peter had returned to New York by November 1739, when he married Mary Alexander.

23. See Menard and McCusker, *Economy of British America*, pp. 309–26.

24. Philip Livingston to Jacob Wendell, 16 Mar. 1741, Livingston Papers, MCNY, box 2; Philip Livingston to Robert Livingston, 20 July 1741, 30 Jan. 1745, Livingston-Redmond MSS., reel 7; Neu, "Iron Plantations," pp. 5–8.

25. Philip Livingston to Jacob Wendell, 16 Mar. 1741, Livingston Papers, MCNY, box 2; Robert Livingston to James Duane, 30 Nov. 1765, Duane Papers, NYHS, box 1. The Livingstons' profits included Robert Livingston's cut of roughly 70 percent, plus his sons' ten percent commission. My calculations are based on the following: Account of Iron Made at Ancram, Livingston Manor, 1750–1756, *Documents Relative to the Colonial History of the State of New-York*, 15 vols., ed. E. B. O'Callaghan and Berthold Fernow (Albany, 1849–1851), 7: 336; Account of Goods Sent to Newyork, . . . for Acct of Robt. Livingston Junr Esqr & Consign'd to Walter and Robt. [Cambridge] Livingston, Mar. 1766–Nov. 1768, Livingston Family Papers, NYHS, reel 28; Walter and Robert [Cambridge] Livingston's account of Sales of 342 Tons pigg Iron, 1767–1768, Robert R. Livingston Papers, NYHS, reel 1; John Stevenson's account with Robert Livingston, 1769–1775, Livingston-Redmond MSS., reel 8; Philip Livingston's agreement with Ebeneezer Loomis, 14 Apr. 1748, Livingston-Redmond MSS., reel 6; Robert Livingston's agreement with Jedidiah Moore, 20 Oct. 1757, Livingston-Redmond MSS., reel 7; Robert Livingstons's agreement with William Smith, et al., 21 Nov. 1775, Livingston-Redmond MSS., reel 8; Diary and Account Book of Charles DeWitt, 1749–1780, Misc. MSS., B. V. DeWitt, NYHS.

26. Robert Livingston to Peter Van Brugh Livingston, 26 June 1751, Welch-Livingston Collection, NYHS.

27. Robert Livingston to James Duane, 22 Nov. 1763, 9 Nov. 1764, Duane Papers, NYHS, box 1; James McLachlan, *Princetonians, 1748–1768: A Biographical Dictionary* (Princeton, 1976), pp. 274–79.

28. See John Henry Livingston to Henry Livingston, 4 Feb. 1766, Livingston Family Papers, New York Public Library.

29. Philip Livingston to Jacob Wendell, 17 June 1746, Livingston Papers, MCNY, box 2. Philip's son William often expressed similar sentiments. See, for example, William Livingston, et al., *The Independent Reflector*, ed. Milton M. Klein (Cambridge, Mass., 1963), pp. 419–20, and William Livingston to Peter R. Livingston, 10 Nov. 1758, William Livingston Papers, Massachussetts Historical Society, reel 2.

30. On the growing regard for education among elites in English America see, for instance, Daniel Blake Smith, *Inside the Great House: Planter Family Life in Eighteenth-Century Chesapeake Society* (Ithaca, NY, 1980), pp. 62–68, 89; Louis B. Wright, *The First Gentlemen of Virginia: Intellectual Qualities of the Early Colonial Ruling Class* (San Marino, Calif., 1940), pp. 38–62; Carl and Jessica Bridenbaugh, *Rebels and Gentlemen: Philadelphia in the Age of Franklin* (New York, 1942), pp. 180–90; Frederick B. Tolles, *Meeting House and Counting House: The Quaker Merchants of Colonial Philadelphia, 1682–1763* (Chapel Hill, 1948), pp. 133–43.

31. Alida Livingston to Robert Livingston, 23 July 1722, in Biemer, ed., "Business Letters," p. 205; Henry Beekman Livingston to Robert

R. Livingston, Jr., 20 Nov. 1778, Robert R. Livingston Papers, NYHS, reel 1.

32. Will of Philip Livingston, 15 July 1748, Livingston-Redmond MSS., reel 6; Robert Livingston to James Duane, 16 Oct. 1762, Misc. MSS., Robert Livingston, NYHS; James Duane to Mary Livingston Duane, 20 Feb. [1781], Duane Papers, NYHS, box 4.

33. William Livingston to Noah Welles, 18 Feb. 1749, Livingston-Welles Correspondence, Yale University; William Livingston to [?], 6 Dec. 1787, William Livingston Papers, Mass. Hist. Soc., reel 9. On the changing clientele of colonial colleges, see Samuel Eliot Morison, *Three Centuries of Harvard, 1636–1936* (Cambridge, Mass., 1946), pp. 59–60, 110–23. Most of the Livingstons were Protestant dissenters, and consequently avoided sending their sons to King's College, an Anglican institution.

Notes to Essay 3/Steffen

1. See Wertenbaker's *Patrician and Plebeian, or the Origin and Development of the Social Classes of the Old Dominion* (New York, 1910) and *Virginia Under the Stuarts, 1607–1688* (New York, 1914). Wertenbaker toned down his devastating critique of the seventeenth century gentry in *The Old South: The Founding of American Civilization* (New York, 1942), chap. 2.

2. Bernard Bailyn, "Politics and Social Structure in Virginia," in James Morton Smith, ed., *Seventeenth-Century America: Essays in Colonial History* (Chapel Hill, N.C., 1959), 90–115.

3. Allan Kulikoff, *Tobacco and Slaves: The Development of Southern Cultures in the Chesapeake, 1680–1800* (Chapel Hill, N.C.,1986), 263–67.

4. Daniel Blake Smith, *Inside the Great House: Planter Family Life in Eighteenth-Century Chesapeake Society* (Ithaca, N.Y., 1980), 246. In certain respects Smith's analysis is similar to that of Philip Greven in *The Protestant Temperament: Patterns of Child-Rearing, Religious Experience, and the Self in Early America* (New York, 1977).

5. Jan Lewis, *The Pursuit of Happiness: Family Values in Jefferson's Virginia* (New York, 1983), chap. 1. For a similar analysis see Michael Zuckerman, "William Byrd's Family," *Perspectives in American History*, vol. 12 (1979), 255–311, and Kenneth A. Lockridge, *The Diary, and Life, of William Byrd II of Virginia, 1674–1744* (Chapel Hill, N.C., 1987).

6. Provincial Court, Inventories, Maryland Hall of Records, Annapolis.

7. Baltimore County Court, Inventories, Maryland Hall of Records.

8. The wills were located in Provincial Court, Wills, and Baltimore County Court, Wills, Maryland Hall of Records.

9. Darrett B. Rutman and Anita H. Rutman, "'Now-Wives and Sons-in-Law': Parental Death in a Seventeenth-Century Virginia County," in Thad W. Tade and David L. Ammerman, eds., *The Chesapeake in the Seventeenth Century: Essays on Anglo-American Society* (Chapel Hill, N.C., 1979), 153–82; Lois G. Carr, "The Development of the Maryland Orphans' Court, 1654–1713," in Aubrey C. Land, Lois Green

Carr, and Edward C. Papenfuse, eds., *Law, Society, and Politics in Early Maryland* (Chapel Hill, N.C., 1979), 206–42.

10. Philip J. Greven, Jr., *Four Generations: Population, Land, and Family in Colonial Andover, Massachusetts* (Ithaca, N.Y., 1970); Robert A. Gross, *The Minutemen and Their World* (New York, 1976); Kenneth A. Lockridge, "Land, Population, and the Evolution of New England Society, 1630–1790," *Past and Present*, vol. 39 (1968), 62–80.

11. Provincial Court, Wills, 27, 280–82.

12. Provincial Court, Wills, 34, 426–28.

13. Baltimore County Court, Wills, 3, 317.

14. Baltimore County Court, Wills, 3, 214–16.

15. Baltimore County Court, Wills, 3, 299–303.

16. Baltimore County Court, Wills, 3, 205–08.

17. In the following analysis of deeds of gifts, I identified every land transaction that the gentry recorded in approximately 50 volumes of deed books. See Baltimore County Court, Land Records, Maryland Hall of Records.

18. Lawrence Stone, *The Family, Sex and Marriage in England, 1500–1800* (New York, 1977), 656.

19. Baltimore County Court, Wills, 27, 280–82; Provincial Court, Wills, 30, 566–67; Baltimore County Court, Land Records, TR # D, 307–08; TR # C, 369–70.

20. This estimate is based on an analysis of the distribution of real property recorded in Baltimore County, Debt Books, 1754, Maryland Hall of Records.

21. Baltimore County Court, Land Records, B # L, 83–88; TR # C, 18–20; AL # A, 672–75.

22. Baltimore County Court, Land Records, AL # B, ff. 27–28; B # H, 420–24; BB # I, ff. 31–33, 210–12.

Notes to Essay 4/Crane

1. See Philip J. Greven, Jr., *Four Generations: Population, Land, and Family in Colonial Andover, Massachusetts* (Ithaca, New York: Cornell, 1970); Daniel Scott Smith, "Parental Power and Marriage Patterns: An Analysis of Historical Trends in Hingham, Massachusetts," *Journal of Marriage and the Family* 35 (August 1973), 419–28; Joseph F. Kett, *Rites of Passage: Adolescence in America, 1790 to the Present* (New York: Basic Books, 1977); John Modell, Frank F. Furstenburg, Jr., and Theodore Hershberg, "Social Change and Transitions to Adulthood in Historical Perspective," *Journal of Family History* (Autumn 1976), 7–32; Robert V. Wells, "Family History and Demographic Transition," *Journal of Social History* 9 (Fall 1975), 1–20; Maris A. Vinovskis, "Angels' Heads and Weeping Willows: Death in Early America," *Proceedings* of the the American Antiquarian Society 86, part 2 (1977), 273–302; Peter D. Hall, "Marital Selection and Business in Massachusetts Merchant Families, 1800–1900," *The Family and Its Structure and Function*, ed. Rose L. Coser (New York: St. Martin's, 1974); Edward N. Saveth, "The American Patrician Class: A Field for Research," *Kinship and Family Organization*, ed. Bernard Farber (New York: John Wiley and Sons, 1966), 257–68;

Randolph S. Klein, *Portrait of an Early American Family: The Shippens of Pennsylvania Across Five Generations* (Philadelphia: University of Pennsylvania, 1975); Peter Laslett and Richard Wall, *Household and Family in Past Time* (Cambridge: Cambridge UP, 1972); Thad Tate and David L. Ammerman, eds., *The Chesapeake Society in the Seventeenth Century: Essays on Anglo-American Society and Politics* (New York, 1979); Robert V. Wells, "Family Size and Fertility Control in Eighteenth Century America: A Study of Quaker Families," *Population Studies* 35 (1971), 73–82; Mary Beth Norton, "The Evolution of White Women's Experience in Early America," *American Historical Review* 89 (1984), 593–619; John Demos, *A Little Commonwealth* (New York: Oxford, 1970); Richard D. Brown, *Modernization: The Transformation of American Life 1600–1865* (New York: Hill and Wang, 1976); Bernard Bailyn, *Education in the Forming of American Society* (Chapel Hill: University of North Carolina Press, 1960); Philippe Aries, *Centuries of Childhood: A Social History of Family Life* (New York: Vintage, 1962); Ross W. Beales, Jr., "In Search of the Historical Child: Miniature Adulthood and Youth in Colonial New England," *American Quarterly* 27 (1975), 379–98; David Hackett Fischer, *Growing Old in America* (New York: Oxford, 1977); David E. Stannard, "Death and Dying in Puritan New England," *American Historical Review* 78 (1973) 305–30; Michael Gordon, ed., *The American Family in Social-Historical Perspective* (New York: St. Martin's, 1978); John Demos, *Past, Present and Personal: The Family and the Life Course in American History* (New York: Oxford, 1986).

2. Thomas Lynch II's grandson James Hamilton, Jr. (governor of South Carolina 1830–1832) had a trunk of family papers at his home in Charleston in 1836 when the house caught fire and burned to the ground, destroying the trunk's contents. Hamilton had accumulated Lynch papers to write a biography of Thomas Lynch, Jr. for John Sanderson's *Lives of the Signers* (1823); he retained possession of those papers until the fire. Hamilton's two aunts had inherited a trunk full of family papers that they usually deposited at a bank when they went into the country. On one fateful occasion, however, they left the trunk with Governor Hamilton instead of at the bank and the house fire consumed the lot. Hamilton and his aunts inherited Lynch silver, linen, portraits and other family possessions, and they divided the Lynch library among themselves. Hamilton's share of the books was saved from the fire because he kept his Lynch library at his plantation on Pennyworth Island in Savannah River. Those books, many with the Signer's signature, were nearly lost when a box fell into the river as the volumes were being transported to Pennyworth. They were damaged from lying in the water for several days, but were eventually pulled out, and survived. Public records, institutional archives, genealogy, references in the papers of contemporaries, and Hamilton's biography of the Signer, drawn as it was from original materials and family tradition, make up most of the extant sources for the family. See James Hamilton to Robert Gilmore, 6 April 1836, S. Gilman to I. K. Kefft, 5 April 1845, S. P. Hamilton to C. C. Jones, 19 December 1881, all in Joseph E. Fields, "A Signer and His Signatures or The Library of Thomas Lynch, Jr.," *Harvard Library Bulletin* 14 no. 2 (Spring 1960), 222, 224, 230.

3. Demos, *Past*, x.

4. Frampton E. Ellis, *Some Historical Families of South Carolina* (Atlanta, 1962), 37–39; Lois D. Hines, *Lynch Families of the Southern States*, ed. Dorothy F. Wolfeck (Naugatuck, Conn., 1966), 159–75; William P. Baldwin, Jr., *Plantations of the Low Country: South Carolina, 1697–1865* (Greensboro: Legacy Publications, 1985), 64; John S. Green, Index to Grants, Warrants and Conveyances 1675–1766, NC: 87, G:182, South Carolina Department of Archives and History, Columbia, S.C.; Index to Land Grants Before 1776, 38: 63, SC Archives; Fields, "Library," 210–19.

5. Ellis, *Families*, 37; Edward McCrady, *The History of South Carolina Under the Proprietary Government, 1670–1719* (New York, 1897), 570–71; Walter B. Edgar and N. Louise Bailey, *Biographical Directory of the South Carolina House of Representatives* (Columbia: University of South Carolina, 1977), 2: 419; Robert M. Weir, *Colonial South Carolina: A History* (Milwood, N.Y.: Kraus-Thomson, 1983), 41, 115,; Fields, "Library," 211; George Rogers, Jr., *Charleston in the Age of the Pinckneys* (Columbia: USC Press, 1980), 9–10; George Rogers, Jr., *The History of Georgetown County, South Carolina* (Columbia: USC Press, 1970), 23, 25; Baldwin, *Plantations*, 71, 75, 77; James Hamilton Jr., "Thomas Lynch," *Lives of the Signers of the Declaration of Independence*, ed. John B. Sanderson (Philadelphia: R. W. Pomeroy, 1823), 5: 2–19; Alberta M. Lachicotte, *Georgetown Rice Plantations* (Columbia: State Printing Company, 1970), 191–94; Green, Index, Book 1701–12: 98; Book 1701–14: 60; H: 130, 236; Index to Land Grants, 38: 413, 424; 39: 100, 111, 322, 178; 1: 86, 87, 88; 2: 348; 3: 258; Index to Plat Books, 1731–1776, 1: 241, 242, 282; 3: 380, 387, SC Archives Photostat.

6. Weir, *Carolina*, 146; Baldwin, *Plantations*, 77; Rogers, *Georgetown*, 77, 95, 96, 112, 41, 43–44, 51, 91, 88, 105–07, 108–10, 125, 111; Ellis, *Families*, 39; L. H. Butterfield, ed., *The Adams Papes: Diary and Autobiography of John Adams* (New York: Atheneum, 1964), 2: 85; *BDHR*, 2: 420–22; Index to Land Grants, 6: 84; 8: 323; 9: 41; 11: 416; 13: 203; 20: 535; 26: 570, 571; 31: 329, 539; 34: 121, 162, 163; Index to Plat Books, 5: 440; 6: 368, 396; 8: 25; 11: 342; 16: 436; Charleston County Wills, WPA Transcripts, 18 (1776–1784), 231–33, SC Archives; Baldwin, *Plantations*, 76–78; Lachicotte, *Georgetown*, 171; Plat Books, Charleston County Register Office of Mesne Conveyances, E4: 47; Hamilton, "Lynch"; Herman P. Hamilton Collection, Chester, South Carolina; George W. Williams, *St. Michael's Charleston 1751–1951* (Columbia: USC Press, 1951), 29; James Hamilton, Jr. to New England Society of Charleston, 8 May 1847, James Hamilton, Jr., Papers, Southern Historical Collection, UNC, Chapel Hill; *Adams Papers*, 3: 307–08, 316; 2: 114, 116, 117, 118, 119, 123, 135; Fields, "Library," 235; Edmund C. Burnett, ed., *Letters of Members of the Continental Congress* (Washington: Carnegie Institute, 1923), 1: 253, 314–15; Mrs. St. Julien Ravenel, *Charleston: The Place and the People* (New York: Macmillan, 1931), 220; R. Nicholas Olsbert, "Ship Registers in the South Carolina Archives, 1734–1780," *South Carolina Historical Magazine* 74 (1973), 201, 220, 258; Inventories of Estates (1736–1739), 286–304, SC Archives.

7. Hamilton, "Lynch," 17, 30, 22, 19; Fields, "Library," 210–19; Joseph E. Fields, "Lynch Autographs in South Carolina," *SCHM*

53 (1952), 129–32; Charles F. Jenkins, "An Account of a New Portrait of Thomas Lynch, Jr., *SCHM* 28 (1927), 1–7; "Historical Notes," *SCHM* 7 (1906), 170; *BDHR*, 3: 450–52; Lachicotte, *Georgetown*, 191; Rogers, *Georgetown*, 106, 113; William E. Hemphill and Wylma A. Wates, eds., *Extracts from the Journals of the Provincial Congresses of South Carolina, 1775–1776* (Columbia: SC Archives Department, 1960), 5, 34, 46, 49, 74, 185, 186, 212, 241, 250, 251; Adams, *Papers*, 2: 241, 244, 246; 3: 379, 381–82, 437; Burnett, *Letters*, 1: lxii–lxiii.

8. Charleston County Wills, 18: 231–32; 20: 152–59.

9. Hamilton, "Lynch" 18–20.

10. The heirs of Thomas Lynch III divided the estate in the 1780s rather than sell it. Sabina and her Bowman heirs got Peachtree and Lynch lands on South Santee; Elizabeth and her Hamilton heirs got a plantation on Lynches Island and lands on North Santee, and unmarried Esther got the residue. Fairfield and Hopsewee were sold out of the family, and the Hamiltons, in straightened financial circumstances, lost their Santee lands in 1811. The Bowmans retained theirs somewhat longer, and Esther Lynch maintained a connection with the Santee until her death. See Rogers, *Georgetown*, 159; Virginia Glenn, "James Hamilton, Jr. of South Carolina," Ph.D. dissertation, UNC, 1964; Secretary of State, Miscellaneous Records, 3C: 204, 3F: 124, 3H: 257, SC Archives; South Carolina Acts and Resolutions for 1812, p. 46, South Caroliniana Library.

11. Material for this analysis was drawn from Weir, *Carolina*, 236, 160, xiii, 135; Saveth, "Patrician," in *Kinship*, ed. Farber, 258, 266; Demos, *Past*, 27–28, 75; Daniel Bell, "The Break-Up of Family Capitalism," *Partisan Review* 24 (Spring 1957), 317–20; Philip Greven, *The Protestant Temperament, and the Self in Early America* (New York: Alfred Knopf, 1980), 265–68; Hamilton to New England Society, 1847; and five articles in Gordon, *American Family*: Hall, "Marital Selection," 191; Kett, "Stages," 176, 186; Demos, "Old Age in Early New England," 248; Greven, "Family Structure in Seventeenth-Century Andover, Massachusetts," 33; Wells, "Transition," 521, 11.

12. Hamilton to New England Society, 1847.

Notes to Essay 5/Kay and Cary

1. Marvin L. Michael Kay and Lorin Lee Cary, "'They Are Indeed the Constant Plague of Their Tyrants': Slave Defense of a Moral Economy in Colonial North Carolina, 1748–1772," *Slavery and Abolition* 6 (1985): 38–39.

2. Kay and Cary, "'They Are Indeed'"; E. P. Thompson , "The Moral Economy of the English Crowd in the Eighteenth Century," *Past and Present*, no. 50 (1971): 78–79. See also Eugene Genovese in *Roll Jordon Roll: The World the Slaves Made* (New York: Pantheon Books, 1974), 125; Herbert G. Gutman, *The Black Family in Slavery and Freedom, 1750–1925* (New York: Pantheon Books, 1977), 318–19. For a recent analysis of slave theft within the context of the slaves' moral economy,

see Alex Lichtenstein, "'That Disposition to Theft, With Which They Have Been Branded': Moral Economy, Slave Management and the Law," *Journal of Social History* 22 (1988): 413–40.

3. For the application of Gramsci's concept of cultural hegemony to problems in American history, see T. Jackson Lears, "The Concept of Cultural Hegemony: Problems and Possibilities" and John Patrick Diggins, "Comrades and Citizens: New Mythologies in American Historiography," both in *The American Historical Review* 90 (1985): 567–93, 614–38, respectively; contributions by Leon Fink, Jackson Lears, John P. Diggins, George Lipsitz, Mari Jo Buhle and Paul Buhle to "A Round Table: Labor, Historical Pessimism, and Hegemony," *The Journal of American History* 75 (1988): 115–61; Michael Kazin, "The Historian as Populist," *The New York Review of Books*, 12 May 1988, 48–50.

4. Kay and William S. Price Jr., "'To Ride the Wood Mare': Road Building and Militia Service in Colonial North Carolina, 1740–1775," *The North Carolina Historical Review* 57 (1980): 361–409; Kay and Cary, "Slave Defense of a Moral Economy," 37–56; "Slave Runaways in Colonial North Carolina," *The North Carolina Historical Review* 63 (1986): 1–39; "'The Planters Suffer Little or Nothing': North Carolina Compensations for Executed Slaves," *Science and Society* 15 (1976): 288–306.

5. Kay and Cary, "A Demographic Analysis of Colonial North Carolina with Special Emphasis upon the Slave and Black Populations," in Jeffrey J. Crow and Flora J. Hatley, eds., *Black Americans in North Carolina and the South* (Chapel Hill: University of North Carolina Press, 1984), 101–02; Philip D. Morgan, "Colonial South Carolina Runaways: Their Significance for Slave Culture," *Slavery and Abolition* 6 (1985): 59–61; Betty Wood, *Slavery in Colonial Georgia, 1730–1775* (Athens: University of Georgia Press, 1984), 104–05.

6. This is developed in our forthcoming book.

7. For a similar, suggestive analysis, see Roger Bastide, *African Civilizations in the New World* (London: C. Hurst & Co., 1971; orig. pbd. 1967), 89.

8. For the development of some of these points, see Michael Mullin, "British Caribbean and North American Slaves in an Era of War and Revolution, 1775–1807," in Jeffrey J. Crow and Larry E. Tise, eds., *The Southern Experience in the American Revolution* (Chapel Hill: University of North Carolina Press, 1978), 37–38.

9. For bride price, see the following in A. R. Radcliffe-Brown and Daryll Forde, eds., *African Systems of Kinship and Marriage* (London: Oxford University Press, 1950): Meyer Fortes, "Kinship and Marriage Among the Ashanti," 279–81; Daryll Forde, "Double Descent Among the Yako," 321–26. Also see: Philip D. Curtin and others, *African History* (Boston: Little, Brown and Co., 1978), 160, 166; John S. Mbiti, *African Religions and Philosophy* (New York: Anchor Books, 1970; orig. pbd. 1969), 183–84; Remi Clignet, *Many Wives, Many Powers: Authority and Power in Polygynous Families* (Evanston: Northwestern University Press, 1970), 23, 50, 250–55; George Peter Murdock, *Africa: Its Peoples and Their Culture History* (New York: McGraw-Hill Book Company, 1959), 24–25, 246, 262, 416, 419; Oyekan Owomoyela, "The Social Significance of Gift-Giving in Yoruba Culture" (unpublished paper), 4–6. Professor Owomoyela, a Nigerian scholar, is a member of the English department at the University of Nebraska at Lincoln.

10. See "The Capture and Travels of Ayuba Suleiman Ibrahima," 49–50, and "The Interesting Narrative of Olaudah Equiano, or Gustavus Vasa, the African," two eighteenth century narratives that refer to bride wealth, in Philip D. Curtin, ed., *Africa Remembered: Narratives by West Africans from the Era of the Slave Trade* (Madison: University of Wisconsin Press, 1967),49–50, 70, respectively. For an informative nineteenth century account of bride price among different ethnic groups in Sierra Leone see "History of the Amistad Captives," 9–15, 26, in Jules Chametzky and Sidney Kaplan, eds., *Black and White in American Culture: An Anthology from the Massachusetts Review*, (Amherst: University of Massachusetts Press, 1969), 291–330.

11. John Brickell, *The Natural History of North Carolina* (Murfreesboro, North Carolina: Johnson Publishing Co., 1968; orig. pbd. 1737), 274.

12. Brickell, *Natural History of North Carolina*, 274.

13. See Kay and Cary, "Demographic Analysis," 86–102.

14. An English slave trader reported in 1788 concerning marital practices in Sierra Leone, "tho polygamy is allowed in ye Country it is practiced only by the rich." See, "Extracts from the Evidence of Jno. Matthews Esqr. given to ye Committee of Privy Council," 4 March 1788, in Long's Collections, Add. MSS 18272, ff. 1–6, British Museum, London, quoted in Daniel C. Littlefield, *Rice and Slaves: Ethnicity and the Slave Trade in Colonial South Carolina* (Baton Rouge: Louisiana State University Press, 1981), 78–79. Ample nineteenth century evidence, also for Sierra Leone, is in Chametzky and Kaplan, eds., *History of the Amistad Captives*, 9–15, 26. Ethnographic studies that note the prevalence of monogamy in West African societies where polygyny was the preferred marital form, include: Forde, "Double Descent Among the Yako," 288; Fortes, "Kinship and Marriage Among the Ashanti," 281; Mbiti, *African Religions and Philosophy*, 188. Harold E. Driver similarly evaluates the practices of American Indians in his *Indians of North America* (Chicago: University of Chicago Press, 1969), 230–32.

15. Brickell, *Natural History of North Carolina*, 274–75.

16. See plantation records listed in *Sources*, Table 1.

17. Kay and Cary, "Demographic Analysis," 72–103. We develop comparative figures concerning the concentration of slaves on large plantations more extensively in our forthcoming book. Also see: Phillip Morgan's analysis of estate inventories in "Black Society in the Lowcountry, 1760–1810" in Ira Berlin and Ronald Hoffman, eds., *Slavery and Freedom in the Age of the American Revolution* (Charlottesville: University of Virginia Press, 1983), 95, Table 9; Allan Kulikoff, "The Beginnings of the Afro-American Family in Maryland," in Aubrey C. Land, Lois Green Carr, and Edward C. Papenfuse, eds., *Law Society and Politics in Early Maryland* (Baltimore: Johns Hopkins University Press, 1977), 171–96; Russell R. Menard, "The Maryland Slave Population, 1658 to 1730: A Demographic Profile of Blacks in Four Counties," *The William and Mary Quarterly*, 3d. ser., 32 (1975): 29–54; U.S. Bureau of the Census, *Historical Statistics of the United States: Colonial Times to 1957* (Washington, D.C., 1960), Series Z 1–19, p. 75b.

18. For discussions of nuclear family development in South Carolina and the Chesapeake, see Morgan, "Black Society in the Low Country," 124–29; Kulikoff, "Beginnings of Afro-American Family in Maryland," 175–80. For slave attempts to maintain or establish marriages and

families on single plantations and how masters responded to these efforts, see: Mary Beth Norton, Herbert Gutman and Ira Berlin, "The Afro-American Family in the Age of Revolution" in Berlin and Hoffman, eds., *Slavery and Freedom*, 184–88; Norton, *Liberty's Daughters: The Revolutionary Experience of American Women, 1750–1800* (Boston: Little, Brown & Co., 1980), 65–70.

19. Gutman, *Black Family*, 190–94. Also see: Cheryll Ann Cody, "Naming, Kinship, and Estate Dispersal: Notes on Family Life on a South Carolina Plantation, 1786–1833," *William and Mary Quarterly*, 3d. ser., 39 (1982): 192–211; Cody, "There was No 'Absolom' on the Ball Plantations: Slave-Naming Practices in the South Carolina Low Country," *The American Historical Review* 92 (1987): 563–96.

20. James M. Robin's Papers, Vol. 1, Massachusetts Historical Society. Pollock Papers, P.C. 31.1; John Walker Papers, P.C. 254.1; Pollock Papers, "Lean by Thomas Pollock to Jacob Mitchell," P.C. 31.1; Avery Family Papers, Miscellaneous, Roll Book of Slaves of the Avery Family, 1766 to 1865, P.C. 294.1; Pollock-Devereaux Papers, Inventory of Slaves in 1797 and List of Slaves, 1806—P.C. 32.1, all in North Carolina State Archives; Gutman, *Black Family*, 172–73, 180.

21. Clement Idun, a Fante and doctoral candidate at The University of Toledo, helped us to understand the traditional residential patterns of the Fante, Asante, and Ga. Also see Fortes, "Marriage and Kinship Among the Ashanti," 261 and A. I. Richards, "Some Types of Family Structure Amongst the Central Bantu," both in Radcliffe-Brown and Forde, eds., *African Systems of Kinship and Marriage*, 246–48, 261.

22. Among the Ibo of southeastern Nigeria, a patrilineal and patrilocal people, each co-wife lives with her children in a separate hut or apartment in her husband's compound. Murdock, *Africa*, 247–48.

23. For discussions of African lineages and clans and how they interrelated with other institutions, see Murdock, *Africa*, 24–32, and the following articles in Radcliffe-Brown and Forde, eds., *African Systems of Kinship and Marriage*: Radcliffe-Brown, "Introduction," 13–23, 39–43; Richards, "Some Types of Family Structure Amongst the Central Bantu," 207–51; Fortes, "Kinship and Marriage Among the Ashanti," 252–84; Forde, "Double Descent Among the Yako," 285–332. See Sidney W. Mintz and Richard Price, *An Anthropological Approach to the Afro-American Past: A Caribbean Perspective* (Philadelphia: Institute for the Study of Human Issues [Occasional Papers in Social Change, No. 2] 1976), 35–36, for an elegant analysis of why cognatic descent, which maximizes the number of effective kin, was considerably more serviceable to American slaves than traditional African unilineal descent patterns.

24. James M. Robin's Papers, Vol. 1, Massachusetts Historical Society; John Walker Papers, P.C. 254.1, North Carolina State Archives.

25. Lien by Thomas Pollock to Jacob Mitchell—Pollock Papers, P.C. 31.1, North Carolina State Archives.

26. See Kulikoff, "The Beginnings of the Afro-American Family in Maryland," 176, for a discussion of the spread of interplantation kinship lines. Such movement is much in evidence in the estate records listed in *Sources*, Table 1.

27. See plantation papers listed in *Sources*, Table 1.
28. Gutman, *Black Family*, 197.

Notes to Essay 6/Beales

1. Research for this article was made possible by a Fellowship for College Teachers from the National Endowment for the Humanities and a sabbatical leave from Holy Cross.

2. Dates in parentheses refer to the diaries of Ebenezer Parkman. The extant portions of the diary through 1755 (except 1736 and 1742, which were recently acquired by the American Antiquarian Society) appear in *The Diary of Ebenezer Parkman, 1703–1782: First Part, Three Volumes in One, 1719–1755*, ed. Francis G. Walett (Worcester, Massachusetts: American Antiquarian Society, 1974). The years 1737 and November 1778 through 1780 are printed in *The Diary of Rev. Ebenezer Parkman, of Westborough, Mass., for the Months of February, March, April, October and November, 1737, November and December of 1778, and the Years of 1779 and 1780*, ed. Harriette M. Forbes ([Westborough:] Westborough Historical Society, 1899). Unpublished portions of the diary are held by the American Antiquarian Society (1736; 1742; 1756–May 1761; June 1764–June 1769; 10–21 November 1772; June 1773–October 1778) and by the Massachusetts Historical Society (August 1771–June 1773; 1781–1782).

3. See Edmund S. Morgan, *The Puritan Family: Religion and Domestic Relations in Seventeenth-Century New England* (rev. ed.; New York: Harper, 1966), 67–68; John Demos, *A Little Commonwealth: Family Life in Plymouth Colony* (New York: Oxford University Press, 1970), 139–42; Joseph F. Kett, *Rites of Passage: Adolescence in America, 1790 to the Present* (New York: Basic Books, 1977), 16; James Axtell, *The School upon a Hill: Education and Society in Colonial New England* (New Haven: Yale University Press, 1974), 97–99; Joseph E. Illick, "Child-Rearing in Seventeenth-Century America," in Lloyd deMause, ed., *The History of Childhood* (New York: The Psychohistory Press, 1974), 303–50; and John F. Walzer, "A Period of Ambivalence: Eighteenth-Century American Childhood," in deMause, 351–82.

4. On Parkman, see the sketch by Clifford K. Shipton in *Biographical Sketches of Those Who Attended Harvard College in the Classes of 1713–1721, with Bibliographical and Other Notes*, vol. 6 of *Sibley's Harvard Graduates* (Boston: Massachusetts Historical Society, 1942), 511–27. On Westborough, see Heman Packard DeForest and Edward Craig Bates, *The History of Westborough, Massachusetts* (Westborough: The Town, 1891), and Harriette Merrifield Forbes, *The Hundredth Town: Glimpses of Life in Westborough, 1717–1817* (Boston: Rockwell and Churchill, 1889).

5. "Nursing and Weaning in an Eighteenth-Century New England Household," The Dublin Seminar for New England Folklife, *Annual Proceedings 1985* (Boston: Boston University, 1987), 48–63.

6. John Cotton, *A Practical Commentary, or An Exposition with Observations, Reasons and Uses upon the First Epistle Generall of John* (London,

1656), 124, as quoted in Morgan, *Puritan Family*, 66.

7. "Meditations Divine and Moral," in John Harvard Ellis, ed., *The Works of Anne Bradstreet in Prose and Verse* (New York: Peter Smith, 1932 [1867]), 41.

8. A catalog of childhood accidents would be bloody. Nine-year-old Billy, for example, almost bled to death after cutting himself with an ax while chopping firewood (30 November 1750). Parkman's grandson Neddy (Edward), age nine, nearly cut off two of his five-year-old brother Lewis's fingers (18 March 1773).

9. The diary for the years from June 1761 through May 1764 is not extant.

10. In the same entry, Parkman also noted that "*John* trades with *Jonas Kenny* for two [sheep] and a Lamb to be received next Fall, but Mr. *Moses Nurse* gives the Note to Me of what John is to receive for his money." Breck and Samuel owned sheep at the ages of 17 and 15, respectively (2 October 1766), as did Elias at the age of 13 (3 November 1774). Parkman's daughter Lucy owned three sheep at the age of 15 (8 January 1750).

11. He departed for Ashburnham on 27 August 1770; returned home on 11 December; and presumably went back to Ashburnham, for his father again noted his return on 9 February 1771.

12. By 1770 three of the 16 Parkman children had died, and seven had married. Of the four remaining sons, Samuel was apprenticed to a merchant in Boston; Breck, trained as a housewright, worked in the towns of Ashby, Brookfield and Upton; John spent much of the year in Brookfield, where he was apprenticed to a saddler; and Elias spent part of the year in Ashburnham. Like Elias, Hannah spent several months in Ashburnham, and thus only Anna Sophia spent the entire year at home.

13. Ebenezer Parkman, Jr., appears always to have had a difficult time providing for his family. Although the elder Parkman's diary is silent with respect to the terms of Elias's stay, perhaps Ebenezer, Jr., felt that Elias's presence in Westborough would provide advantages which were not available in Brookfield. By 1772, however, he could not afford to be without Elias's help and sent for his son. This was, the minister wrote, "very Contrary to my Expectation, but his Father is unable to go on with his Business and Sends for him" (19 May 1772).

14. Morgan, *Puritan Family*, 78. See also Lawrence Stone, *The Family, Sex and Marriage in England, 1500–1800* (New York: Harper & Row, 1977), 107–09; and Alan Macfarlane, *The Family Life of Ralph Josselin, a Seventeenth-Century Clergyman: An Essay in Historical Anthropology* (Cambridge: At the University Press, 1970), 205–10.

15. Class of 1761.

16. "I teach my Sons Alexander, Breck and Samuel at home and little John begins to learn to write" (2 January 1761).

17. See 8, 10 April, 6 May 1771; 27 May, 28 June 1772.

18. Class of 1770.

19. See 19, 30 May 1774.

Notes to Essay 7/Robson

1. Whatever their original location, copies of these letters are available at Dickinson College, the indispensible repository for study of Nisbet.

2. There is no detailed modern study of Charles Nisbet's alienation from life in early national Pennsylvania, an omission I hope soon to remedy. For facets of Nisbet's unhappiness, see Samuel Miller, *Memoir of the Reverend Charles Nisbet, D. D.* (New York: Robert Carter, 1840); James H. Smylie, "Charles Nisbet: Second Thoughts on a Revolutionary Generation," *Pennsylvania Magazine of History and Biography* 98 (1974): 189–205; James D. Tagg, "The Limits of Republicanism: The Reverend Charles Nisbet, Benjamin Franklin Bache, and the French Revolution," *Penn. Magazine of History and Biography* 112 (1988): 503–43; Charles Coleman Sellers, *Dickinson College: A History* (Middletown, CT: Wesleyan University Press, 1974); and Boyd Lee Spahr, "Charles Nisbet, Portrait in Miniature," *Bulwark of Liberty: Early Years at Dickinson*, Boyd Lee Spahr Lectures in Americana, 1947–1950 (New York: Fleming H. Revell Company, 1950), 55–73.

3. Edmund S. Morgan, *The Puritan Family: Religion and Domestic Relations in Seventeenth-Century New England* (Rev. ed., New York: Harper & Row, Publishers, 1966); Peter Laslett, *The World We Have Lost: England Before the Industrial Age* (New York: Scribners, 1966).

4. See, for example, John Demos, *A Little Commonwealth: Family Life In Plymouth Colony* (New York: Oxford University Press, 1970); Philip J. Greven, *Four Generations: Population, Land and Family in Colonial Andover, Massachusetts* (Ithaca: Cornell University Press, 1970); Kennth Lockridge, *A New England Town: The First Hundred Years* (1st ed., New York: W. W. Norton & Co., 1970); Stephanie Graumann Wolf, *Urban Village: Population, Family, and Community in Germantown, Pennsylvania* (Princeton: Princeton University Press, 1976); Lorena S. Walsh, "'Till Death Us Do Part': Marriage and Family in Seventeenth-century Maryland" and Darrett B. and Anita H. Rutman, "'Now Wives and Sons-in-Law': Parental Death in a Seventeenth-Century Virginia County," Thad W. Tate and David L. Ammerman, eds., *The Chesapeake in the Seventeenth Century* (Chapel Hill: University of North Carolina Press, 1979).

5. Philip J. Greven, *The Protestant Temperament: Patterns of Child Rearing, Religious Experience, and the Self in Early America* (New York: Oxford University Press, 1977); Lawrence Stone, *The Family, Sex and Marriage in England, 1500–1800* (New York: Harper & Row, Publishers, 1977).

6. See, for example, Daniel Blake Smith, *Inside the Great House: Planter Family Life in Eighteenth-Century Chesapeake Society* (Ithaca: Cornell University Press, 1980); Jan Lewis, *The Pursuit of Happiness: Family and Values in Jefferson's Virginia* (New York: Oxford University Press, 1983); Darrett B. and Anita H. Rutman, *A Place in Time: Middlesex County, Virginia, 1650–1750* (New York: W. W. Norton & Co., 1984).

7. Greven, *Prot. Temperament*, chaps. 2, 4, 6; Stone, *Family, Sex and Marriage*, chaps. 3, 5, pts. ii–v, 9, 13, pt. i.

8. Greven, *Prot. Temperament*, chap. 6; Stone, *Family, Sex and Marriage*, chaps. 9, 13, pt. i.

9. Stone, Chaps. 9, 13, pt. i.

10. Mary Beth Norton, *Liberty's Daughters: The Revolutionary Experience of American Women, 1750–1800* (Boston: Little, Brown, 1980), pt. II; Linda K. Kerber, *Women of the Republic: Intellect and Ideology in Revolutionary America* (Chapel Hill: University of North Carolina Press, 1980), chaps. 7–9; Nancy F. Cott, *The Bonds of Womanhood: "Women's Sphere" in New England, 1780–1835* (New Haven: Yale University Press, 1977); Joy Day and Richard Buel, Jr., *The Way of Duty: A Woman and Her Family in Revolutionary America* (New York: W. W. Norton & Co., 1984).

11. John Demos, *Past, Present and Personal: The Family and the Life Course in American History* (New York: Oxford University Press, 1986), chap. 2; E. Anthony Rotundo, "American Fatherhood: A Historical Perspective," *American Behavioral Scientist* 29 (1985): 7–25; E. Anthony Rotundo, "Manhood in America: The Northern Middle Class, 1770–1920," (Ph.D. Dissertation, Brandeis University, 1982).

12. Demos, *Past, Present and Personal*, 44–48; Rotundo, "American Fatherhood," 8–9.

13. Greven, *Prot. Temperament*, 32–43, 49–55, 151–52, 159–70.

14. Demos, *Past, Present and Personal*, 49–55; Rotundo, "American Fatherhood," 10–13.

15. Samuel Miller, *Memoir of Nisbet*, 15–19, 29–30; R. Wallace White, *A Family Chronicle. Book One, Charles Nisbet* (Carlisle, PA: Privately printed, 1980), 1–4.

16. White, *Fam. Chronicle*, 3; J. H. S. Burleigh, *A Church History of Scotland* (London: Oxford University Press, 1960), 278–303.

17. Miller, *Memoir of Nisbet*, 24; Charles Nisbet to Mary Nisbet Turnbull, 7 Mar. 1798 (Founders' Papers, Dickinson College Archives [All Nisbet letters to Mary Turnbull cited in this article are from this repository]).

18. Stone, *Family, Sex and Marriage*, 451.

19. Miller, *Memoir of Nisbet*, 74–78.

20. Smylie, "Nisbet: Second Thoughts," 189–205.

21. Greven, *Prot. Temperament*, 341–47.

22. For a more detailed description of Nisbet's relations with Tom than is presented here, see David W. Robson, "'My Unhappy Son': A Narrative of Drinking in Federalist Pennsylvania," *Pennsylvania History* 52 (1985): 22–35.

23. Charles Nisbet to Jedediah Morse, 24 Oct. 1799 (Historical Society of Pennsylvania, Philadelphia).

24. Charles Nisbet to Alexander Addison, 6 Aug. 1795 (Special Collections, University of Pittsburgh Library [All Nisbet letters to Addison cited in this article are from this repository]).

25. Charles Nisbet to Alexander Addison, 9 Sept. 1797; for Morgan's hypothesis, see *The Puritan Family*, 77–78.

26. Charles Nisbet to Alexander Addison, 12 Aug., 5 Nov. 1797.

27. Charles Nisbet to Alexander Addison, 19, 24 Feb. 1798.

28. Miller, *Memoir of Nisbet*, 302.

29. Charles Nisbet to Mary Nisbet Turnbull, 25 Oct. 1791.

30. Charles Nisbet to Mary Nisbet Turnbull, 12 Nov., 27 Dec. 1791; 30 July, 20 Oct. 1792.
31. Charles Nisbet to Mary Nisbet Turnbull, 30 July, 20 Oct. 1792.
32. Charles Nisbet to Mary Nisbet Turnbull, 20 Oct., 10, 15 Nov. 1792; 16 Apr., 8 Nov. 1793.
33. Charles Nisbet to Mary Nisbet Turnbull, 7 Mar. 1798.
34. Charles Nisbet to Mary Nisbet Turnbull, 1 June, 16 Nov. 1799.

Notes to Essay 8/Rosenzweig

1. E. S. Martin, "Mothers and Daughters," *Good Housekeeping* 64, (May 1917): 27.
2. For overviews of the changes in women's lives, see Carl Degler, *At Odds: Women and the Family in America from the Revolution to the Present* (New York, 1980); Margaret G. Wilson, *The American Woman in Transition; 1870–1920* (New York, 1979); and Mary P. Ryan, *Womanhood in America* (New York, 1975). On anger, see Carol Z. Stearns and Peter N. Stearns, *Anger; The Struggle for Emotional Control in America's History* (Chicago, 1986), especially chap. 4.
3. "The Female World of Love and Ritual;" "Hearing Women's Words; A Feminist Reconstruction of History;" and "The New Woman As Androgyne: Social Disorder and Gender Crisis, 1870–1936," in Carroll Smith-Rosenberg, *Disorderly Conduct; Visions of Gender in Victorian America* (New York, 1985) 53–76, 11–52, 245–96.
4. "Maybell," *Ladies Home Journal* 1 (October 1884).
5. Ruth Ashmore, "My Girls' Mothers," *Ladies Home Journal* 7 (October 1890): 12; Alan Cameron, "A Woman's Most Grievous Mistake," *Ladies Home Journal* 14 (October 1897): 10.
6. Fanny Fern, "Tell Your Mother," *Ladies Home Journal* 5 (June 1888).
7. Ruth Ashmore, "A Girl's Best Friend," *Ladies Home Journal* 8 (May 1881): 12.
8. "How Girls Deceive Their Parents," *Ladies Home Journal* 1 (November 1884); M. E. W. Sherwood, "How Shall Our Girls Behave?", *Ladies Home Journal* 5 (October 1888): 2; "What is a Lady," *Ladies Home Journal* 5 (November 1888): 13; 17; Ella Wheeler Wilcox, "An Evil of American Daughters," *Ladies Home Journal* 7 (April 1890): 3; Edward Bok, Editorial, "The American Skeleton," *Ladies Home Journal* 20 (May 1903): 14.
9. William Lee Howard, M.D., "Why Didn't My Parents Tell Me," *Ladies Home Journal* 24 (August 1907): '32; Editorial, "Where One Girl Began," *Ladies Home Journal* 34 (January 1917): 7; "My Mother Didn't Tell Me," *Harper's Bazaar* 46 (October 1912): 484, 523; Alice Bartlett Stimson, "When the College Girl Comes Home," *Harper's Bazaar* 42 (August 1908): 797–99; Charles Edward Jefferson, "A Sermon to Grown-up Daughters," *Woman's Home Companion* 43 (February 1916): 7; "The Case of the Elderly Mother," *Ladies Home Journal* 36 (March 1919): 112; Harriet Brunkhurst, "The Girl Whose Mother is 'Old',"

Ladies Home Journal 35 (June 1919): 132.

10. Ruth Ashmore, *Ladies Home Journal* 11 (September 1894): 16; "Antagonism Between Mothers and Daughters," *The Independent* 53 (26 September 1901): 2311.

11. While the periodical literature is certainly suggestive, as Jay Mechling has pointed out, there can be no assumption of direct correspondence between popular advice literature of any sort and actual family behaviors and experiences. "Advice to Historians on Advice to Mothers," *Journal of Social History* 9 (Fall 1975): 44–63.

12. Even these sources may not provide totally accurate data regarding family interactions. Mothers and daughters do not necessarily write to one another about hostile feelings. Autobiographers typically record their lives as older adults, and their recollections may be faulty and/or distorted by their own biases. For these same reasons, oral histories are not always dependable sources for the historical study of family relationships.

13. Degler, *At Odds*, 82–83.

14. 7 August 1886, Series III, Box 25, Folder 397, Annie Winsor Allen Papers, Schlesinger Library, Radcliffe College.

15. 11 November 1893, Series III, Box 25, Folder 400, Allen Papers.

16. Fragment, c. 1899, Series III, Box 24, Folder 390, Allen Papers.

17. See extensive mother-daughter correspondence, Series III, Boxes 23, 24, 25 and 27, Allen Papers.

18. 11 January 1879, in *The Making of a Feminist; Early Journals and Letters of M. Carey Thomas*, ed. Marjorie Dobkin (Kent, Ohio, 1979), 152.

19. Dobkin, ed., *The Making of a Feminist*, 152; "The New Woman As Androgyne," 257.

20. 16 July 1875, *The Making of a Feminist*, 100. An earlier journal entry also documents Mrs. Thomas's commitment to education: "An English man Joseph Beck was here to dinner the other day and he don't believe in the Education of Women. Neither does Cousin Frank King and my such a disgusson [sic] they had. *Mother of course was for. . . .*" [emphasis added] 26 February 1871, 50.

21. Dobkin, ed., *The Making of a Feminist*, 263.

22. 11 December 1903, Box 3, Volume 60; 16 May 1907, Box 3, Volume 64, Book 6, Hilda Worthington Smith Papers, Schlesinger Library,Radcliffe College.

23. 3 October 1909, Box 2, Folder 49, Smith Papers.

24. See, for example, 9 January 1915, Box 4, Volume 78, Book 20, Smith Papers: "It seems as if I should never get anywhere, but should stay at home with Mother. *She* hasn't enough to do, & realizes it sadly."

25. 25 December 1917, Box 4, Volume 81, Book 23, Smith Papers.

26. Box 10, Folder 171, Smith Papers.

27. Vida Scudder, *On Journey* (New York, 1937) 66–67, 88.

28. Mary Simkhovitch, *Neighborhood* (New York, [1938]), 47.

29. 3 December 1902, Carton 1, Folder 42; 8 August 1912, Carton 1, Folder 63, Louise Marion Bosworth Papers, Schlesinger Library, Radcliffe College.

30. Joyce Antler, "'After College, What?': New Graduates and the Family Claim," *American Quarterly* 32 (Fall 1980): 428.

31. See letters to Katharine Dummer Fisher, Box 45, Folder 925 and

letter to "Happy" (Ethel) Dummer Mintzer, 8 July 1920, Box 10, Folder 165a, Ethel Sturges Dummer Papers, Schlesinger Library, Radcliffe College.

32. For an interesting discussion of the positive contribution of families, particularly mothers, to the continuing growth and development of college-educated daughters, see Antler, "'After College, What?': New Graduates and the Family Claim," cited above, note 30. Additional examples of mothers who supported daughters' untraditional aspirations include the mothers of Ethel Puffer Howes, Boxes 1 and 7, Morgan-Howes Family Papers; Florence Luscomb, "The Twentieth Century Trade Union Woman: Vehicle for Social Change Oral History Project," Institute of Labor and Industrial Relations, University of Michigan-Wayne State University, 1978; and Ella Lyman Cabot, Ella Lyman Cabot Papers, Series III, Box 3, Folder 65, all in the Schlesinger Library, Radcliffe College. See also Joyce Antler, *Lucy Spraque Mitchell; The Making of a Modern Woman,* (New Haven, 1987), and Sharon O'Brien, *Willa Cather: The Emerging Voice,* (New York, 1987).

On the other side of the issue, for an example of unmitigated mother-daughter conflict, see Margaret Anderson, *My Thirty Years' War* (New York, 1969), first published in 1930. The papers of Clara Savage Littledale clearly document both conflict and caring, e.g., her letters to her sister, 18 February 1915 and 2 August 1918, Box 3, Folders 55 and 56, and journal entries, 15 February 1915, 23 February 1915, and 3 April 1915, Box 1, Volume 17., Schlesinger Library, Radcliffe College.

33. For an analysis of the effects on the family of the emphasis on outside expertise, see Christopher Lasch, *Haven in a Heartless World; The Family Besieged* (New York, 1977).

34. See, for example, Margo E. Horn, *Family Ties: The Blackwells. A Study in the Dynamics of Family Life in Nineteenth Century America,* Dissertation, Tufts University, 1980, and Mary E. Bulkley, "Grandmother, Mother and Me," mimeographed manuscript, Schlesinger Library, Radcliffe College. Examples of less than perfect earlier mother-daughter interactions are also cited in Nancy F. Cott, *The Bonds of Womanhood* (New Haven, 1977), 178; and Nancy M. Theriot, *The Biosocial Construction of Femininity; Mothers and Daughters in Nineteenth-Century America* (Westport, Connecticut, 1988), 77.

35. Carroll Smith-Rosenberg has commented on the lack of congruence between the perspectives of male authors and the experiences of women: "I ceased to search in men's writings for clues to women's experiences." "Hearing Women's Words: A Feminist Reconstruction of History," in *Disorderly Conduct,* 27, cited above, note 2.

36. Peter Filene suggests that mothers lived vicariously through their daughters' rebellious and emancipated behavior during the late nineteenth century. *Him/Her/Self; Sex Roles in Modern America,* 2nd ed. (Baltimore, 1986), 23.

37. Ethel Sturges Dummer, for example, was involved in a wide variety of activities outside her home. See Degler, *At Odds,* chap. 13 for a discussion of women's world beyond the home. Smith-Rosenberg also comments on the activities of women outside the confines of domesticity. "The New Woman As Androgyne," 256–57.

38. See Peter N. Stearns with Carol Z. Stearns, "Emotionology:

Clarifying the History of Emotions and Emotional Standards," *American Historical Review* 90 (October, 1985): 813–36. On the control of anger in American society, see Stearns and Stearns, *Anger*, cited above, note 2.

39. Joan Jacobs Brumberg, *Fasting Girls; The Emergence of Anorexia Nervosa as a Modern Disease* (Cambridge, 1988), 126–140 and Theriot, *The Biosocial Construction of Femininity*, 119–132.

40. Nancy M. Chodorow, *The Reproduction of Mothering; Psychoanalysis and the Sociology of Gender* (Berkeley, 1978).

41. See, for example, Nancy Friday, *My Mother My Self* (New York, 1977).

42. Theriot, *The Biosocial Construction of Femininity*, 12.

43. Hannah Whitall Smith, aunt of M. Carey Thomas, to Mary Berenson, her daughter, 28 Septermber 1910, in Logan Pearsall Smith, ed., *Philadelphia Quaker: The Letters of Hannah Whitall Smith* (New York, 1950), 210.

Notes to Essay 9/McBride

1. George Rosen, *The Structure of American Medical Practice 1875–1941*, ed. Charles E. Rosenberg (Philadelphia: University of Pennsylvania Press, 1983).

2. Harry F. Dowling, *City Hospitals: The Undercare of the Underprivileged* (Cambridge, Mass.: Harvard University Press, 1982).

3. George Rosen, "The First Neighborhood Health Center Movement: Its Rise and Fall," *From Medical Police to Social Medicine: Essays on the History of Health Care*, ed. G. Rosen (New York: Science History Publications, 1974), 304–27.

4. E. Franklin Frazier, *The Negro in the United States* (New York: Macmillan, 1957), 191.

5. Carl V. Harris, *Political Power in Birmingham, 1871–1921* (Knoxville, Tenn.: University of Tennessee Press, 1977), 160.

6. U.S. Bureau of the Census, *Bulletin 129—Negroes in the United States* (Washington, D.C.: GPO, 1915), 43–44; John W. Trask, "The Significance of the Mortality Rates of the Colored Population of the United States," *American Journal of Public Health* (hereafter abbreviated *AJPH*), vol. 5, (March 1916), 256.

In both the urban North and South, black death rates tended to be double those of whites. In 1913, for instance, Washington's (D.C.) white mortality rate was 14.4 compared to 24.4 for the city's blacks; the same figures for Mobile were 16.9 to 25.7; for Charleston, 15.7 to 37.2; and for Norfolk, 13.4 to 29.9.

7. Monroe Lerner and Odin W. Anderson, *Health Progress in the United States* (Chicago: University of Chicago Press, 1963), 118. Rates for blacks are those for "nonwhites," about 99 percent of whom were blacks or "Negroes." (115–16).

8. E. M. Kitagaw and P. M. Hauser, *Differential Mortality in the United States: A Study in Socioeconomic Epidemiology* (Cambridge, Mass.: Harvard University Press, 1973), 2–3, 28–29, 175; John M. Last, "Epidemiol-

ogy and Health Information," *Maxcy-Rosenau—Public Health and Preventive Medicine* (Norwalk, Conn.: Appleton-Century-Crofts, 1986), 23.

9. U.S. Bureau of the Census, *Negro Population—1790–1915* (Washington, D.C.: GPO, 1918), 334.

10. U.S. Bureau of the Census, *Negroes in the United States, 1920–1932* (Washington, D.C.; GPO, 1935), 457. While infant mortality rates for both whites and blacks decline throughout the rest of the century, a significant racial variation prevails. On this long-term trend, see Carl L. Erhardt and Joyce E. Berlin, *Mortality and Morbidity in the United States* (Cambridge, Mass.: Harvard University Press, 1974), 189–93.

11. For discussion of the concept of racialism and related classic documents regarding its development, see Louis L. Snyder, *The Idea of Racialism* (Princeton, N.J.: D. Van Nostrand, 1962). For a recent critique of the notion of racial-biological determinism and diseases susceptibility, see Richard Cooper, "Race, Disease and Health," in *Health Race & Ethnicity*, ed. by Thomas Rathwell and David Phillips (London: Croom Helm, 1986), 21–79.

12. For example, see Thomas W. Murrell, "Syphilis and the American Negro: A Medico-Sociologic Study," *Journal of the American Medical Association*, vol. 54 (12 March 1910), 847; H. M. Folkes, "The Negro as a Health Problem," *Journal of the AMA*, vol. 55 (8 October 1910), 1246–47; William F. Brunner, "The Negro Health Problem in Southern Cities," *AJPH*, vol. 5 (March 1915), 183–90; and Gordon Wilson, "Diseases in Apparently Healthy Colored Girls," *New York Medical Journal*, vol. 103 (25 March 1916), 585–88. Murrell, Folkes, Brunner and Wilson were doctors from Richmond, Biloxi (Mississippi), Savannah and Baltimore, respectively.

13. Murrell's "Syphilis and the American Negro," for instance, argued that under slavery blacks had thrived, but now they were "crushed" by their uncontainable promiscuity, alcohol consumption and preference for unclean living conditions. This research admonished that within a few decades the entire black population would be overrun with syphilis. Other southern medical opinion emphasized that members of the black race had incredible physical protection against common ailments. In 1911 a prominent hospital physician of a deep South city published "Immunity of the Negro to Alcoholism." It is filled with social opinion posed as fact: "The negro continually gets drunk"; "since emancipation [blacks] indulge at will and to any extent in the use of alcohol"; "among pure-blooded African descendants, such as laborers congregated at railroad camps [whiskey's] ultimate effects on the individual are almost nil." He reached this conclusion because only 17 of the 594 patients at his hospital treated for alcoholism were black. G. Farrar Patton, "The Relative Immunity of the Negro to Alcoholism," *New Orleans Medical and Surgical Journal*, vol. 64 (September 1911), Tulane University Medical Library, New Orleans, 201–03; quote on p. 203. This physician, of course, was disregarding one of the elementary principles of health statistics by drawing universal judgements about incidence in a large population from the characteristics of one hospital's subset of patients. For a classic explanation of this statistical error, see A. Bradford Hill, *Principles of Medical Statistics*

(ninth edition—New York: Oxford University Press, 1971), 291–92.

14. J. S. Fulton, "Discussion [of] J. W. Trask, 'The Significance of the Mortality Rates of the Colored Population of United States,'" *AJPH*, vol. 6 (March 1916), 259–60; quote on p. 260.

15. E. F. Frazier, *The Negro in the United States*, 567; S. J. Holmes, *The Negro's Struggle for Survival: A Study in Human Ecology* (Berkeley, Calif.: University of California Press, 1937), 15–16. In 1896 Hoffman wrote his influential treatise, *Race Traits and Tendencies of the American Negro*, asserting that the black's "extreme liability to consumption alone would seal its fate." Eggleston's 1913 book, *The Ultimate Solution of the American Negro Problem*, argued that the constitutional weaknesses of the black race meant certain elimination for this portion of America's population. Some years later, Dr. Pearl wrote: "Just in proportion as the Negro becomes anything but an agricultural laborer in the Southern States [sic] does he hasten the time of his final extinction in this country." (Holmes, *The Negro's Struggle for Survival*, 15–16; quote on p. 16).

16. Virginia Department of Health, "Morbidity and Vital Statistics," *Virginia Health Bulletin*, vol. 7, Extra No. 1 (5 February 1915), Virginia State Library, Richmond, Va., 49.

17. Brunner, "The Negro Health Problem in Southern Cities," 186, 189.

18. Rosemary Stevens, *American Medicine and the Public Interest* (New Haven, Conn.: Yale University Press, 1973), 200.

19. Ira V. Hiscock, et al., "Infant Hygiene," United States Public Health Service, *Municipal Health Department Practice for the Year 1923 Based upon Surveys of the 100 Largest Cities in the United States, Public Health Bulletin* no. 164, July 1926 (Washington, D.C.: GPO, 1926), 245–46; Samuel C. Prescott and M. P. Horwood, *Sedgwick's Principles of Sanitary Science and Public Health* (New York: Macmillan, 1935), 510–12; Richard H. Shryock, *The Development of Modern Medicine* (Madison, Wisc.: University of Wisconsin Press, 1979), 329.

20. Mayhew Derryberry, "The Significance of Infant Mortality Rates," United States Public Health Service, *Public Health Reports* [hereafter abbreviated *PHR*] vol. 51 (May 1936), 545–46.

21. Harry F. Dowling, *Fighting Infection: Conquests of the Twentieth Century* (Cambridge: Mass.: Harvard University Press, 1978), 64; Stevens, *American Medicine and the Public Interest*, 200; Paul Starr, *The Social Transformation of American Medicine* (New York: Basic Books, 1982), 260–61.

22. J. H. M. Knox, Jr. and Paul Zentai, "The Health Problems of the Negro Child," *AJPH*, vol. 16 (August 1926), 805–09; quote on p. 805.

23. J. H. M. Knox, Jr., "The Preschool Child in Rural Maryland," *Transactions of the Medical and Chirurgical Faculty of Maryland* (1924) cited in Knox and Zentai, "The Health Problem of the Negro Child," 809, n. 13.

24. *Official Proceedings of the White House Conference on Child Health and Protection, Supplement to the United States Daily, vol. 5, no. 228, section 11 (28 November 1930), [General Statement],* Papers of the Bureau of Social Hygiene, Box 10, Folder 212, Rockefeller Archive Center, Pocantico, N. Y., 12.

25. For a study of the role and impact of black medical professionals on twentieth century urbanization and public health movements, see David McBride, *Integrating the City of Medicine: Blacks in Philadelphia Health Care, 1910–1965* (Philadelphia: Temple University Press, 1989).

26. T. Parran, Jr., "Public Health in New York State," *Proceedings of the Forty-Seventh Annual Meeting of State and Provincial Health Authorities of North America, Washington, D. C., June 23, 1932*, 95.

27. Jones cited Chicago as a primary example. There 86 percent of the black families had only "immediate" and or "distant relatives" in the household, while at least ten percent "of the householding group was made up of persons who were in no way related." *Official Proceedings of the White House Conference on Child Health and Protection*, 45.

28. *Official Proceedings*, 44.

29. In 1915 Booker T. Washington, the nationally prominent black educator and political leader, established Negro Health Week. Centered at his college, the Tuskegee Institute, black public health and community workers throughout the nation's black neighborhoods organized local Negro Health Week campaigns to encourage public awareness of effective preventive health and sanitation practices. However, it was not until 1930 that the U. S. Public Health Service formally incorporated this movement under the title "National Negro Health Movement," N. A., *National Health Agencies—A Survey With Especial Reference to Voluntary Associations* (Washington, D. C.: Public Affairs Press, 1945), 234–35.

30. M. J. Bent, "Health Education Programs of Government Agencies," *Journal of Negro Education*, Yearbook, vol. 6 (July 1937), 500.

31. Statement by James H. Robinson, supervisor of State Negro Welfare of the Tennessee Department of Institutions, quoted by John M. Gibson, "The Black Man and the Great White Plague," *Social Forces*, vol. 14 (May 1936), 585–90; quote on p. 587.

32. M. O. Bousefiled, 'Major Health Problems of the Negro," *Hospital Social Service*, vol. 38 (1933), 544–45.

33. Elizabeth C. Tandy, "Infant and Maternal Mortality Among Negroes," *Journal of Negro Education*, Yearbook, vol. 6 (July 1937), 332. See also, Derryberry, "The Significance of Infant Mortality Rates"; and Dorothy E. Holland and G. T. Palmer, "Improving the Value of the Infant Mortality Rate as an Index of Public Health Effort," *American Journal of Diseases of Children*, vol. 36 (December 1928), 1237–249.

34. E. H. Beardsley, *A History of Neglect: Health Care for Blacks and Mill Workers in the Twentieth Century South* (Knoxville: University of Tennessee Press, 1987), 163, 165; James T. Patterson, *America's Struggle Against Poverty 1900–1980* (Cambridge, Mass.: Harvard University Press, 1981), 67.

35. George St. J. Perrott, et al., "The National Health Survey: Scope and Method of the Nation-Wide Canvass of Sickness in Relation to its Social and Economic Setting," *PHR*, vol. 54 (15 September 1939), 1–3.

36. "Statement of Dr. W. Montague Cobb, Representing the National Medical Committee of the NAACP," *United States Senate, Hearings Before the Committee on Education and Labor U. S. Senate Seventy-Ninth Congress Second Session on S. 1606—A Bill to Provide for a National Health*

Program, Part 1, April 2–5, 9–11, 16th, 1946 (Washington, D. C.: GPO, 1946), 502. See also, Frazier, *The Negro in the United States*, 573–74, 587. The NAACP medical group could have relied on any of dozens of studies growing out of the National Health Survey. One classic National Health Survey study revealing the "extreme intricacy of the whole question of the relation between housing and health," is Rollo H. Britten and Isidore Altman, "Illness and Accidents Among Persons Living Under Different Housing Conditions—Data Based on the National Health Survey," *PHR*, vol. 56 (28 March 1941), 30. The NAACP used the findings of the National Health Survey in its lobbying effort in behalf of a national health insurance program. The NAACP emphasized two points in its support of the wider access to medical care that would result from such an insurance program. First, the survey had proven irrevocably that most of the excess black mortality and morbidity were caused by preventable ailments such as infections diseases that were related to the black population's generally lower economic level and the resultant "overcrowding, poor nutrition, bad sanitation and lack of medical care." Secondly, the survey demonstrated that the health status of blacks improved when their standard of living improved.

37. M. J. Bent, "Health Education Programs of Government Agencies," 503. Dr. Bent was a professor of bacteriology and preventive medicine at Meharry.

38. Gibson, "The Black Man and the Great White Plague," 590, 586.

39. [New York Tuberculosis and Health Association], "Statistical Survey Completed for 1939 Shows Mortality Rise in Urban Centers," *New York Tuberculosis and Health Association Journal*, vol. 4 (December 1940), 3; William J. Brown *et al., Syphilis and Other Venereal Diseases* (Cambridge, Mass.: Harvard University Press, 1970), 112–13. Tuberculosis deaths among blacks, for instance, rose in New York City from 1938 to 1939 and remained discouragingly high in other large cities. In 1939 blacks comprised 50 percent of the TB mortality in Baltimore, New Orleans, 58; Washington, 72; Birmingham, 78; Atlanta, 78; Memphis, 79.44. Syphilis rates for blacks nationwide in 1940 were over five times those of whites.

40. Paul B. Cornely, "Race Relations in Community Health Organization," *AJPH*, vol. 36 (September 1946), 984–92; P. B. Cornely, "Segregation and Discrimination in Medical Care in the United States," *AJPH*, vol. 46 (September 1956), 1074.

41. On the rise of national interest in nutrition policy resulting from mobilization for World War II, see Paul Adams, *Health of the State* (New York: Praeger, 1982); and National Research Council, Commission of Life Sciences, Food and Nutrition Board, Committee on Nutrition in Medical Education, *Nutrition Education in U. S. Medical Schools* (Washington, D. C.: National Academy Press, 1985).

42. U. S. Department of Labor, Children's Bureau, Division of Health Services, "Types of Health Activities Benefitting Negro Mothers and Children Under the Federal-Aid Programs for Maternal and Child-Health Services and Services for Crippled Children, December, 1943," [mimeo], Philadelphia Free Library, Fischer Government Documents Collection; quotes on pp. 3 and 5.

43. Morris Gleich, et al., "A Review of Twenty Years of Premature

Infant Care at Harlem Hospital," *The Harlem Hospital Bulletin*, vol. 5 (June 1952), 11–17.

44. Dept. of Labor, "Types of Health Activities," 10.

45. Cornerly, "Race Relations in Community Health Organizations," quote on p. 990.

46. Cornerly, 984–87.

47. Dowling, *City Hospitals*, 160; Quentin Young, "The Urban Hospital," *Reforming Medicine; Lessons of the Last Quarter Century*, eds. V. W. Sidel and Ruth Sidel (New York: Pantheon, 1984) 34.

Notes to Essay 10/Altenbaugh

1. This represents a tentative, synthetic essay, exploring a potential conceptual framework for a larger study comparing Italian and Mexican responses to the assimilation process. I hope that such a comparative historical analysis will serve as an informed basis for a rational and sensitive policy response to the ongoing and dynamic Mexican immigration.

2. Leonard Dinnerstein and David M. Reimers, *Ethnic Americans, A History of Immigration and Assimilation* (New York: Harper and Row, 1982), 88; National Commission on Secondary Education for Hispanics, *"Making something happen": Hispanics and urban high school reform* (Washington, DC: Hispanic Policy Development Project, 1984), 3.

3. Guadalupe San Miguel, "Status of the Historiography of Chicano Education: A Preliminary Analysis," *History of Education Quarterly* 26 (Winter 1986): 523–51. Also see Joan Moore, *Mexican Americans*, Englewood Cliffs, N.J.: Prentice Hall, 1976).

4. Richard D. Alba, *Italian Americans: Into the Twilight of Ethnicity* (Englewood Cliffs, NJ: Prentice-Hall, 1985); Humberto S. Nelli, *From Immigrants to Ethnics: The Italian Americans* (New York: Oxford University Press, 1983); Virginia Yans-MacLaughlin, *Family and Community: Italian Immigrants in Buffalo, 1880–1930* (Ithaca: Cornell University Press, 1977); Rudolfo Acuña, *Occupied America: A History of Chicanos* (New York: Harper and Row, 1981); Dinnerstein and Reimers, 43–45, 88–101, 142.

5. Dinnerstein and Reimers, 142. Refer to Milton M. Gordon's classic definition of ethnicity, especially his treatment of "ethclass," in *Assimilation in American Life: The Role of Race, Religion, and National Origins* (New York: Oxford University Press, 1964). Also, see John Bodnar, *Immigration and Industrialization: Ethnicity in an American Mill Town, 1870–1940* (Pittsburgh: University of Pittsburgh Press, 1977), 152–55; John J. Bukowczk, "The Transformation of Working-Class Ethnicity: Corporate Control, Americanization, and the Polish Immigrant Middle Class in Bayonne, New Jersey, 1915–1925," *Labor History* 25 (Winter 1984): 53–82; Andrew M. Greeley, *Ethnicity in the United States: A Preliminary Reconnaisance* (New York: Wiley, 1974) see especially chap. 4, "Does Ethnicity Matter?" Michael Novak, *The Rise of the Unmeltable Ethnics* (New York: MacMillan, 1973), xviii.

6. Lawrence A. Cremin, *Traditions of American Education* (New York:

Basic Books, 1977), viii. Also see Bernard Bailyn, *Education in the Forming of American Society: Needs and Opportunities for Study* (Chapel Hill: University of North Carolina Press, 1960).

7. Thomas Bender, *Community and Social Change in America* (Baltimore: Johns Hopkins University Press, 1978), 7.

8. S. F. Brumberg, "Tales Out of School: Reports of East European Jewish Immigrants in New York City Schools, 1893–1917," *Issues in Education* 2:91–109; J. Higham, "Integrating America: The problem of Assimilation in the Nineteenth Century," *Journal of American Ethnic History* 1:7–25; Rudolph J. Vecoli, "Contadini in Chicago: A Critique of *The Uprooted*," *Journal of American History* 51 (December 1964): 404–17; William J. Reese, "Neither Victims nor Masters: Ethnic and Minority Study," in John H. Best, ed., *Historical Inquiry in Education: A Research Agenda* (Washington, DC: American Educational Research Association, 1983).

9. Oscar Handlin, *The Uprooted: The Epic Story of the Great Migrations that Made the American People* (New York: Grosset and Dunlap, 1951), 4; Vecoli, 404–417; Talcott Parsons, "The Kinship System of the Contemporary United States," *American Anthropologist* 45 (Jan.–Mar. 1943): 22–38.

10. Yans-McLaughlin, 18–20, is most insightful on this point. Also refer to Gutman, *Work, Culture and Society* and Hoffman, "The Writing of Chicano Urban History: From Bare Beginnings to Significant Studies," *Journal of Urban History* 12:199–205.

11. Peter Laslett, *The World We Have Lost: England Before the Industrial Age* (New York: Charles Scribner's, 1971), 248–49.

12. Yans-McLaughlin, 23. Refer to Clifford Geertz, "Ritual and Social Change: A Javanese Example," *American Anthropologist* 59 (February 1957): 32–54.

13. John Bodnar, *The Transplanted: A History of Immigrants in Urban America* (Bloomington: Indiana University Press, 1985), 71.

14. Charles H. Mindel and Robert W. Habenstein, *Ethnic Families in America: Patterns and Variations* (New York: Elsevier Science Publishing Co., 1981), 8.

15. Bodnar, *The Transplanted*, 72.

16. Bodnar, 68. See Tamara K. Hareven's pioneer analysis of the history of the family and networking in *Family Time and Industrial Time: The Relationship Between the Family and Work in a New England Industrial Community* (New York: Cambridge University Press, 1982).

17. Jill S. Quadagno, "The Italian American Family," in Charles H. Mindel and Robert W. Habenstein, eds., 63.

18. Yans-McLaughlin, 60–61, 63, 66.

19. Yans-McLaughlin, 68–69.

20. Yans-McLaughlin, 69–70.

21. David Alvirez, Frank D. Bean and Dorie Williams, "The Mexican American Family," in Charles H. Mindel and Robert W. Habenstein, eds., 274; Richard Griswold del Castillo, *La Familia: Chicano Families in the Urban Southwest, 1848 to the Present* (Notre Dame: University of Notre Dame Press, 1984), 61.

22. Quoted in Albert Camarillo, *Chicanos in a Changing Society: From Mexican Pueblos to American Barrios in Santa Barbara and Southern Califor-*

nia, 1848–1930 (Cambridge: Harvard University Press, 1979), 146.

23. Griswold del Castillo, 53, 54, 55.
24. Camarillo, 147.
25. Alvirez, Bean, and Williams, 275.
26. Bodnar, *The Transplanted*, 82–83.
27. Yans-McLaughlin, 257; Quadagno, 71.
28. Yans-McLaughlin, 81; 84, 87.
29. Quadagno, 63.
30. Quoted in Qadagno, 64.
31. Alvirez, Bean and Williams, 282; Camarillo, 60–65; Griswold del Castillo, 71, 121–22.
32. Griswold del Castillo, 30.
33. Griswold del Castillo, 32, 34.
34. Griswold del Castillo, 96–97.
35. Griswold del Castillo, 99–100.
36. Griswold del Castillo, 102, 104.
37. Griswold del Castillo, 79; Alvirez, Bean and Williams, 277; Acuña, 318.
38. Bodnar, *The Transplanted*, 76; E. R. L. Gould, *The Social Condition of Labor* (Baltimore: Johns Hopkins Press, 1893), 25.
39. Margaret Byington, *Homestead: The Households of a Mill Town* (New York: Russell Sage Foundation, 1910; reprint ed., Pittsburgh: University of Pittsburgh Press, 1974), 142; Bodnar, *The Transplanted*, 87.
40. Byington, 201–02.
41. U. S. Department of Labor, Bureau of Labor Statistics, *Summary of the Report on Conditions of Women and Child Wage Earners in the United States*, Bulletin 57 (Washington, DC: U. S. Government Printing Office, 1916), 30.
42. Yans-McLaughlin, 159, 169, 171, 188–89.
43. Yans-McLaughlin, 172, 195.
44. Yans-McLaughlin, 176–77.
45. Camarillo, 91, 93.
46. Acuña, 209; Alvirez, Bean and Williams, 283; Griswold del Castillo, 125.
47. Acuña, 205–206, 282; Camarillo, 220–21.
48. Griswold del Castillo, 109.

Notes to Essay 11/Litoff and Smith

1. Charles E. Taylor to Barbara Wooddall, later Wooddall Taylor, 27 August 1941. Hereinafter cited as CET and BWT.
2. Charles and Barbara's first date was arranged by Charles's cousin, Virginia Edwards Kitchens, who lived in Fairburn. Charles's grandparents, Edna and Charles Lancaster, were also Fairburn residents. Fairburn is located 20 miles southwest of Atlanta.
3. BWT to CET, 16 July 1942.
4. Ellen K. Rothman, *Hands and Hearts: A History of Courtship in America* (New York: Basic Books Inc. 1984), 12. For a general introduction to wartime romance, see John Costello, *Virtue Under Fire: How*

World War II Changed Our Social and Sexual Attitudes (Boston: Little, Brown and Company, 1985), esp. chap. 1. Recently, we sent an author's query, in the form of a letter to the editor, to the approximately 1,400 daily newspapers published in the United States as well as to over 100 magazines, soliciting the letters women wrote to service personnel during World War II. Judging from the more than 600 responses that we have received thus far, many couples across North America courted by mail. We are presently working on a book based on the letters written by women during the Second World War.

5. The letters of CET and BWT are part of a private collection that the letter writers have very generously made available to the authors in the preparation of this paper.

6. BWT to CET, 6 January 1942.

7. BWT to CET, 22 April 1942.

8. CET to BWT, 9 January 1942.

9. BWT to CET, 16 July 1942.

10. CET to BWT, 24 February, 2 March 1942.

11. BWT to CET, 4 February 1942.

12. BWT to CET, 11 February 1942. Good advice on protocol when out with a serviceman is in Henrietta Ripperger, "Are You Going With A Serviceman?" *Good Housekeeping*, June 1941, p. 121. See also Jo Anne Healey, "Nice Girls Go On Military Weekends," *Good Housekeeping*, June 1942, p. 4 and Henrietta Ripperger, "Gone With the Draft," *Good Housekeeping*, November 1941, pp. 70, 225.

13. A good general introduction to the history of dating in the twentieth century is John Modell, "Dating Becomes the Way of American Youth," in *Essays on the Family and Historical Change*, eds. Leslie Page Moch and Gary D. Stark (College Station, Texas: Texas A&M University Press, 1983), 91–125. On dating practices in the 1920s, see Paula S. Fass, *The Damned and the Beautiful: American Youth in the 1920s* (New York: Oxford University Press, 1977), esp. 262–63. Emily Post, *Etiquette* (New York: Funk and Wagnalls Company, 1922, 1929, 1939, 1945, 1960). Also useful are Beth L. Bailey, *From Front Porch to Back Seat: Courtship in Twentieth-Century America* (Baltimore: Johns Hopkins University Press, 1988) and Joseph F. Kett, *Rites of Passage: Adolescence in America: 1790 to the Present* (New York: Basic Books, 1977).

14. Frederick Lewis Allen, *Only Yesterday* (New York: Harper and Brothers, 1931); Robert S. Lynd and Helen Merrell Lynd, *Middletown in Transition: A Study in Cultural Conflicts* (New York: Harcourt, Brace and Company, 1937); and Willard Waller, "The Rating and Dating Complex," *American Sociological Review*, 2 (1937): 727–34. For rejoinders to Waller, see Samuel Harman Lowrie, "Dating Theories and Student Responses," *American Sociological Review*, 16 (June 1951): 334–40 and Michael Gordon, "Was Waller Ever Right? The Rating and Dating Complex Reconsidered," *Journal of Marriage and the Family*, 43 (February 1981): 67–75. Another source on dating and courtship in this era is Francis E. Merrill, *Courtship and Marriage: A Study in Social Relationships* (New York: William Sloane Associates Inc., 1949).

15. CET to BWT, 25 February 1942. A debate on dating between Philip Wylie and Sarah-Elizabeth Rodger appeared in *Cosmopolitan*, November 1942, "The Girls They Left Behind Them: Should They Have

Dates?", 32–33. Also of interest is Florence Howitt, "How to Behave in Public Without an Escort," *Good Housekeeping*, September 1943, pp. 40, 160–61.

16. BWT to CET, 12 April 1942.

17. BWT to CET, 13 April 1942.

18. BWT to CET, 13 July 1942.

19. BWT to CET, 20 July 1942.

20. BWT to CET, 20 February 1942.

21. BWT to CET, 11 December 1941. On the cancellation of Christmas furloughs after Pearl Harbor, see "Soldiers Say Farewell to Girls as Christmas Leaves Are Cancelled," *Life*, 15 December 1941, p. 40. Information on the unheralded military movement at this time is discussed in "Troops on the Move," *Life*, 29 December 1941, pp. 22–23.

22. CET to BWT, 25 December 1941.

23. CET to BWT, 5 March 1942.

24. CET to BWT, 12 March 1942.

25. BWT to CET, 2 June 1942.

26. "Love in Wartime," *Collier's*, 25 July 1942, p. 70; Gretta Palmer, "Marriage Under the Microscope," *Collier's*, 15 May 1943, pp. 12, 74, 76; Walter John Marx, "What About Marriage," *Commonwealth*, 10 July 1942, pp. 270–72; Eleanor Harris, "Don't Stop, Don't Look, Just Marry," *Cosmopolitan*, April 1941, pp. 28–29, 95; Gretta Palmer, "ABCs of Love in War," *Cosmopolitan*, April 1942, pp. 34–35; Dean Jennings, "Cinderellas of War," *Cosmopolitan*, September 1943, pp. 62–63, including information on special counseling at the San Francisco YWCA; William C. Headerick, "To Wed or to Wait?" *Current History*, October 1943, pp. 115–20; J. F. Nelson, "War Brides," *Independent Woman*, January 1942, pp. 7–8; "Marriage and War," *Ladies' Home Journal*, March 1942, pp. 110–11; Leslie B. Holman, "Married Strangers," *Ladies' Home Journal*, October 1944, pp. 156–57; K. W. Taylor "Are They Too Young to Marry?" *Parent's Magazine*, January 1944, pp. 16–17; "Will War Marriages Work?," *Reader's Digest*, November 1942, pp. 14–18. "I Married My Soldier Anyway," *Good Housekeeping*, June 1942, p. 33; A. Maxwell, "Should Marriages Wait?" *Woman's Home Companion*, November 1942, pp. 58–60; Elizabeth Gordon, "The Triumph of Little Things," *House Beautiful*, March 1943, pp. 35–37; Randolph Ray, "For Better or For Worse," *Atlantic*, March 1944, pp. 62–65; P. Popenoe and D. Eddy, "Can War Marriages Be Saved?" *American Magazine*, November 1944, pp. 40–41; Elizabeth Shepley Sergeant, "What is War Doing to Modern Marriage?" *Cosmopolitan*, December 1944, pp. 64–65, 173; Samuel Tenenbaum, "The Fate of Wartime Marriage," *American Mercury*, November 1945, pp. 530–36; "Soldiers' Wedding: Seven Couples Marry All at Once," *Life*, 4 May 1942, pp. 82–87; "Life Visits New York's Marriage License Bureau," *Life*, 21 June 1943, pp. 98–101; and Harry Henderson and Sam Shaw, "Marriage in a Hurry," *Collier's*, 17 July 1943, pp. 22–24.

27. "War Brides," *Saturday Evening Post*, 12 June 1943, pp. 28–29, 84; Dorothy Marsh, "Here Comes the War Bride," *Good Housekeeping*, June 1943, pp. 82–85; Martha Strout, ed., "Fashions: Destinations Matrimony," *Good Housekeeping*, March 1944, pp. 45–51; Nancy Shea, "A Call to Arms," *Woman's Home Companion*, June 1942, pp. 96–97; Alexander

S. Potts, "How to Get Married," *Collier's*, 19 May 1945, pp. 66, 68; Dr. Joseph R. Sizoo, "Faith in Wartime," *Woman's Home Companion*, October 1942, pp. 15, 74; Louise Andrews Kent, "Mrs. Appleyard . . . 'Masterminds a' Service Wedding," *House Beautiful*, March 1944, pp. 92–93, 126; Louise Andrews Kent, "Mrs. Appleyard Plans a . . . Wartime Wedding Breakfast," *House Beautiful*, pp. 50–51, 123, 125, 127; June Rainard Hunting, "Comfort for All In-An-Uproar Brides," *House Beautiful*, April 1944, pp. 78–79, 83, 93; and "Furlough Brides: The Newest Fad in Bridal Bouquets is the Victory Stamps Corsage," *Life*, 22 June 1942, pp. 37–40.

28. From a volcano of romantic fiction, good examples include Vina Delmar, "The Home Front," *Cosmopolitan*, August 1942, pp. 26–29, 75–77, 79; Eleanor Mercein, "School for Wives," *Cosmpolitan*, October 1943, pp. 67–70, 73–76, 78, 80, 82, 86, 88–89, 91–92, 94, 96, 98, 101–02; Leona Mattingly, "G. I. Wedding," *Saturday Evening Post*, 21 August 1943, pp. 14, 52, 54, 56, 59; 13, 74–78; Sarah-Elizabeth Rodger, "War Bride," *Woman's Home Companion*, February 1943, pp. 28, 110, 112–24. Will F. Jenkins, "Crazy Marriage," *Collier's*, 2 October 1943, p. 17; Hope Hale, "Straight Answer," *Collier's*, 27 May 1944, pp. 14, 65; and Max Hampton; "Army Wedding," *Collier's*, 16 June 1945. The February 1944 issues of *Collier's* contained a novel-length piece, "War Wedding," by Margaret Culkin Banning.

29. James H. S. Bossard, "War and the Family," *American Sociological Review*, 6 (June 1941): 330–44; Ernest W. Burgess, "The Effect of War on the American Family," *American Journal of Sociology*, 48 (November 1942): 343–52; and H. J. Locke, "Family Behavior in Wartime," *Sociology and Social Research*, 27 (March–April 1943): 277–84. On the increase in the marriage rate during the early war years, see Karen Anderson, *Wartime Women: Sex Roles and Family Relations During World War II* (Westport, CT: Greenwood Press, 1981), 76–79.

30. E. M. Mudd and M. M. Everton, "Marriage Problems in Relation to Selective Service," *Family*, 22 (June 1941): 129–30; Ruth Zurfluh, "Impact of the War on Family: Wartime Marriages and Love Affairs," *Family*, 23 (December 1942): 304–12; Evelyn Millis Duvall, "Marriage in Wartime," *Marriage and Family Living*, 4 (November 1942): 73–76; Katherine Whiteside Taylor, "Shall They Marry in Wartime?" *Journal of Home Economics* 34 (April 1942): 213–19; and Robert G. Foster, "Marriage During Crisis," *Journal of Home Economics*, 35 (June 1943): 329–32. The importance of this topic was further highlighted, in September 1943, when the prestigious *Annals of the American Academy of Political and Social Science* devoted an entire issue to "The American Family in World War II." Ray H. Abrams, "The American Family in World War II," *Annals of the American Academy of Political and Social Science*, 229 (September 1943), entire issue. See especially John F. Cuber, "Changing Courtship and Marriage Customs," 30–38; Gladys Gaylord, "Marriage Counseling in Wartime," 39–47; and Ernest R. Mower, "War and Family Solidarity and Stability," 100–06. The topic of war marriages was even the subject of university debate teams. E. M. Phelps, ed., "War Marriage," *University Debater Annual* (1942–1943), 159–91.

31. CET to BWT, 4 January 1942.

32. BWT to CET, 29 January 1942.

33. CET to BWT, 25 February 1942.
34. CET to BWT, 12 March 1942.
35. BWT to CET, 19 March 1942.
36. CET to BWT, 5 April 1945, provides an account of the events of the night they were married.
37. BWT to CET, 29 April 1942.
38. BWT to CET, 22 June 1942.
39. BWT to CET, 22 June 1942 (second letter of the day). CET to BWT, 18, 19 June 1942. In June 1942, Congress had enacted the Servicemen's Dependents Allowance Act. For more information on this subject, see John D. Millett, *The Army Service Forces: The Organizational Role of the Army Service Forces* (Washington, DC: Department of the Army, 1954), 107; Denzel C. Cline, "Allowances to Dependents of Servicemen in the United States," *Annals of the American Academy of Political and Social Science*, 27 (May 1943): 51–58 and Phyllis Aronson, "The Adequacy of the Family Allowance Systems as It Effects the Wives and Children of Men Drafted into the Armed Forces," (M. A. thesis, Wayne University, 1944). Discussion in the popular press includes Harry Henderson and Sam Shaw, "Pay for Soldier's Families," *Collier's* 22 May 1943, pp. 18, 76; Gretta Palmer, "Army's Problem Wives," *Reader's Digest*, July 1944, pp. 66–68; J. C. Furnas, "They Get 'Em Paid," *Saturday Evening Post*, 5 June 1943, pp. 22, 105, 106; Brig. Gen. Harold N. Gilbert, "Green Checks for the Folks Back Home," *American Magazine*, January 1944, pp. 94–97; and Nell Giles, "That Army-Navy Paycheck: Answers to Many Problems," *Ladies' Home Journal*, March 1944, pp. 4–5.
40. BWT to CET, 18 June 1942.
41. CET to BWT, 10 July 1942.
42. BWT to CET, 29 July 1942.
43. BWT to her parents, 4 August 1942. *The Atlanta Journal*, 2 September 1942, carried the announcement of their "official" marriage. Barbara and Charles kept the knowledge of their first marriage a secret for more than 40 years. Not until the early 1980s, when these letters began to be discussed as the possible source of a forthcoming book, did they reveal the full details of their first and second marriages.

Notes to Essay 12/Hunter

1. Dorothy Cameron Disney, "My Thirty Years with 'Can This Marriage Be Saved?'", *Ladies Home Journal* (hereafter *LHJ*), 100:1, (Jan. 1983), 19–20.
2. The original four articles turned into nine that year, and for the next eleven years, "Can This Marriage Be Saved?" appeared an average of eight times a year as a special feature. Its popularity is indicated by the fact that it was highlighted on the cover most months. In 1964 it became a regular feature, appearing at least 11 times a year. Disney wrote the vast majority of the columns, and it was not until the early seventies that the files of other marriage counseling agencies were used on a regular basis. Until that time, Popenoe wrote an introduction to

each article, commenting on the general problem found in the case.

3. "Can This Marriage Be Saved?" remains one of the most popular features in the magazine and has always ranked in the top ten when it comes to reader response as determined by letters to the editor. Interview with Marge Rosen, current editor of the feature, November 1986.

4. The basic premise of the feature was that marriages *could* be saved. In the 232 cases reviewed between 1953 and 1977, only four described marriages that could *not* be saved. The first was the case of a totally reclusive scientist who had no time for his family. (*LHJ*, 71:9, [Sep. 1954], 61ff.) The second described a marriage between two childish and irresponsible people who lacked any commitment to anything but their own selfish needs, (*LHJ*, 76:10 [Oct. 1959] pp. 49ff.) In both instances, the counselors insisted that with a little more effort, the marriages could have been saved. The third presented a woman whose husband of 19 years had informed her that he was a homosexual. (*LHJ*, 92:1, [Jan. 1975], 12ff.) The final failed marriage was that of a woman who had married a father figure and then had proceeded to outgrow her husband. (*LHJ*, 94:6, [June 1977], 16ff.

5. One clue to the emphasis on marriages that could be saved can be seen in the incidence of alcohol abuse in the cases discussed. While Popenoe himself in his comments admitted that surveys indicated that drinking problems were singled out by wives as the second (and sometimes the first) most serious issue in marriages, only 30 cases (13 percent) dealt with drinking problems and only three dealt with cases of true alcoholism. Likewise, there were only a handful of cases involving even minor physical abuse. There was, however, a great deal of what is currently regarded as psychological abuse, of incessant criticism and belittling on the part of the husbands. This was always strongly condemned. Only 31 cases included infidelity among the problems (13 percent), while three dealt with gambling, two with the wife's obesity, two with drugs, and two with homosexuality.

6. Only one of the 232 cases was identifiably about a black couple, while two dealt with Mexican–Americans, possible because of the Los Angeles locale of so many of the cases.

7. Elaine Tyler May, *Homeward Bound: American Families in the Cold War Era*, (New York: Basic Books, 1988) connects the lack of security that faced Americans in the public arena with the new emphasis on the home and family. "The self-contained home held out the promise of security in an insecure world. It also offered a vision of abundance and fulfillment" (3). See pp. 8–9 for May's explanation of how the family of the fifties was in fact nontraditional. See p. 185 for figures on the shortfall in the expected divorce rate. May suggests some of the reason for the popularity of "Can This Marriage Be Saved?" in the fifties and early sixties in her chap. 8, "Hanging Together: For Better or for Worse." She notes that men and women in the fifties, despite their high expectations about married life and their inevitable disappointment, "stayed married to a remarkably high degree." Partly, she attributes this to the power of prevailing norms, but also to "sheer determination" (185). She also points out that the reliance on experts such as those represetned by "Can This Marriage Be Saved?" was very widespread. Such experts "offered a distinctly apolitical means of

solving problems that were often the result of larger social restraints" (187). Certainly, the message of the feature was that through hard work, determination and good will, individuals could solve their marital problems. Counselors frequently recognized that societal constraints caused families problems, but called on individuals to adapt rather than calling for social change.

8. The upshot of the demonstration was a section prepared by the New York Women's Collective in the August 1970 issue of the *Journal* which included articles on all aspects of women's unhappy position in society. The article on marriage was a take-off on "Can This Marriage Be Saved?" The marriage wasn't saved, but the wife was.

9. The cases described were never unidimensional, and many times the complaints of husbandly or wifely failures covered more than one of the categories. There was obviously a high correlation between husbands who overworked, did not help around the house, and were inadequate fathers. Likewise, there was a similar correlation between domineering husbands and those who controlled the family finances. The figure of 72 percent achieved by eliminating the duplicates. Hence, in 167 cases, the husband was found to have failed to meet his role responsibilities in one way or another.

10. *LHJ*, 70:11 (Nov. 1953), 69ff.

11. *LHJ*, 75:11 (Nov. 1958), 53.

12. *LHJ*, 70:11 (Nov. 1953), 126–27.

13. Nineteen cases (8 percent) described husbands who refused to allow their wives any say in the household finances. For examples, see the features in February 1953, April 1962, May 1967, October 1970 and November 1973.

14. When the husband's earning power was the source of dispute, it generally had less to do with his ability to find a job and more to do with the general unsteadiness of his work patterns. Also, in about one-third of the cases, the problem had to do with the unrealistic expectations of the wife.

15. *LHJ*, 88:11 (Jan. 1971), 10ff.

16. *LHJ*, 83:7 (Jul. 1966), 34ff.

17. *LHJ*, 72:10 (Oct. 1955), 61ff.

18. *LHJ*, 78:10 (Oct. 1961), 24ff.

19. *LHJ*, 72:8 (Aug. 1955), 61.

20. *LHJ*, 78:10 (Oct. 1961), 34.

21. *LHJ*, 78:9 (Sep. 1961), 24ff.

22. *LHJ*, 74:9 (Sep. 1957), 83ff. See also, *LHJ*, 74:5 (May 1957), 76ff.

23. *LHJ*, 86:8 (Aug. 1969), 16ff.

24. Occupations were clear for 80 of the wives in these cases. Of these, 40 were employed and three were students. Ten had worked in the past. Twenty-seven were homemakers. For a discussion of the change in editorial policy, see Jean E. Hunter, "'A Daring New Concept': The *Ladies' Home Journal* and Modern Feminism," *Journal of the National Women's Studies Association*, forthcoming.

25. *LHJ*, 88:6 (June 1971), 10ff.

26. *LHJ*, 90:1 (Jan. 1973), 12ff.

27. *LHJ*, 90:6 (June 1973), 16ff.

28. *LHJ*, 92:7 (July 1975), 14ff.

29. See *LHJ*, 90:4 (April 1973), 8ff.; 90:5 (May 1973), 12ff.; 90:8 (Aug. 1973), 16ff.; 90:12 (Dec. 1973), 14ff.; 91:10 (Oct. 1974), 29 for examples of wives who went to work to help their marriages.

30. *LHJ*, 87:11 (Nov. 1970), 12ff.

31. *LHJ*, 93:5 (May 1976), 20ff.

32. See note 7 above for a fuller description of May's thesis.

33. Barbara Ehrenreich, *The Hearts of Men*, (Garden City, N.Y.: Doubleday & Co., 1983).

About the Contributors

RICHARD J. ALTENBAUGH is associate professor of history at Northern Illinois University. He received his Ph.D. from the University of Pittsburgh in 1980. Dr. Altenbaugh is the author of *Education for Struggle: The American Labor Colleges of the 1920s and 1930s* (Temple University Press, 1990) and the editor of *The Teacher's Voice: A Social History of Teaching in Twentieth-Century America* (Falmer Press, forthcoming).

ROSS W. BEALES, JR. is associate professor of history at the College of the Holy Cross. Dr. Beales, who earned his Ph.D. in history from the University of California at Davis in 1971, is currently working on a book-length study, *The Worlds of Ebenezer Parkman: Family, Religion and Community in Eighteenth-Century Westborough, Massachusetts.*

STEFAN BIELINSKI is founder and director of the Colonial Albany Social History Project, a model community history program sponsored by the New York State Museum. He is also the author of *Abraham Yates, Jr. and the New Political Order in Revolutionary New York* (1975) and *Government by the People: The Story of the Dongan Charter and the Birth of Participatory Democracy in the City of Albany* (1986).

LORIN LEE CARY, professor emeritus, taught labor history at the University of Toledo for 22 years. Dr. Cary, who received his Ph.D. from the University of Wisconsin-Madison in 1968, was also a Fulbright Senior Scholar at the University of New South Wales in Sydney, Australia in 1980. He is the coauthor of *No Strength Without Union: An Illustrated History of Ohio Workers, 1803–1980* (Ohio Historical Society, 1983), and he is president of the Southwest Labor Studies Association.

VIRGINIA G. CRANE is professor of history at the University of Wisconsin-Oshkosh. She earned her Ph.D. in southern history from the University of North Carolina in 1964. The author of various articles, Dr. Crane is also a member of the Organization of American Historians and the Southern Historical Association.

JOHN DEMOS is professor of history at Yale University. His work as a social and family historian includes *A Little Commonwealth: Family Life in Plymouth Colony*, *Entertaining Satan: Witchcraft and the Culture of Early New England* and *Past, Present and Personal: The Family and the Life Course in American History*.

JEAN E. HUNTER is professor of history at Duquesne University and directed the Duquesne History Forum from 1988 through 1990. She received her Ph.D. in British history from Yale University in 1970, but in recent years has turned her attention to the history of women and the family in 20th century America. Her current research centers on the role that the *Ladies' Home Journal* played in modernizing the American woman.

MARVIN L. MICHAEL KAY is professor of history at the University of Toledo. He is also the former editor of *Studies in Burke and His Time*. Currently, Dr. Kay is completing a book on slavery in colonial North Carolina (coauthored with Lorin Lee Cary), and he is collaborating on a study of the North Carolina Regulators. Dr. Kay received his Ph.D. at the University of Minnesota.

CYNTHIA A. KIERNER is assistant professor of history at the University of North Carolina at Charlotte. Dr. Kierner, who earned her Ph.D. in early American history from the University of Virginia in 1986, is the author of *Traders and Gentlefolk: The Livingstons of New York, 1675–1790* (Cornell University Press, forthcoming).

JUDY BARRETT LITOFF is professor of history at Bryant College. Dr. Litoff is the coauthor of *Miss You: The World War II Letters of Barbara Wooddall Taylor and Charles E. Taylor* (University of Georgia Press, 1990) and *Since You Went Away: Letters from the Home Front by American Women, 1941–1945* (Oxford University Press, forthcoming). She received her Ph.D. in history in 1975 from the University of Maine.

PAUL T. MASON is professor of history at Duquesne University. He has edited a book on totalitarianism and has published articles and reviews on historiography. A Ph.D. in history from St. Louis University in 1964, his research interests have moved from the Enlightenment, to Fascism, to his present interest in using the methods and insights of psychoanalysis to understand the post-war era in the United States.

DAVID MCBRIDE is associate professor of history at the State University of New York at Binghamton. He is the author of *Integrating the City of Medicine: Blacks in Philadelphia Health Care, 1910–1965* (Temple University Press, 1989).

DAVID W. ROBSON is associate professor and chair of history at John Carroll University. Previously, Dr. Robson has taught at Agnes Scott College, Emory University and the University of Wyoming. He earned his Ph.D. in early American history from Yale University in 1974. Dr. Robson is the author of *Educating Republicans: The College in the Era of the American Revolution, 1750–1800* (Greenwood Press, 1985).

LINDA W. ROSENZWEIG is associate professor of history and education at Chatham College. She is also the editor of *Developmental Perspectives on the Social Studies* (1982) and the coauthor of *Themes in Modern Social History* (1985). Dr. Rosenzweig earned her Ph.D. in history from Carnegie-Mellon University, and she is currently working on a book discussing late nineteenth and early twentieth century American mother-daughter relationships.

DAVID C. SMITH is professor of history at the University of Maine. He earned his Ph.D. in history from Cornell University in 1965. Dr. Smith is the coauthor of *Miss You: The World War II Letters of Barbara Wooddall Taylor and Charles E. Taylor* (University of Georgia Press, 1990) and *Since You Went Away: Letters from the Home Front by American Women, 1941–1945* (Oxford University Press, forthcoming).

CHARLES G. STEFFEN is associate professor of history at Georgia State University. He has also served as a Fullbright Lecturer at the University of Buenos Aires in Argentina. Dr. Steffen, who received his Ph.D. from Northwestern University in 1977 in early American history, is the author of *The Mechanics of Baltimore: Workers and Politics in the Age of Revolution, 1763–1812* (1984).